# THE
# WELL-TRAINED
# COMPUTER

### DESIGNING SYSTEMATIC
### INSTRUCTIONAL MATERIALS
### FOR THE CLASSROOM
### MICROCOMPUTER

# THE
# WELL-TRAINED
# COMPUTER

### DESIGNING SYSTEMATIC
### INSTRUCTIONAL MATERIALS
### FOR THE CLASSROOM
### MICROCOMPUTER

## MYNGA K. FUTRELL & PAUL GEISERT

## EDUCATIONAL TECHNOLOGY PUBLICATIONS
## ENGLEWOOD CLIFFS, NEW JERSEY 07632

Library of Congress Cataloging in Publication Data

Futrell, Mynga K.
   The well-trained computer.

   Bibliography: p.
   Includes index.
   1. Microcomputers--Programming. 2. Computer-assisted
instruction. I. Geisert, Paul. II. Title.
QA76.6.F87   1984      371.3'9445      84-1629
ISBN 0-87778-190-7

Printed in the United States of America.

Library of Congress Catalog Card Number:
84-1629.

International Standard Book Number:
0-87778-190-7.

First Printing: April, 1984.

# Preface

A microcomputer has the potential for becoming many things—an entertainer, an accountant, an analyst, or . . . *a teacher's aide*. To become a teacher's aide, the computer must be directed (trained) by a computer program to do certain tasks. As in any training endeavor, the training of a computer may be good or bad, resulting in a teacher's aide that is absolutely marvelous or one as destructive as the sorcerer's apprentice. The focus of this book is the well-trained microcomputer. The well-trained computer will be directed in its performance by a computer program based on sound and systematic instructional design.

Our goal is to provide a classroom teacher with a systematic approach to the design of educational materials for the microcomputer. With this knowledge, the teacher can evaluate instructional materials developed for the microcomputer, and can make enlightened decisions as to whether the computer has been well-trained or poorly-trained to perform its responsibilities as a teacher's aide. In addition, if the teacher knows or learns some computer programming skills, he or she can couple knowledge of good instructional design with programming to systematically develop his or her own effective educational computer materials.

Conceptually, the book is divided as follows:

- Chapters 1 and 2 present the architecture, characteristics, and potentials of the classroom microcomputer.
- Chapters 3 through 8 present principles and strategies of lesson design for a well-trained instructional computer.
- Chapters 9 and 10 present the concepts associated with the computer's role in classroom management (computer-managed instruction).
- Chapters 11 and 12 present two aspects of securing good computer courseware—programming and evaluating.

- The Appendices list various resources to help in using the microcomputer in the classroom.

It should be noted that there is no section of the book devoted to the various brands and models of microcomputers available for use in the classroom. There are two major reasons for this purposeful omission.

First, the microcomputer industry is growing at a phenomenal rate. New computers are constantly being brought out and old models updated. This flux is so great that any book that attempts to cover the field would be out of date within a few months of publication. A book is not the appropriate source of information on the merits of various computers; such information is best obtained directly from computer vendors (see Appendix B) or from magazines and periodicals that specialize in reviewing such products on an ongoing basis (see Appendix C).

Second, almost all microcomputers, regardless of their brand name, perform the same electronic tasks. An analogous situation exists with television sets. No matter what brand name you purchase, you know that each TV will receive the same set of stations and perform the same basic function—receiving a station's television signal and transforming it into pictures and sound. So it is with microcomputers, with one major exception. Instructional programs developed for one model microcomputer may not, and probably will not, run on any other type of computer.

When a specific microcomputer is chosen, the purchaser is locked into a discrete corresponding body of instructional materials. Therefore, it is essential that the first major decisions concerning which microcomputer is to be obtained for the classroom be made regarding the *instructional programs to acquire*, not the *microcomputer to purchase*. Before a microcomputer is purchased for classroom use, a thorough survey of the programs available for such use must be made, and decisions developed concerning which major programs are suitable for use in the given classroom. Then, and only then, can a logical decision be reached as to which computer should be purchased to give access to the specific body of instructional programs chosen.

The well-trained instructional microcomputer could certainly result in a revolution in the classroom. It has the potential to become the most effective and efficient teacher's aide ever to have come into existence. Whether or not that potential is realized will be in large part a function of the computer's training. Just as people can be well or poorly educated by their schools, so educational computers can be well or poorly trained by their designers and programmers. It is the intent of this book to help teachers develop, or at least recognize, materials that will produce well-trained instructional microcomputers, and to help teachers keep poorly-trained computers out of their classrooms.

Mynga K. Futrell
Paul Geisert

July, 1983

# Table of Contents

Preface ................................................................ v

### Part I—Introduction to Microcomputers in the Classroom

Chapter 1:     Microcomputers .............................................  5

Chapter 2:     Microcomputer Classroom Capabilities ............ 25

### Part II—Designing Lessons

Chapter 3:     The Well-Trained Computer-Teacher ............... 51

Chapter 4:     Defining Lesson Purpose ................................ 67

Chapter 5:     Developing Performance Measures ................... 95

Chapter 6:     The Processes of Instruction ........................... 109

Chapter 7:     An Example Computer Tutorial Lesson .......... 129

Chapter 8:     Fine-Tuning the Processes of Instruction ......... 149

### Part III—Managing Learning

Chapter 9:     The Well-Trained Computer-Manager .............. 171

Chapter 10:   Preparing a CMI System ................................... 193


### Part IV—Acquiring Effective Courseware

Chapter 11:   Programming Courseware ............................... 211

Chapter 12:   Evaluating Courseware ................................... 227


### Appendices

Appendix A:  Readings in Instructional Development ........... 253

Appendix B:  Computer Manufacturers ................................ 257

Appendix C:  Computer Magazines ....................................... 259

Appendix D:  Periodicals of Professional Organizations ......... 261

Appendix E:  Books on Computers ....................................... 263

Appendix F:  Sources of Information on Educational Soft-
             ware ............................................................... 267


Index ................................................................................ 271

# THE
# WELL-TRAINED
# COMPUTER

## DESIGNING SYSTEMATIC
## INSTRUCTIONAL MATERIALS
## FOR THE CLASSROOM
## MICROCOMPUTER

# PART I
# INTRODUCTION TO MICROCOMPUTERS
# IN THE CLASSROOM

Chapter 1: Microcomputers

Chapter 2: Microcomputer Classroom Capabilities

# Chapter 1

# Microcomputers

## Introduction

*Instructional Intent.* This chapter will help you to do the following:

1. View microcomputers as simple machines which teachers can easily learn to operate.
2. Adopt the position that one does not need to know how a computer *works* in order to be able to *operate* it effectively.
3. Identify and name all the main components of a microcomputer, and state the function of each.
4. Identify three ways to communicate with a microcomputer.
5. Relate the factors of hardware, memory, and software to the computer's ability to function in a classroom.

If you are already familiar with the form and function of computers commonly used in the classroom, you may want to quickly review the parts illustrated in the figures in this chapter, or you may skip directly to Chapter 2.

*Knowledge Prerequisites.* No previous experience with computers is required in order to reach the objectives of this chapter. No special knowledge is prerequisite to this chapter.

-------------------------------------------------------------------------

## Computer!

For some reason or other, the word "computer" has come to mean to many people a thing complex and mysterious, having powers that can only be controlled by experts. Nothing is further from the truth. The computer is a "simple machine" that can be easily understood and controlled by almost anyone. Why, even monkeys have been taught to use computers to communicate their needs and desires to their caretakers!

Why do computers elicit awe and discomfort in some people? It may be because large and sophisticated computers do large and sophisticated things that the average person has trouble comprehending. For example, people have difficulty understanding how computers can be made to play chess with champions, and in many cases, to be the winners. Computers are renowned for their ability to hold and manipulate large amounts of information. How they do this is a mystery to many. But all of this is (or can be) irrelevant to you. You do not need to know how a computer *works* in order to *use* one. In fact, you need to know very little in order to make very good use of a microcomputer in your classroom. And that "very little" you need to know is relatively easy to learn.

Here is a simple analogy that will make it easier to understand that you do not need to know how a microcomputer works to use the computer. Most schools now have photocopy machines, such as a Xerox, IBM, or 3M. These machines are used routinely by teachers, becoming in some cases indispensable to their daily classroom activities. But, few teachers know how a photocopy machine makes a duplicate copy of a printed page! In truth, all a teacher needs to know about a duplicator is a few simple rules, such as: what button must be pushed to set the number of copies wanted; what button starts the machine; how the paper should be loaded; and who should be called if the paper gets jammed.

So it is with a microcomputer. You need to know a few simple rules about which computer buttons to push and who to call if the paper in the printer jams.

There really is not all that much that you need to learn about microcomputers before you employ one to work with you in your classroom. We hope this awareness of the relative ease of using microcomputers encourages you to forge ahead to use one. In fairness, however, we must warn you of one difficulty you will probably encounter at times, which may tend to discourage you or make your learning experience somewhat uncomfortable. The difficulty is this—a barrage of "computereze."

Computereze is our term for the jargon of computer users, and with the rapid development of computers and their proliferation within society over the past decade, it has been growing by leaps and bounds. Like any jargon (pilots have theirs, surfers theirs), it consists of technical terms used by an "in" group. This body of jargon makes the topic look formidable to an outsider. As you move beyond reading this book (in which we try to keep computereze to a minimum) to acquaint yourself with other materials on microcomputers, you will meet and talk with a variety of individuals more familiar with microcomputers than you, almost all of whom will bombard you with their impressive mastery of computer lingo. We want to alert you in advance that this tendency is quite prevalent among the "in" group of computer users. The aware novice is not quite so easily intimidated or made uncomfortable as is the one who meets speakers of computereze unawares. If you ask a fellow teacher, who "knows all about computing," some simple question, do not be surprised if you receive an explanation which might as well be in Swahili. As you gain experience, computereze will make sense to you.

In this book, we try to keep our discussions and explanations as free of computereze as possible. You will encounter in the book words and phrases commonly used by computer salespersons, fellow teachers, other computer books, and computer magazines, but we have tried to keep our use of terminology to a minimum and to introduce each new term we do use in plain English. To read most of the computer magazines commonly found on bookstore shelves, however, you will need to become somewhat proficient at translating computereze into regular English.

By the end of this chapter, you will have learned a good deal of computereze. You will know about software, courseware, hardware, floppy disks, and microprocessors, all basic vocabulary for computereze. To this extent, you will be gradually moving toward joining the "in" group whether you want to or not. We want to help you make the movement comfortably.

### Microcomputer Basics

Let's start off with an introduction to the machine itself. How formidable does the computer pictured in Figure 1.1 look to you?

This little item is an example of a simple but powerful microcomputer. It certainly does not look like a device which

*Figure 1.1*

*A Simple Microcomputer*

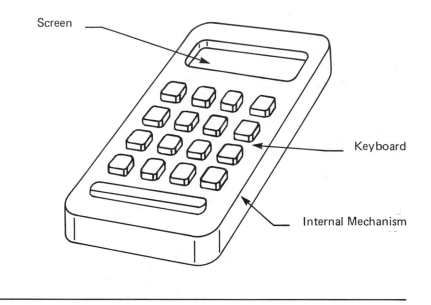

Screen

Keyboard

Internal Mechanism

---

should strike fear in the heart of a teacher. This computer has three important components:

(1) a *keyboard* for putting information into the computer;
(2) a *screen* to display information going into and coming out of the computer; and
(3) an *internal mechanism,* including the *microprocessor* and the *memory,* which manipulates and stores information between the time the information goes in via the keyboard and comes out via the screen.

You really do not need to know anything about how these three items "work." That is, there is no reason for us to go into a lengthy explanation of what happens when your pressing a key causes a character to appear on the screen. It is of little or no value to you as a teacher to know how the various components of a computer function. (Of course, if you are interested, there are books that will provide this explanation.) What you do need to know are the operations it takes to make a computer work for you in the classroom. There is a world of difference between knowing how to operate a computer, and knowing how a computer operates. You only need to learn how to operate a computer, and leave the other aspects to computer technicians, repairpersons, and others interested in the internal workings of the machine.

At the same time, it is clear that computers range in complexity from simple programmable calculators through personal computers to complex military computers that monitor information from hundreds of satellite computers all over the world. As you progress in your expertise as a user of computers in education, you will recognize the various levels of expertise associated with computers, and you will be able to decide which level is comfortable for you at a given time.

A three-year-old child can run a "Speak and Spell" computer purchased from a toy store, and that is one level of computer competence. An eight-year-old may have a complete command of an arcade game of great skill and complexity, and that is another level of competence. A high school teacher may have a microcomputer in his or her classroom and know nothing more than how to utilize an attendance and grading program for classroom recordkeeping. An elementary teacher may purchase and use a math drill-and-practice program for independent study by his or her fifth-grade students on a microcomputer located in the school's library. A home economics teacher may develop and write an instructional program on how to store foods, and have it "translated" to the computer by a curriculum developer. A chemistry teacher may develop an instructional program that simulates on the screen a chemical experiment. An instructional designer working for a large company may develop a year's course in algebra for use in individualized instruction on a large central computer. All of these levels of expertise represent valuable educational endeavors, and there is no reason to believe that everyone should be a "computer expert." It is possible to learn to operate a microcomputer and have it in full classroom operation in one day, utilizing prepackaged computer instructional materials.

In this book, we will be staying at the level of "user of classroom microcomputers." That is, we will deal with the sorts of computers commonly found in schools and classrooms, known as "personal computers" or "microcomputers," and having such trade names as Apple, Radio Shack TRS-80, Atari, Commodore, Franklin, and IBM.

Of course, not all microcomputers are as simple in form as the model presented in Figure 1.1. Most computers generally have a full typewriter keyboard. They usually have a large screen for viewing text, and they may be attached to a printer (typewriter) so that the computer can print as well as display text on the screen. Figure 1.2 is an illustration of a computer which has all the components we have mentioned. With this computer, each component is in its own enclosure. Pretty simple!

### Getting Information to a Computer

Providing information and instructions to the computer so that they can be manipulated by the microprocessor is known in computer lingo as "entering" the data or commands into the computer (your first sampling of computereze). Suppose you want to provide your students with 25 practice problems on a topic. You want to make up your own problems to cover the topic. How do you get the problems into the computer?

*Keyboard Data Entry.* One way of getting information into a microcomputer is through the keyboard. As you invent the problems, you can type them directly into the computer using the keyboard (with the help of a special "authoring program," which you will learn about later). The problems go directly into the computer's memory, which is where the microcomputer stores information to be acted on by the microprocessor. The problems you wrote are stored for use by your students that day. Later, when a student uses the computer, the microprocessor can retrieve each stored problem and present it to the student.

If, at the end of the day, you decide that the problems were valuable and you would like to have them available for use again the next day, you will face a choice: either leave the microcom-

*Figure 1.2*

*Basic Microcomputer Components*

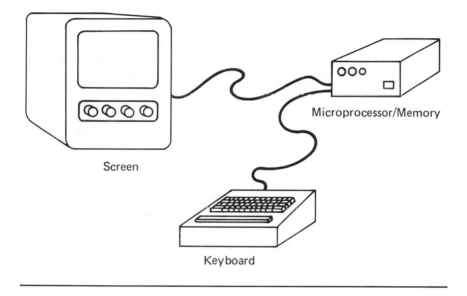

Microprocessor/Memory

Screen

Keyboard

---

puter on overnight to save the problems, or save them using an "accessory device." If you turn off the computer, the computer will simply "forget" the problems, and you would have to type them in again in order to "remind" the microcomputer. This dilemma derives from the nature of the microcomputer's memory.

*Memory.* Memory is an important aspect of computer operation, and you will often see a memory designation embedded in the name of the computer, e.g., a 64K Apple IIe microcomputer. The "64K" part of the name is translated to plain English to mean 64,000 units of memory. A memory unit is an electronic unit of the computer that can store one piece of information. For example, a 64K computer can store 64,000 letter A's. Storing 64,000 letter A's would be a rather trivial use of a computer, but it illustrates the concept. There are about 500 words on one double-spaced typed page, with an average of five letters per word, so the 64K memory of a microcomputer could hold about 24 full pages of typed information. In reality, the 64K will store all sorts of information. It may store text to be printed on a printer, it may store instructions for making various decisions, and/or it may store statements of what to put on the screen, when to put it there, and how long it should stay there.

Computers can be purchased with as little as 1K memory capacity. This is too little memory for many practical applications. Memory can be purchased for essentially all computers, and added until the maximum for the given computer is reached. For example, you may purchase a computer having 2K, work with it for a month or two, and then find you need more memory. You can then add more memory, normally in 16K "packages." Sometimes these memory additions simply plug into the computer; other times they must be installed inside of it.

The limits imposed by internal computer memory can be overcome by the fact that it is rather easy to utilize accessory memory units outside of the computer. Although there are some very real technical differences between internal and external information storage, for all practical purposes, the teacher can consider them together.

*Using Accessory Information Storage Devices.* Microcomputers have a finite amount of built-in electronic memory. The fact is *all* computers have a limited amount of electronic memory. Because of the nature and limitations of a computer's electronic memory, there is a need for having "accessories" to store computer information. The solution to the problem of the microcomputer's internal memory, from which information vanishes as soon as the computer is turned off, is in the provision of accessory external, and essentially unlimited, information storage. Computers have the power to save information in an easily readable form (readable by the computer, that is).

Some microcomputers can record information much like a tape recorder can record music on a tape. If your microcomputer is of this type, you can save the problems composed for your students on regular audiotape. At a simple command, the microprocessor can take any information previously entered from the keyboard and move it onto a cassette tape located in a cassette recorder. The cassette tape and recorder are exactly the same ones commonly used to record sound. In fact, if you or your school has a cassette recorder/player for recording sound, you may be equipped already to save computer information. (Note, though, that not all tape recorders are compatible with specific computers, due to variations in electronic components; check the information booklet supplied with your computer.)

To reiterate an earlier concept, there is no need for you to know how a cassette recorder stores computer information. You only need to learn the rules of how to operate a cassette recorder in order to have it store information from your computer for you.

Another common method of storing information for use in the computer is with a disk. The disk looks like a thin plastic record in a case, and it stores information like a cassette tape, that is, in the form of recorded electronic messages.

The computer disk is placed in a "player" called the disk drive, and information may be sent to the microcomputer from the disk, or from the microprocessor to the disk for storage. If the disk is small and flexible, it is called a floppy disk (or mini-disk or diskette), and it is used in a disk drive (see Figure 1.3). If the disk is hard and not flexible, it is called a hard disk and drive, and is generally located in a sealed cabinet.

*Other Computer Accessories.* Various attachments for the computer have developed rapidly. Devices for receiving and producing sound, controlling lights, monitoring temperature, and otherwise getting information into and out of the computer are currently available. These accessories generally have specific applications, some of which are valuable to the classroom use of the computer.

Some screens are able to receive information from a *light pen*. The light pen puts the learner in contact with the computer via the screen. It is used to touch the screen at any location, and the computer can sense where the pen is touching. For example, the computer could present a map of the U.S. and ask the student to touch the light pen to the state of Ohio. The computer would then

*Figure 1.3*

*Floppy Disk and Disk Drive*

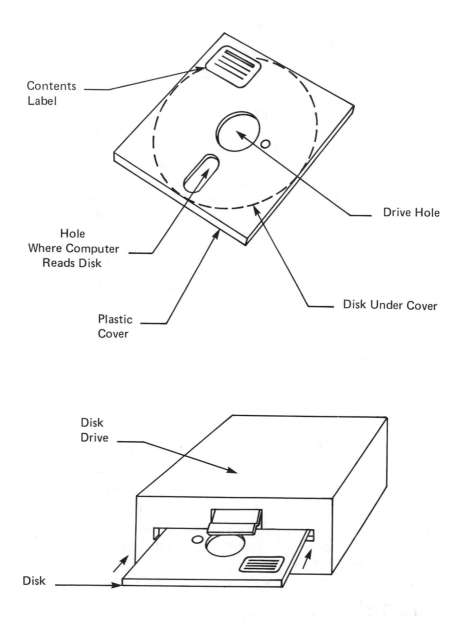

sense the student's response and act on it. Other screens, called *touch screens*, can sense the direct pressure of a finger pushing against the surface of the screen.

*Paddles, joysticks,* and *mouses* are all devices that translate movements of the hand into computer signals. This type of information entry is commonly used in playing video games and in drawing graphics. The student moves a device to the right or left, up or down, and the computer can interpret the signals.

The *graphics tablet* is a drawing surface and a stylus, which is analogous to a light pen. The stylus is used to draw shapes and graphic figures on the tablet. When the desired shape has been completed, a button on the stylus is pressed, and the computer accepts the image that has been drawn on the tablet.

The *keypad* is simply a set of special function keys with the numerals 0 through 9 arranged as on a calculator, making for convenient use when typing a series of numbers, or in certain games.

A *printer* produces printed materials, such as worksheets, tests, and grade records.

Figure 1.4 is an illustration of a microcomputer with several of the components we have mentioned so far.

## Computers Communicating with Other Computers

Once computers were in common use, people found it convenient to have one computer send messages to another computer. Now for school use, some companies produce micro-computers organized into classroom "networks." A network configuration generally involves a central "teacher computer" connected via wires to a group of "student computers." In this manner, the teacher may command a more sophisticated micro-computer and have control of what information is sent to the students, while the students work on less sophisticated (and less expensive) peripheral computers.

Classroom microcomputers can be "networked" with large central computers a few miles or even thousands of miles away. The advantage is the same as with classroom networks: a large, sophisticated, and expensive computer can service many smaller, inexpensive computers. The teacher thereby gains computing power in a cost-effective manner.

*Figure 1.4*

*Computer Components*

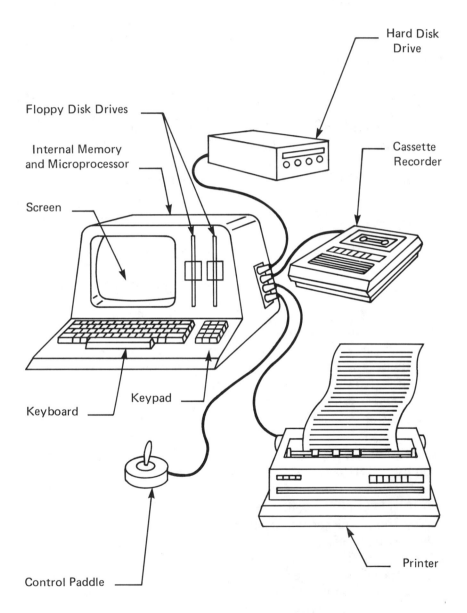

Often, one computer is connected to a second computer via an instrument called a *modem*. The modem is an electronic device that allows a computer to send electronic information over standard telephone lines to another computer, which receives the information through its own modem (see Figure 1.5). The use of the modem translator permits computer information to be sent from computer to computer in an efficient and effective manner.

## All Computers Are Similar

At first, different brands of computers look very different from each other. The various styles of cases and screens and keyboards tend to present a picture of great diversity. But, as a comparison, think about all of the brands of TVs that are on the market. Although there is a great deal of diversity in their appearance, everyone knows that all TVs operate basically the same. Structurally, microcomputers are even more similar than TVs, often having the same microprocessors, memories, disk drives, and electronic components under different brand names. As you "get to know" various brands of computers, they will take on the same aura of familiarity that the TV now possesses, and you will be at ease when meeting a new model or brand of computer.

Functionally, too, all microcomputers are almost the same. They may vary in the type of keyboard they have, or in the color of the screen, or in the shape of the enclosure, or in whether or not they use a cassette recorder or a disk storage device, or have a modem attached, but for all practical purposes, they are the same. That is, the basic operating components we have described are common to almost all computers except in regard to cosmetic form. If you learn to operate one computer, you will have the knowledge to quickly learn to operate others.

To utilize the photocopy analogy again, once you learn the main ideas of using a Xerox photocopy machine, it is easy to walk up to a 3M copier and use it, even if you have never seen a 3M copier before. You may have to look around on the copier a little to determine which keys do what, but there is no need to get panicky about being confronted by a new machine. You know they all work in the same or similar ways. So it is with microcomputers.

*Figure 1.5*

*Computer-to-Computer Communication*

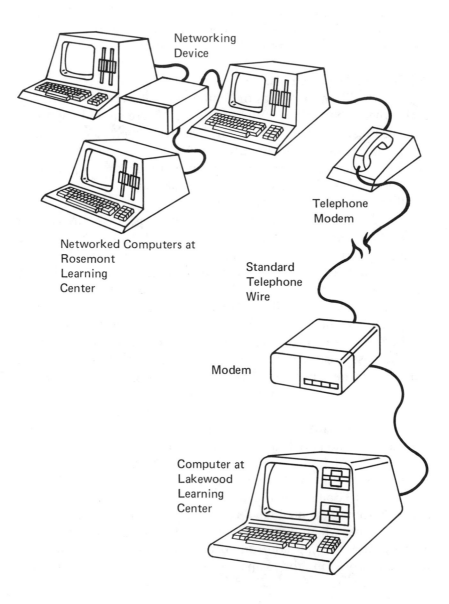

Networking
Device

Networked Computers at
Rosemont
Learning
Center

Telephone
Modem

Standard
Telephone
Wire

Modem

Computer at
Lakewood
Learning
Center

Look at the three computer systems in Figure 1.6, and locate on each picture the following items: (1) the screen, (2) the keyboard, and (3) the disk drive. You will notice that the computers, although superficially different, are operationally very similar.

### Computer "Wares"

So far, you have learned mostly about computer *hardware*. The physical and electronic parts of the computer are the computer's hardware. The screen is a piece of hardware, as is the microprocessor, the keyboard, and the printer. Hardware is machinery. The set of instructions to operate the machinery is called *software*.

A microcomputer is simply an assembled, but inert, piece of machinery, until the electronics of the machine are put into appropriate patterns to do specific jobs. This is done by providing the computer with command statements telling it what to do. These command statements are organized using a *computer program*.

The program is simply a series of statements, written in a language that is often similar in form to a human language like English. The program governs the computer's electronic patterns thereby telling the computer when to do a specific task. Computer programs are also called computer software, to contrast the hardware of the computer which does a task and the program (software) of the computer that directs which tasks will be done, and when.

The program is in essence the heart and soul and personality of a computer. For, as we have explained, all computers do essentially the same tasks. If you were to ask which model of computer to purchase on the basis of hardware, the answer would be "it really does not matter." *But software does matter!* The computer programs you use with your computer become the basic determiners of your computer's classroom behavior. The computer will not do anything except what the program directs it to do. Ergo, the major factor in any computer system's performance lies in the software.

One major problem with software is that it is (in general)

*Figure 1.6*

*A Variety of Computer Shapes*

hardware-specific. That is, a program written for an Apple computer will not run on an Atari computer. The same problem exists for almost any computer you can name. This means that you do not have the freedom to purchase any computer that looks good to you, and then expect necessarily to have appropriate educational programs which you can use with that computer.

Software can be secured in two major ways. First, you can purchase programs from commercial sources. Second, you can write your own programs. Your future decisions on how to secure software will be a matter of the level at which you will wish to use microcomputers. At one level, you may wish to purchase all the programs you will ever need, and never consider writing one yourself. At another level, you may wish to learn to write exactly the programs you want. It is simply a matter of how much time and interest you want to invest in custom-making your computer programs.

Normally, a teacher purchases the programs that serve his or her needs. Later, when a teacher finds that commercial programs do not serve all his or her needs, the teacher learns how to write computer programs.

A special form of software is *courseware*. Courseware is any computer program that directs the electronics and hardware of a microcomputer such that the computer operates in some *instructional* (thus, *course*-related) manner. Courseware is an extremely important determiner of the classroom computer's behavior, and much of the rest of this book is devoted to explaining the principles of how to develop (or recognize) good courseware.

### Getting a Microcomputer Up and Running

Perhaps you are still a little leary about having a computer in your classroom. Maybe you are not convinced of its simplicity, and feel that it just may give you no end of trouble. Let us present a scenario that will describe to you what it takes to get a microcomputer in operation in your classroom. We prefer to leave the details concerning the selection of software and hardware for later chapters, so here we will simply skip over the criteria for purchase of the various items described in the scenario.

The principal has just given a teacher the go-ahead to get a microcomputer for his classroom. First, the teacher searches out all sources of software for his classroom. He goes to various computer stores (if nearby), he reads computer magazines found on bookstore shelves, and he contacts his local and national professional organizations for suggestions as to sources for software.

After reviewing software that can be applied directly in his classroom, he makes a selection. In this scenario, the teacher places a purchase order to buy, from a local dealer, a set of comprehensive programs that teach the arithmetic skills required for his grade level. Since this is a major package, the teacher will purchase the software first, via mail-order from the publisher, and then purchase the computer that will run the software.

The teacher has found in his reading that software is, in many cases, linked to one specific computer. That is, software developed for the Apple computer does not run on an Atari computer. Sometimes software developers write their programs for one computer, such as an Apple, and then rewrite the program for a second or third computer, therefore making it available on multiple machines. In the case of the teacher's choice of a math package, he finds that the program he really wants is available only for the TRS-80 Model 4 computer. He makes a decision to purchase this machine.

Our teacher decides to purchase his machine from a store in his community. He places a purchase order for a TRS-80 Model 4 computer, with two disk drives, and a printer. Soon two boxes are delivered.

Opening the larger of the boxes, the teacher discovers the microcomputer. The instruction book included in the box directs the teacher to simply unbox the computer and plug it in. The smaller box is opened, and the instructions show where to plug the printer into the computer, and how to load the paper and test the printer. One hour after the materials arrive, the microcomputer system is operable.

The teacher takes one of the mathematics program disks received earlier in the mail and slips it into a slot in the front of the computer (the disk drive opening). A push of one button activates the computer, and the disk takes over. The computer follows the electronic instructions written on the disk, the screen lights up, and the computer screen takes over the task of teaching mathematics. Everything the student needs to know appears on the screen.

The screen tells the student what buttons to push, how to enter numbers, when to push the ENTER key, how to quit the program, etc. The student only needs to follow the screen's written instructions. If an error is made, there rarely is a large consequence. The teacher may feel comfortable letting the student freely learn to use the program, since *there is no way to harm the computer by using the keyboard*.

Mere hours after the arrival of the computer boxes, a student is busy using the mathematics program in the classroom!

## Summary

By now you should know the major parts of all personal microcomputer systems presently used in classrooms and the function of each part. You should know the importance of software (courseware) to the microcomputer's functioning. In addition, you should be at ease with the concept of using a microcomputer in the classroom, since it is a machine that almost anyone can learn to operate. It is easy to learn to operate because, contrary to common belief, you do not need to know how a computer works in order to operate a computer.

With this foundation of knowledge of computers and computer programs, you are ready to learn some of the things microcomputers can do and cannot do in the classroom.

# Chapter 2
# Microcomputer Classroom Capabilities

### Introduction

*Instructional Intent.* Now that you know about the architecture of microcomputers, we can move on to examining the power and capabilities of the classroom computer. This chapter will help you to reach the following five objectives:

1. State seven major technical capabilities of the classroom computer.
2. Define two or three classroom capabilities of the computer for each of its seven technical capabilities.
3. Compare and contrast the microcomputer's two major instructional roles—CAI and CMI.
4. State the non-instructional roles the classroom microcomputer can play, along with their values and limits.
5. Discuss the limitations of the computer in the classroom.

In this chapter, we will identify and define the important characteristics of the computer that allow it to play instructional and non-instructional classroom roles. If you have a good understanding of CMI and CAI and what the computer can and cannot do in the classroom, you may want to go on to Chapter 3 and the topic of using systematic instruction with the computer.

*Knowledge Prerequisites.* It is important that you know the form and function of the microcomputer in order to understand the technical capabilities that provide the power for instructional and non-instructional classroom tasks. You should have reached the objectives of Chapter 1 before proceeding into this chapter.

------------------------------------------------------------------------

## The Power of the Computer

The best way for you to get a good overview of the technical power of the computer is to put down this book and go to an arcade that features "video games," those ubiquitous machines that go beep/beep/beep and are coming to occupy space in all your favorite stores, eating places, and movies. A video game is nothing more than a computer with a keyboard and screen, a microprocessor programmed for a game, and a speaker system for sound.

*Are you still reading?* Then we assume that you have not left for the arcade and you wish for us to describe to you the technological power of the microcomputer. Let us take you on the video game tour. As you read the next few paragraphs, be alert to the various capabilities of this ordinary "arcade computer."

As you enter the arcade, the first game you pass is calling to you with beeps and flashes. It is bidding for attention. The screen is in full color and is presenting synopses of the game to be played. On the screen is a written summary: "The highest possible score for this game is 40,000. The last player scored 25,575. The highest score ever made on this game was 38,595." The "keyboard" in front of you consists of two sticks, one for each hand, and two buttons for each thumb. The ends of the sticks rotate a full 360 degrees.

Upon your insertion of a coin, your mobile "player" appears on the screen. It is under full attack by some sort of space creature, and you can use one of the sticks to help it flee, and the button to resurrect it when escape fails. You can use the other stick and button to fire a weapon in various directions. There is a whole set of rules about who can attack what, when, how, and how many times. Creatures are moving. Colors are changing. Sounds are emanating from the bowels of the machine. The attacking creatures are "intelligent." As you learn methods to destroy them, they "remember" how you did it and never make the same mistake twice. They get smarter and smarter and move faster and faster as the game is played. Will you get smarter and smarter and move faster? No? Then you are doomed. Your player will be destroyed.

A flash of red and green signals that your 25 cents is gone. The creatures have won again. But you have scored 7,675 points during your stand.

The screen now reads, "The last player scored 7,675 points." (How is *that* for a gradebook?) You cannot let such a score stand. After all, you have learned a lot about the space creatures and how they can be destroyed, so you will definitely get a better score next time. And so goes the night. And your quarters.

**Technical Power**

Just think of the things that the video game-computer can do! It can store records, such as player scores, and display them as text. It has a full-color display, just like a color TV. It has stereo sound. The characters on the screen are not text, but are moving images and pictures. The game characters learn. An enemy space invader can watch your moves and learn how to avoid your actions, improving its performance as the game progresses. How does it do this? The computer has a memory which possesses the rules by which the game is played. Most importantly, the computer can make decisions. During the game, the computer must continuously decide if you are playing within the rules, whether your "shots" have or have not destroyed an invader, and so forth. Built into the computer may be some sort of electronic clock which times the game and regulates it in terms of progressive hardness by placing limits on the time spent by the microprocessor with any particular set of game rules.

All of these features of the arcade computer, and more, are available for the classroom computer. To date, educators have not been nearly as successful in the development of instructionally powerful microcomputer materials as developers of video games have been in tapping the microcomputer's technical power to produce materials with high entertainment value. But most limitations on the potential of the microcomputer for classroom instructional purposes do not presently lie within the *computer*.

The seven major technical capabilities of the computer of primary interest to the teacher are its ability to:

- produce and manipulate images on a screen that may include color and motion;
- produce and record sound directly;
- store in memory and retrieve from memory tremendous amounts of verbal and numerical information;
- tell time;
- compute any mathematical functions;
- make logical decisions; and
- control external devices.

**Classroom Competencies**

The technical capabilities of the microcomputer can be directly related to teacher and classroom activities. Let's take a brief look at some "classroom competencies." The following listing is not intended as a comprehensive cataloging of skills which the microcomputer can offer the teacher. It is intended simply as an illustrative sampling of the range and diversity of activities the microcomputer and its peripherals can perform.

*Visual Skills.* The computer's technical ability to manipulate images provides a number of classroom capabilities. It can:

- present text in any language;
- present images in any color;
- move images around in a pattern;
- fade, blend, merge, and flash images; and
- present moving pictures (stored on a videotape or video-disc).

*Auditory Skills.* The computer's ability to respond to and generate sound provides the following auditory capabilities. The computer can:

- present computer-generated speech;
- present music and sound effects;
- listen to and respond to spoken words; and
- coordinate the presentation of sound and image.

*Memory Skills.* The computer's memory capabilities provide, among other things, the following classroom capabilities:

- to store enormous amounts of verbal and numerical information;
- to know who is using the computer;
- to record all moves made or answers given by a student during a session or lesson;
- to keep records of test scores;
- to keep class records of lessons finished; and
- to store any type of written records—student files, listings of instructional materials, reference materials, etc.

*Time-Telling Skills.* The capability of the computer to tell time gives it these classroom abilities:

- to know/record the date a student uses a computer;

- to know/record how long a student uses a computer;
- to know/record how long it takes a student to work a problem or respond to a question; and
- to vary the speeds of visual/auditory presentations based on time data collected during sessions.

*Mathematical Skills.* The ability of the computer to perform math calculations enables the classroom microcomputer to:

- be used as a calculator; and
- simulate situations based on relationships between variables.

*Decision-Making Skills.* The capability of the computer to make decisions provides it with these classroom capabilities:

- to decide if a student's performance meets a given criterion;
- to decide how well a student is progressing through a lesson;
- to decide the level at which a student is answering questions;
- to decide if a student should continue studying a lesson or stop; and
- to decide which students have finished which lessons.

*Manipulation Skills.* A microcomputer can not only control its own functioning, but also it can direct other machines or devices in the performance of their tasks. This technical capability provides a number of additional classroom competencies:

- to direct a printer in printing on paper tests, lessons, or other information stored or produced by the computer;
- to direct the sending of messages from place to place—city to city or school to school—by telephone transmission through a telephone modem;
- to direct the presentation of recorded music or other sounds to students in lessons or tests by manipulating a record player or electronic musical instrument or noise-maker; and
- to direct the presentation of moving pictures with sound in lessons or tests by manipulating a videodisc player or other videotape recorder.

All in all, the microcomputer has skills which, if put to use, would make it a powerful classroom tool. In what ways could the classroom teacher make use of these classroom capabilities?

### Teacher Roles That the Classroom Computer Can Play

A teacher wears many hats. The teacher may be an instructor, teaching a given lesson. The teacher may also be a class manager, making decisions concerning what is to be taught, the sequence of lessons to be taught, how long to remain on a given lesson before moving on to the next, etc. Of course, the teacher may also be associated with many (too many?) tasks which are peripheral to teaching. For example, the teacher may act as a shopkeeper collecting money for books and milk, a nurse to sick children, a custodian, a secretary recording test scores in a gradebook, an entertainer to students, a psychologist to disturbed pupils, etc.

The microcomputer's technical abilities enable it, like the teacher, to play a number of roles in the classroom. In fact, the utilization of the computer in the classroom can be thought of as directly paralleling the activities of the teacher. The computer may be utilized to teach a specific lesson. It may be called upon to manage student progress by making decisions on the topics certain students should study; determine how long a student should study; decide when a student has completed studies on a given topic, etc. The computer can also be involved in tasks peripheral to "teaching," such as recordkeeping, housekeeping, producing study sheets, and other tasks to which all teachers devote considerable energy.

For purposes of discussion, the microcomputer's classroom roles will be divided into *instructional roles* and *adjunct classroom roles*. Instructional roles relate directly to the process of promoting learning and managing students' learning experiences. Adjunct roles include all those activities which commonly occur within a classroom, but which may not be directly involved in teaching new learning *per se*. As you will read, these two roles are not always discrete. We will first take a look at the main instructional roles. You will see how the microcomputer's technical capabilities can provide valuable assistance to the teacher in promoting and guiding a student's learning.

A number of acronyms have established themselves in the jargon of educational computing. "CAI" and "CMI" are two of the most prevalent, and we will be referring to these often throughout the book.

### Instructional Roles

*CAI.* CAI refers to computer-assisted instruction. A near relative to CAI is CAL, computer-assisted learning, a term commonly used in England and Canada for the same type of activity. CAI is the concept that the computer can present to the student instruction which will help the student to learn a fact or concept, or solve a problem. In the CAI mode, the computer is "teaching" something to the student. It is engaging in a direct attempt to cause the student to learn. This attempt generally takes place within the framework of a "computer lesson," and in this book we will try to limit our use of the term CAI to this sort of endeavor on the computer's part.

Just as there are various means by which a teacher can teach, there are a variety of ways that a computer can teach. The computer might present a lesson teaching students how to discriminate the letters "a,e,i,o,u" from each other in print. It could engage in promoting concept learning, teaching the child such concepts as "hot and cold," "near and far," etc. It could present the student with reading-comprehension lessons. A computer lesson could offer the student a simulation of a science experiment on the screen, and ask the student to take data in order to solve a problem. The computer could be programmed to conduct many of the same sorts of teaching activities that the teacher would conduct.

The most powerful CAI mode occurs when the computer is acting as a tutor. In this mode, the computer interacts with the student in a give-and-take process during the lesson. The student is active in the learning process. The CAI tutorial presents information and questions, and has the student react to the presentation. The computer then reacts to the student's input in ways which, if appropriately designed by the instructional developer, will promote learning. The computer-tutor is patient, organized, and demanding. The effective CAI tutorial function can be an important aspect of the classroom computer's instructional role.

*CMI.* CMI refers to computer-managed instruction, and connotes the utilization of the computer to manage student progress through a learning sequence. The lessons in the sequence may or may not be CAI. (In other words, the lessons may be conducted by the computer, but they could just as well be conducted by other means independent of the classroom computer, such as by the teacher or through other typical classroom activities.) Computer management of instruction can include presenting to the student learning goals and objectives, testing to determine student progress toward these goals and objectives, recordkeeping to illustrate and document student progress (for both teacher and student), and diagnosis and prescription of what the student should study next, based on his or her performance on previous objectives.

CMI may prove to be the most powerful application of the computer in the classroom! When the computer takes over the diagnosis and prescription aspects of classroom management, the teacher is freed to concentrate on what he or she does best—teach. Of course, the computer does not simply take over the management of learning in a class by being plugged into the wall. The computer must "know" the goals and objectives it is to manage. It needs to learn the names of all the students in the class. And it needs to have criteria for making decisions about how a student should progress along a learning pathway. But the research seems to indicate that the gains in learning earned by setting up a CMI system can be well worth any efforts required in providing the computer with the information it needs to manage the students' learning programs.

Just as teachers rarely separate their teaching and management roles, the CAI and CMI functions of the computer are often found in integrated forms. Computer courseware can include both a management function and an instructional function. In some instances, this dual function is called computer-based instruction (CBI) or computer-based training (CBT), but these are rather loose terms which very often refer to almost any function the computer may have in the classroom setting. In some courseware that is available, a teacher can choose whether to utilize only the teaching aspect of the program (CAI), only the CMI aspect, or both CAI and CMI.

### Adjunct Classroom Roles

There are numerous roles other than instruction *per se* for the computer in the classroom. It can present students with games (very valuable to the teacher for reward purposes) or with simulations (instructional as well as non-instructional), and can also be employed for student use as an artistic canvas or a musical instrument, and as a playground. It also can be used by the teacher as a tool for attitude development, or for assisting the handicapped. The adjunct roles of the computer will be expanding as teachers find new ways to have microcomputers act as their aides. We will examine here a number of the most valuable of these adjunct roles.

*Drill-and-Practice.* One of the most common types of computer programs found on the educational software market is the "drill-and-practice" routine. The computer is admirably suited to such a role, in which it presents to students lists of words for definition, mathematical problems for all sorts of calculation practice, and graphics and pictures for identification.

Most commercial drill-and-practice programs are basically non-instructional routines, since the computer really does not have the responsibility of teaching any new information. Drill-and-practice generally connotes a process of reviewing learning which has already been gained through some *other* instructional means, not necessarily a computer lesson. It means making sure that a given piece of learning is practiced sufficiently to maintain an appropriate student performance level. As most classroom teachers know, the need for appropriate drill-and-practice routines at the start of school after a long summer is significant. The microcomputer can be of tremendous benefit to the teacher in meeting this particular challenge.

There are a number of "stand-alone" computers available in toy stores which sell for a few dollars and feature drill-and-practice routines, including some which present words to students (actually say the word and then check the students' spelling of the words). Others present simple arithmetic drill-and-practice routines.

The strength of the computer in providing drill-and-practice lies in its ability to generate (or store) enormous numbers of practice problems and their answers. For example, in addition and subtraction the computer can present, for all practical purposes, *all* possible addition and subtraction problems. The computer can be programmed to generate the problems from a random set of numbers, calculate the answers, present the problems to the student, check his or her answers, and then provide prestored comments to the student concerning their acceptability.

There are a number of computer programs available which allow the teacher to create "flashcards" for student use, on specific topics pertinent to current classroom study. These programs require no computer programming skill. The program asks the teacher (or student) to enter the "flashcard words" and their complementary "answers" and, in an instant, the program is ready to run. The teacher can present arithmetic facts (12 x 3 = ? on one "side" of the flashcard, and 36 on the other "side"), or language drill (the French word ALLER means TO GO).

The drill pattern can be varied in a number of ways. Games can be established around the pattern in which the student earns points for doing questions at a certain performance level or at a certain speed (remember that the computer can monitor the student's speed as well as his or her performance level). Since a student's records can be kept by the computer on how many items the student gets right and wrong, the teacher can have the computer decide when the student has had enough drill on a specific topic.

*Values of computer drill-and-practice:*
- *it helps make student performance automatic;*
- *it can keep student's skills up-to-date;*
- *it is easy to program courseware; and*
- *the drill pattern is simple to use.*

*Limits of computer drill-and-practice:*
- *it can be boring;*
- *it rarely offers detailed feedback to the student as to why the answer is wrong; and*
- *it is seldom useful for promoting new learning.*

*Objective Testing.* The computer can be utilized to give objective tests to students, grade the tests, record the students' scores, analyze the test questions to determine if they are reliable, and store records until the teacher is ready to view them.

Some very sophisticated testing, which cannot be done with paper and pencil, can be accomplished on a computer. For example, the computer can utilize randomly-chosen questions from a bank of questions to produce unique, but parallel, tests for a class. Hundreds of children can take the same test yet not see the same sets of questions, or one child can take many different forms of the same test.

Computer tests are generally objective in nature. Multiple-choice, true/false, matching, short answer, and word correction are examples of such testing formats. Some programs have been developed to analyze written passages, but presently these are more in the experimental stages than ready for implementation in the typical classroom.

One example—a "quick quiz"—illustrates how a microcomputer can help the teacher in testing students. This program allows the teacher to type into the program up to 40 multiple-choice questions with four answer options per question. The program automatically stores the questions and answers. A student then sits at the computer, and it presents him or her with the teacher's questions. The computer corrects the student's answers using the teacher-determined correct answer, and it stores the score. The program can store up to 50 student scores. At the end of a testing period, the teacher can then request the computer to present him or her with the list of scores, showing how the students performed on the quiz. The quiz affords the teacher a simple, but effective, way to make sure that students have learned a given topic of study. Of course, the quizzes produced are stored on disk (or perhaps tape), can be used from year to year, and can be edited at a later time to change and improve them.

With the "quick quiz" sort of program, the teacher becomes an instant computer programmer, but *one who does not need to know anything about actual computer programming itself.* His or her "programming skills" consist only of the ability to put a disk in the microcomputer and type on a keyboard. Following the simple directions of the program, the teacher supplies the questions and the answers, and the computer does the rest.

Mastery-learning techniques are facilitated through the use of the computer to generate multiple tests on the same topic. A student can study, take a test, and if the student receives a "not-passed-yet" evaluation, can restudy and take another test. This procedure can be continued until the lesson is mastered, and the student will never receive the same test twice.

Another sophisticated computer testing technique is one in which the teacher establishes sets of questions that are arranged in hierarchies. The testing procedure starts in the middle of the hierarchy. If a student gets the first questions right, the computer makes the decision to move upward to a harder set of questions. If, on the other hand, the student gets these questions wrong, the computer moves downward to a simpler set of questions. In this fashion, the computer can quickly and easily decide exactly what level a student is at in a series of learning objectives. This type of testing is difficult to provide without a computer because of the large numbers of decisions and testing pathways which must be available during the decision-making process.

*Values of objective testing on computers:*
- *it can be used for new students for placement purposes;*
- *it can be used for off-line diagnosis for placement;*
- *it can present very complex types of testing procedures;*
- *multiple tests on one topic can easily be made;*
- *printed tests can readily be made available;*
- *banks of test questions can be established;*
- *it provides easy revision of test items; and*
- *it provides easy implementation of the mastery learning cycle.*

*Limits of objective testing on computers:*
- *it may be easy to cheat, if the same test is used for all students;*
- *it is limited to objective questions; and*
- *an objective test may not cover all the teacher's objectives for a unit.*

*Recordkeeping.* Aside from keeping records of a student's progress on a specific drill or lesson or on a test, the computer can keep for the teacher all the traditional classroom records. There are a number of programs on the market that provide such "recordbook" functions as maintaining daily attendance, keeping test scores and grades, and performing end-of-semester tasks such as summing and averaging of grades.

The computer can also be an electronic file cabinet, storing any kind of "papers" the teacher wants to store, such as tests, worksheets, grades, letters to parents, memos to other teachers, outlines of lessons, and lesson plans. The electronic filing system allows the teacher to keep all of these documents on a handy tape or disk for future reference or use. They can be read, or printed out, at the teacher's convenience.

*Values of recordkeeping on computers:*
- *it is easy to edit and/or update;*
- *it provides a private record;*
- *it is easy to store; it requires little space; and*
- *its programs perform all necessary calculations.*

*Limits of recordkeeping on computers:*
- *it requires the computer to look at the record; and*
- *it may double the bookkeeping effort if the school requires written records and the computer does not have a printer.*

*Word Processing.* The teacher can tap the ability of the computer to manipulate symbols and use the computer as a word processor. Word processing simply means handling text in efficient, electronic ways. When a word processing program is loaded into the computer, the computer screen turns into an electronic "sheet of paper." That is, a teacher can simply type text onto the screen, rather than onto a piece of paper.

Although this sounds like a simple concept, it is a powerful one. Imagine that a teacher wants to write a three-page lesson for a field trip his or her class will be taking. He or she wants to develop a brief outline of the trip, set expectations of what the students are to learn, and give some key words regarding the place the students will visit. Using traditional methods, the teacher might write the materials first by hand or on a typewriter and then revise them, re-doing a couple of paragraphs or pages, to add a few ideas. The written pages would then need to be prepared to get them to the students, so the material would be transferred onto a ditto page, either by copying the page or typing it onto the ditto, which would then be duplicated.

The word processing capability of the computer allows the teacher to type the original three pages into the microcomputer. The teacher can then revise, add, or eliminate materials, as desired. With word processing, this is extremely easy to do. When the document is "finished," it can be stored on a disk or tape under a specific name. When the teacher is satisfied that the document is ready for printing, he or she simply tells the computer to type it onto a ditto (depending on the type of printer connected to the computer) or other duplicating sheet. Next year, when the field trip will be repeated, the document can be retrieved and revised to represent the current situation (with the new date, the place, etc., easily substituted for those of the previous year).

The preparation of reports, storage of printed materials that are required from time to time, revision and duplication of the teacher's resume, storage of letters to parents (such as permission to take the field trip), etc., are all carried out effectively and quickly using the word processing capability of the computer.

Students can also make use of the word processing function. They would have at their command the ability to write reports and papers with ease and facility. The student-generated reports could be stored in the computer, and subsequently read and discussed by other students. Comments could be added by the teacher, and then removed later by the students as changes were made in the original. When the report reached a final stage, it could be edited by the computer for spelling and grammar, and then printed out. Very high-quality student papers would be the result.

In science, a teacher could create a science report form with a basic outline and explanation of what the report was to contain, i.e., purpose of the study, methods, results, data, and conclusions. The student would use the form outline to complete the report, deleting the teacher's instructions as he or she proceeded. Provision for such "skeletons" for students to flesh out is useful for compositions in many subject areas. The word processor has the capacity of duplicating the basic form for each student who needs to develop a report, a story, or other composition.

*Value of word processing:*
- *ability to develop and revise written text.*

*Limits of word processing:*
- *students and teacher must learn to use the word processing program; and*
- *the computer requires a printer.*

*Computer Games.* Many computer games have no instructional component, other than the simple motor skills of moving a stick to respond to changing variables on the computer screen. Many games, however, are designed to teach specific objectives; and, in some cases, game formats are appended to some other instructional tasks, such as when game points are given for accomplishments on drill-and-practice. In game interactions, one or more students participate, taking turns or working in groups. The formats of the game vary greatly, just as their paper or game board cousins vary, so no description will be attempted here. Most of the time, the games are competitive; fewer in number are those which require class cooperation to win. In all cases, the teacher should look carefully at a game to determine its *instructional* purposes and values.

*Values of computer games:*
- *they are highly motivational;*
- *some can be used with groups;*
- *they can help people dispel fear of the computer; and*
- *they can be used as a reinforcer for other activities.*

*Limits of computer games:*
- *they may not have any instructional meaning;*
- *some students may resent competition;*
- *some students may not like specific games;*
- *they are often created on the basis of violence; and*
- *they often require hard-to-program graphics.*

*Computer Simulation.* Simulations are a type of interaction not routinely employed in classrooms. In general, it is difficult to set up and perform a classroom simulation. The computer, however, does this task with relative ease.

A computer simulation is a situation in which the microcomputer establishes a set of conditions that are like some parallel set of conditions in the "real world." For example, the computer may depict a pond in which five types of animals and seven types of plants are living. The computer then allows the student to change certain variables concerning the pond, change the amount of pollution in the pond water, for instance, or have one of the plants destroyed by harvesting. The computer then changes the simulated pond in the same way that a real pond would change, given the new conditions.

This type of computer activity can be extremely valuable because it allows the student to experiment with the world in the safety of the classroom. It lets the student change parts of the universe that no one could ever really change, and it shows the results of his or her actions.

*Values of computer simulation:*
- *it encourages student thinking at a high level;*
- *students can perform experiments on the universe;*
- *it allows maximum student freedom in thinking patterns;*
- *it is highly motivational to some students; and*
- *it is a change from normal classroom procedures.*

*Limits of computer simulation:*
- *it is sometimes very difficult to program;*
- *it generally serves one student at a time;*
- *it may be time-consuming;*
- *the outcome may not be easily measurable;*
- *reasons for simulation changes may not be apparent; and*
- *a simulation may be a poor model for the real world.*

*Information Inquiry.* The power is growing to access information of likely value to the student in his or her studies. Encyclopedia companies are now providing such a service in the form of a series of disks which the student can use to access large amounts of factual information. Almost unlimited information is presently available through a number of wire services, which can be contacted if the microcomputer has a modem and access to the service (generally for a fee). Universities are providing more and more field services to classrooms, and a number have computer information available for student access.

*Values of information inquiry via the computer:*
- *it makes great amounts of information accessible right in the classroom; and*
- *the student can learn information research techniques.*

*Limits of information inquiry via the computer:*
- *it may be difficult to learn retrieval techniques; and*
- *the facts retrieved may be of little value.*

*Diagnosis and Prescription.* Another major form of student/ computer interaction is diagnostic/prescriptive interaction. The student and the computer interact to make a determination of what the student has accomplished, and what he or she should do next to accomplish more.

One area of diagnostic/prescriptive interaction is the choosing of a career or college. Computer programs are available that will diagnose and then prescribe which colleges could best serve the student's needs and interests. The computer explores all the parameters of attending college, such as the student's interests, how far he or she wants to travel, type of college desired (large, small), whether the student needs a scholarship, the student's academic performance, and his or her extracurricular activities. Next, the computer assigns weightings to those factors and makes decisions on which colleges best fit the student's situation. The computer then presents to the student a listing of colleges and their characteristics for his or her review.

Of course, the computer can also perform the more traditional role of diagnosis and prescription. For example, there is a program that tests students on their foundation abilities for the Scholastic Aptitude Test. It then prescribes exactly what they should study in order to insure they have all their basic language and math skills under control before they take the exam. Diagnosis and prescription can also play a major role in regular classroom learning as well, especially in computer-managed instruction.

*Values of diagnosis and prescription:*
- *it provides valuable decision-making information;*
- *it has easy administration and analysis; and*
- *it is fast.*

*Limit of diagnosis and prescription:*
- *its validity may be limited, resulting in poor advice.*

*Computer Dialog.* There are now computer programs which can talk with students, and can carry on a sensible (and, in some cases, profound) conversation. One such program is "Eliza." Eliza was developed by Dr. Joseph Weizenbaum in 1966 during his studies with artificial intelligence. This program is sufficiently sophisticated that some people suspect that it is not a computer at the other end of the conversation. Others have found Eliza to be a warm and sympathetic counselor, who almost always "says the right thing" to help students solve personal problems.

Computer dialogs are beyond the average programmer to produce, and there are not many available for classroom use, but the potential for this type of interaction is great enough that the teacher may consider having a dialog program in the classroom, especially in conjunction with computer awareness programs for children.

*Values of the computer dialog:*
- *it is very motivational for some students;*
- *it can capture students' interest in computers; and*
- *it has therapeutic possibilities.*

*Limit of the computer dialog:*
- *there is no firm evidence of what the dialog really accomplishes.*

*Applications Packages.* There are available for the microcomputer a number of types of materials that are not necessarily designed for classroom use, but that may play a valuable role in a classroom. "Applications packages" include such things as statistical programs, graphing programs, courseware on computer languages, graphics production software, and accounting programs.

Few of these programs are purely instructional, although most have instructional components pertaining to how to use the package. In many cases, the applications packages are extremely well-programmed to do specific tasks, and if that task fits into the teacher's broad classroom picture, they can be of definite worth.

*Values of computer applications packages:*
- *they fit specific tasks; and*
- *they are very useful when pertinent to a need.*

*Limits of computer applications packages:*
- *each is only good for one thing; and*
- *they are generally written for adults.*

## Limitations of the Computer

The computer is a machine, designed to do specific things. Although the lists of computer capabilities presented earlier in the chapter may have given the impression that the computer's power is unlimited, this certainly is not the case. There are a number of limitations to its power in the environment of the classroom, and the teacher should be aware of these.

### Computers Are Not Intuitive

The computer is extremely systematic in nature. It simply does not operate intuitively. This means that a microcomputer cannot do a teaching task, or any other classroom task, intuitively. In contrast to teachers, who may have great intuitive insight into what is and is not happening in the classroom, the computer has no intuition at all. *Computers do what they are programmed to do.* They will perform their classroom roles precisely as they are programmed to do—doing neither more nor less than they are instructed by their programs to do. To the extent that the classroom microcomputer has been told how to perform every aspect of every task it is assigned, it will be able to do a good job, but it will not be able to depart from its prespecified "behavior options" to behave differently or "better," as a teacher would be able to do when circumstances seem to call for it. Intuitive behavior is not part of the computer's nature.

Let's put this idea another way. A computer could be programmed to present a "perfect lesson," as determined by some set of criteria. For example, the lesson could be perfect in the sense it uses the most modern research about teaching and learning to present the lesson in a systematic manner. The computer would then present a perfect lesson to every student who sat at the computer. But no matter how perfectly the computer was programmed, it would have been programmed for planned actions and, limited by its nature, could not at any point switch to intuitive functioning.

### Computers Have Communication Problems

The average classroom computer has severe limitations in the ways it can communicate with students. Most of its communication will occur through its screen, and that screen typically will contain words.

In principle, of course, the microcomputer is not so limited. Demonstration computers have been set up which have the power to talk, respond to words, present moving pictures in color, and even control robots that are used to move objects. In principle, the microcomputer can do most of the essential things a classroom teacher does when fulfilling classroom responsibilities, albeit not as well. But, "in principle" is very far from "classroom reality." At this time, in the general sense, classroom microcomputers do not talk, listen to speech, present moving pictures in color, or move. These capabilities may be packaged into the "classroom robot" of the future, but they can be excused from our present thinking about using computers in the classroom—today.

The typical microcomputer available for classroom use today will communicate with students through its screen, which will most likely be a black-and-white (or green-and-white) one. Color and graphics are, of course, components of many computer programs used in classrooms, but both capabilities present financial and programming problems. It presently costs much more to develop computer programs which effectively use color and/or graphic images; hence, most programs designed for classroom use are primarily verbal in nature.

Sound from (and to) computers is in its infancy stage, and any available programs for the classroom in this domain will typically be simple and primitive; and, in general, will tend to feature sound for sound's sake. Interestingly enough, some of the best sound features can be found in the very inexpensive "toy" computers.

Communication via print (production of hard copy) is an important classroom feature, and this aspect is well within the realm of microcomputers now in classrooms. That is, printers of a very simple and inexpensive nature can be secured that are extremely reliable and durable.

But communication via the printer is often of more value to the teacher than to the student. Printers are in general quite slow, and utilizing the printer for large volumes of student materials creates logistical problems.

## Computers Can Be Incompetent

The microcomputer limitations mentioned above derive from the microcomputer's own nature and from current state-of-the-art development of microcomputer hardware and programming technology. All too often overlooked is the profound limitation on the microcomputer's capabilities of the state-of-the-art in instructional design for computers. Just because computers have the capabilities of being great teachers (or at least great teachers' aides), that does not mean these capabilities will be appropriately utilized. The most powerful computer in the world can be humbled by poor courseware design. And, if anything is true, it is true that there is a lot of poor instructional programming being sold for use in classrooms. In fact, just as a teacher who is unorganized, bumbling, absent-minded, or distracted will not be effective in promoting efficient and effective classroom learning, neither will a classroom computer be able to perform classroom roles effectively, unless its courseware has been carefully designed to provide it with a systematic way of handling its instructional responsibilities.

As a teacher, you will want to take steps to ward against the presence in your classroom of a bumbling, ineffective microcomputer. The key, of course, is to see to it that your computer's performance is not limited by poor programming or sloppy courseware design.

Quality programs do exist, and you will want your microcomputer to be told how to behave in your classroom by such programs. You may find the search for well-designed courseware somewhat frustrating, but it is important to assure that your computer is competent in performing the classroom tasks that you assign to it. Although you may find that quality computer programs which fit your exact needs are not currently in abundance, this problem should be alleviated as the teacher demand for specific programs increases and more developers devote energy to the careful design of such programs.

### Computers Can Be Costly

The average classroom teacher, or school principal, may find the cost of the microcomputer to be a limiting factor in its use in the classroom. Although the power of the computer may be great, an expenditure of hundreds of dollars to thousands of dollars for a piece of classroom equipment may be prohibitive. Even if the money is there for the purchase of one or more microcomputers, the teacher may find that an individual student can use up a lot of computer time on a given lesson, thus reducing the cost-effective use of the computer, and creating logistical problems.

Research has clearly shown that computer installations can be cost-effective in terms of comparing the amount of learning which is provided by the computer and that provided by other means, such as a teacher. Research has also clearly shown that computer installations can be inordinately expensive. Sometimes they are merely expensive classroom toys. Whether or not the classroom microcomputer is cost-effective depends on how it is used. Good instructional programming can make the computer in the classroom an inexpensive learning tool. Again, the key to good computer applications lies in the courseware, which will govern the application of the computer.

### Summary

It is clear that the computer can be a powerful classroom tool, whether used as a computer-teacher (CAI), as a computer-manager

(CMI), or for performing adjunct classroom tasks, such as keeping records of the milk-money fund or printing parent reports. The computer has many technical capabilities that can be utilized to augment and supplement the teacher's roles in the classroom. The computer can handle a range of responsibilities from mundane drill-and-practice tasks through the teaching of problem-solving, and do it well.

At the same time that the computer has great potential as a classroom assistant, however, it has great potential for being a flop. The computer is severely limited, and the extent to which these limitations are not recognized and compensated for is the extent to which the computer may be a "dud" as a teacher's helper or a plain "disaster" as a teacher itself.

Computers are new to classrooms, and, in some ways, they are presently "visitors." That is, the state-of-the-art for computers has not yet reached a level where the average teacher has a great deal of trust that the computer can truly teach, at least not without the expenditure of much more energy than the result is worth. The rest of this book will speak to this point. It will present a systematic approach to the development of microcomputer instructional materials, in the hope that thoughtful design and development can be utilized to produce effective and efficient classroom computers, truly deserving of teacher confidence, and welcome in classrooms as permanent residents.

# PART II
# DESIGNING LESSONS

Chapter 3: The Well-Trained Computer-Teacher

Chapter 4: Defining Lesson Purpose

Chapter 5: Developing Performance Measures

Chapter 6: The Processes of Instruction

Chapter 7: An Example Computer Tutorial Lesson

Chapter 8: Fine-Tuning the Processes of Instruction

# Chapter 3

# The Well-Trained Computer-Teacher

### Introduction

*Instructional Intent.* This chapter presents the concept of a well-trained instructional computer. The goals and objectives of the chapter are:

1. Compare and contrast the strengths and weaknesses of the human teacher and the microcomputer.
2. Describe three phases in the computer-teacher's training process.
3. Discuss the rationale behind developing systematic instruction for the computer.
4. State the three boundary conditions of the instructional computer's teaching capability.
5. Discuss in terms of developing quality computer instruction the following three terms: (1) purpose, (2) measures, and (3) processes.
6. State three general design steps to be taken when developing a systematic computer lesson.

*Knowledge Prerequisites.* This chapter builds on the concepts of the first two chapters. Teaching experience is helpful in understanding the presentation of the computer as a "student teacher." More specifically, it might be helpful to think back to practice teaching experiences, including the first day you walked into a classroom. Your skills and competencies as a teacher then were probably far below those you possess today. Just as a neophyte student teacher has a great deal of enthusiasm, but not necessarily practical teaching skills, the neophyte computer has a great deal of technical power, but does not necessarily have a great deal of instructional power. A good teacher is the result of capability and an effective training program. It is the same pattern with a computer.

---------------------------------------------------------------

## The Teaching Responsibility

There are many definitions of teaching. Some limit the concept to a human endeavor; others are broader. Our conception is that the teaching responsibility is to cause a desired change in a learner's attitudes, skills, or knowledge. Any of these changes would be evidenced by some modification of the student's behavior. The keyword in our definition is "change." Without a change in a student's behavior, learning has not taken place. Whether performed by a human or a computer, *teaching is the purposeful attempt to help students to learn.* The better the teaching, the more successful is the attempt in achieving the changes in student behavior that are desired.

There are many things a teacher can teach better than a computer. (There are also many things a computer can teach better than a teacher.) One of the things that teachers do in a marvelous fashion (compared to a computer) is to teach intuitively.

### The Versatile Human Teacher

One great strength of the human teacher is the teacher's ability to operate in a classroom in both a systematic (planned) and an intuitive fashion.

The average teacher is a blend of intuitive and systematic teaching behaviors. Most teachers do not simply walk into the classroom and start to teach. Much of the day is systematically planned utilizing course guides, school syllabi for various subjects, and weekly and daily lesson plans. At the start of a new unit, the teacher may sit down and write out a set of goals and objectives for the new unit. He or she searches out all the learning materials for the unit, both in his or her classroom and in the learning resource center. He or she finds appropriate films and audiotapes, and plans activities to make the unit more interesting. He or she may even write tests ahead of time that will allow him or her to decide if and when the students have learned the unit. After all the plans are made, the unit is presented to the student.

But the intuitive teacher knows when to abandon a given plan if he or she senses things are not going right. While "teaching according to plan," the teacher can sense the climate of the classroom and make instructional decisions based on many subtle clues. On a given day, the teacher may sense that the students are working as a team and that it is a good time for group study of a given topic. On another day, the teacher may find the class is not acting as a cohesive group, and that an attempt to organize them into a group instructional activity would be doomed to failure. It may be the day, the lesson, the students, or the teacher who is going wrong, but the intuitive teacher can sense problems and depart from the plan.

### The Not-So-Versatile Computer-Teacher

Alas, the computer, being composed of a number of circuits and wires, operates only in a planned fashion. *It has no power to behave intuitively*.

It is not our intent to get deeply involved in the semantics of whether a computer can or cannot behave "intuitively." For the purposes of this book, we will simply state that the computer does *not*. Computers cannot modify their own planned behaviors (except in *planned* ways). We do consider computers to have definite "behaviors," however, and it is not anthropomorphizing to write in this manner. Throughout this book, we will describe computers in terms of their having the capability of exhibiting certain behaviors that are "trainable," i.e., capable of being brought under control through the use of an appropriate instructional design and computer program. Just for the fun of it, on occasions, we will blatantly anthropomorphize to emphasize the role of instructional design and programming in determining what the computer will do in the classroom.

Certain inherent rules govern computer behavior, rules built in by electronic engineers. These rules force onto the computer certain parameters, thus establishing the arena within which the computer can be a good (even great) teacher. It is possible to maximize the computer's teaching capability by paying appropriate attention to the computer's basic constitution—recognizing its inability to behave intuitively and taking advantage of its ability to behave exactly as it is trained to behave.

### The Computer as a Student Teacher

Your new computer has arrived and sits on the table in front of you. It has the potential to be a good teacher, but at the moment it is a blank slate. It is ignorant of the teaching behaviors it will be expected to display when it assumes the responsibility of teaching a student. In essence, it is the ultimate in a student teacher. The computer comes to you with no preconceived notions of what a teacher is, or should be. It has no prejudices, no fear of principals, no guilt for subjects poorly learned, and no concern for working long hours at low pay. You can make this electronic Eliza Doolittle into a great teacher. How?

The computer must be trained exactly what to teach, how to teach, and how to know when a student has learned something. Actually, training a computer how to do these things is much easier than educating student teachers. Many of the rules on how to teach the computer to teach are clearly and exactly known. Who can say the same for the training of student teachers?

Your *tabula rasa* teacher brings to you one great behavioral trait. It is completely willing to listen to what you want it to do, and then unquestioningly, to do it. Within the limitations of its mechanical and electronic capabilities, *it will teach exactly the way you train it to teach*.

### Training the Computer

There are three major phases in the process of training your computer to teach: (1) instructional design, (2) computer programming, and (3) running the program (see Figure 3.1).

1. *Instructional Design.* The instructional design phase is the heart of the computer's training program, for it is here that decisions are made about what and how the computer will teach. The outcome of the decision-making is a complete design for the instructional pattern the computer will use when it is teaching.

2. *Computer Programming.* The instructional design must be translated into a computer program. This means putting the design into a form that the computer can understand. This task must, of course, be performed by someone who knows how to write computer programs.

3. *Running the Program.* Last in the series of training steps is the actual communication of the commands to the computer,

*Figure 3.1*

*Phases in Computer-Teacher Training*

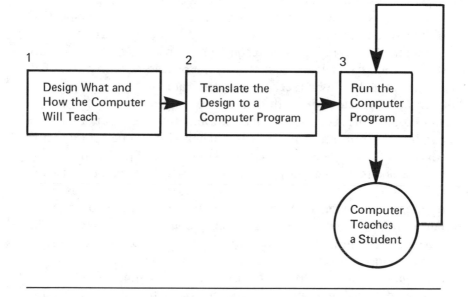

translating into action the original instructional design. The computer program is "loaded" into the computer from the disk or tape on which it has been stored, and when the program is "run," commands are given to the computer that control its teaching behaviors. In other words, the original instructional design is at last made functional by the running of the computer program on the machine in the classroom.

Now that you understand some basics about how to work a microcomputer, you will recognize that the actual training process, at least from the computer's point of view, really occurs in the last of the three steps. In fact, knowing what you do about the computer's "short-term memory," you will probably see quite readily that this last training step will be repeated each time you decide you want your computer to take over a teaching task. It is the nature of the computer that it needs "reminding" by a computer program of what it is to do. Running the program again and again is, in effect, repeatedly training the computer to perform its teaching responsibilities.

Of course, the computer's perspective on its training is not the focus in this book. We must view the process from the perspective of the teacher, who is looking to the computer to assist in the classroom by assuming some teaching responsibilities. When we do so, we find that it is the first step in the process—the instructional design—that should be receiving our attention.

In fact, we can look to those last two steps as simple translation and communication steps necessitated by the fact that the computer is not a human student teacher who can be told directly what and how to teach. These steps are simply required so that we can "speak to the computer" and tell it what we expect it to do. Once an instructional design for computer instruction has been developed, the step of translating it into a computer program is fairly straightforward, albeit a possibly complicated task. We will leave the teaching of how to program computers to the many books and courses on the subject, although the topic of programming is explored in Chapter 11. And, as we have explained, providing the computer program to the computer by way of a tape or disk will be an everyday event for you if you invite a microcomputer into your classroom. So, it is that first step in the computer's training process that you will need to know about if you are concerned about the quality of your microcomputer's performance in its teaching role.

### Training for Competence

You are aware that your computer will not be able to use teaching intuitions while it teaches, but you can still expect it to competently perform those teaching responsibilities to which it is assigned, relying on its capabilities in the systematic arena. After all, computers can perform many planned tasks beautifully. Poor design of computer instructional materials and/or poor programming, however, can result in a computer which exhibits teaching behaviors that are not systematic at all. A computer which is neither systematic nor intuitive is plain and simply operating in a haphazard or random fashion. Such a computer could never be a good teacher, and in some ways may be harmful.

Sadly, much of the computer courseware presently on the market, although usually well-programmed (Figure 3.1, Step 2), quite clearly permits (trains) computers to display sloppy teaching behaviors. It is Step 1 in the training process which most often determines the computer's instructional performance. It is the quality of the instructional design itself that must be questioned when a computer performs poorly as a teacher, and it is to this phase of your computer's training that you must look if you want your computer to be a good teacher.

The focus of this book is on the question of how computer-teachers should act in order to be good teachers, and on how to translate the answer to that question into the appropriate design of computer instruction. We propose that you see to it that your computer is trained by appropriate design to conduct its teaching in an extremely systematic fashion. In this way, you will know exactly how the computer is supposed to behave in its teaching role. You will know what the computer is supposed to teach, how it will accomplish its instructional tasks, and how the computer will know when it has finished its job. Appropriate instructional design to promote systematic teaching behaviors will ensure that your computer performs its teaching not in haphazard or ineffective ways but in the manner which can be expected of a well-trained computer-teacher.

### A Systematic Framework for a Computer's Training Program

To have maximum effectiveness as a teacher, a computer must be carefully trained to teach in a systematic manner. The design of systematic instruction for the computer is founded on three major premises.

1. Computers are most effective when dealing with measurable student performance. Computer instruction is most productive when the purpose of a lesson is to teach content which is measurable using a computer, i.e., knowledge and skills which can be measured with an objective test.

2. The computer needs tools to measure when and if a student needs a lesson or has completed a lesson. To be a good teacher, the computer must be provided with valid and adequate measurement tools for the assessment of student performance.

3. The computer needs to be given specific instructions as to how to help students reach a lesson's learning goal. Effective computer instruction requires that these instructions be guided by this lesson goal, and that they present the student with those events of instruction which will best help the learner reach the goal.

These three concepts—appropriate and precise purpose, valid and adequate measurement tools, and specified instructional processes consistent with lesson purpose—are the hallmarks of quality computer instruction. They are completely interrelated with each other; hence, one good way of illustrating the three ideas is with a triangle. (See Figure 3.2.)

### Training the Computer-Teacher

Let's take a better look at how to produce a good computer-teacher by carrying out the instructional design part of its training according to the criteria illustrated in the systematic framework, and in this sequence: (1) defining lesson purpose, (2) providing measurement tools, and (3) defining processes of instruction.

### Defining Lesson Purpose

The first step in the design of computer instruction is symbolized by the *purpose* corner of the triangular framework. To create any lesson, you must know where you want the lesson to go. In other words, you must define your educational intent. To create a good computer lesson, you must define that intent in terms of the learning that the lesson is supposed to produce.

Learning is a change in behavior; hence, the teaching job of a computer is to change student behaviors. If a biology student walks up to a computer and is unable to list any major parts of the cell, and walks away from the computer being able to list three parts, the computer has created a change in the way the student

*Figure 3.2*

*A Framework for Systematic Instruction*

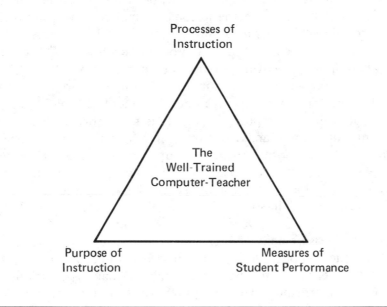

Processes of
Instruction

The
Well-Trained
Computer-Teacher

Purpose of                                   Measures of
Instruction                          Student Performance

acts. The computer has altered the student's behavior. The computer has taught something, and the student has learned something.

Due to the nature of a computer, you must define the purpose of any computer lesson you plan to design in terms of the precise student behavior that you want the lesson to produce. This purpose must be explicitly stated. (You may or may not choose to provide such an explicit statement of lesson purpose to the student during the lesson, but it needs to be in explicit form before the instructional design process proceeds.) You must precisely describe the terminal or end behavior that you want the student to have after completing the lesson. In this way—and only in this way—will you be able to design a way for the computer to know how to tell when a student has successfully completed a lesson. Remember, the computer is not capable of intuition.

When you precisely describe the desired student behavior in writing, you have identified the *performance objective* for the lesson. A student completes a computer lesson when the student can exhibit to the computer the behavior specified in the performance objective of the lesson. In Chapter 4, we will present the procedures for defining and writing a lesson's purpose in the form of such objectives, so that you can do this important first step in training your own classroom computer.

To the extent that a lesson offered on a computer has no terminal performance objective underlying and guiding its design, it is not really a computer lesson. It is some sort of "computer presentation," and is analogous to something which appears on TV and has little aim other than to occupy an individual's time with some moving pictures and sound. A precise description of the terminal behavior desired for the student must be the focus of an effective computer lesson.

### Providing Measurement Tools

Once the computer lesson's purpose is defined, you must make clear to the computer how to go about making decisions on student performance. The computer must have some means of deciding when a student is displaying the behavior the lesson is supposed to teach. It may need to decide at some point during the lesson presentation, or perhaps even before the lesson is presented. Whatever the case, the means for making the decision must be provided in the computer's training. In simpler terms, the computer must be able to measure student performance before, during, and after the lesson in order to make computer decisions on the student's study and learning performance. The second aspect of training a computer to conduct a good lesson is to provide it with the tools to make computer decisions. The computer needs *measurement tools*.

As you know, you cannot expect the computer to make an intuitive judgment that the student "really knows the lesson" and to give you a report. It must rely on objective measurements made of student test performance if it is to provide you with an accurate statement of student accomplishment. Using test performance data, it can indicate for any student whether or not a lesson objective has been mastered or remains to be mastered.

The appropriate measurement tools for systematic computer instruction are a special kind of objective test. It is composed of a set of available objective test items for each performance objective to be taught by the computer. Such *objective-referenced tests* are quite different from typical objective tests used in the classroom. The objective-referenced test is written specifically to measure one and only one performance objective. When you write such a test, you then can indicate to the computer the level at which the student should pass the test to show that he or she has achieved the desired behavior given in the objective.

### Defining Processes of Instruction

The third aspect of the computer lesson framework is concerned with the series of steps a computer must take to lead a student from the start of the lesson to the end of the lesson. This series of steps starts when the student begins the lesson and ends when the student can perform the set of behaviors which the lesson was designed to produce. A computer lesson is successful when these processes get the student's performance to the level specified as the desired terminal performance.

Therefore, with the desired performance specified and the tools for measuring whether or not the performances are satisfactory, you must in this last instructional design step specify for the computer those *events of instruction* which will promote the desired learning, so that it can provide the instruction to the student. The successful lesson design will provide those instructional events which do indeed move students from their beginning performance level to mastery of the lesson objective (as demonstrated on an objective-referenced test of the objective).

If the student is learning on the computer and is restricted to instruction presented on the computer, the instruction must be complete and effective enough to be entirely successful. The instruction must be very comprehensive so that the student can successfully acquire the performance desired as a result of having interacted with the computer. As a developer of instructional computer lessons, you will need to attempt to make the events of instruction foolproof, so that most students studying the lesson on the computer will be able to achieve the objectives of the lesson.

**Another Look at the Systematic Framework**

The triangular framework provides a good model for illustrating the interrelationship between the three components of a systematically-designed computer lesson.

The *purpose* of a lesson can only be achieved through having an effective process of teaching and some method of measuring whether or not the purpose has been achieved.

Purpose ⟶ *Processes—Provide Means to Achieve Purpose*
*Measures—Determine if Purpose Is Achieved*

The *processes* of a lesson can be developed only if the reason for the lesson is clearly defined and there is some method of determining if, during the course of a lesson, a student has or has not completed a lesson.

Processes ⟶ *Measures—Determine if Processes*
*Continue or Stop*
*Purpose—Provides Direction for Processes*

*Measurement* is of little value in and of itself. The computer-teacher utilizes measurement to make two decisions: first, whether the purpose of the lesson has or has not been reached, and second, during the presentation of the lesson, whether to continue the teaching steps (processes of lesson) or stop them (lesson completed).

Measures ⟶ *Purpose—Has It Been Reached?*
*Processes—Should Processes Continue?*

With the three integrated concepts, you have a triad for good computer instruction and the basis for producing systematic computer lessons that fully exploit the capabilities of the microcomputer to be effective.

**Computer Lesson Design**

Let us show you how the framework of systematic instruction will be used in the chapters immediately following as we present the techniques to be employed in the design of instruction for the microcomputer.

Chapter 4 will cover the designing and writing of a performance objective to define a lesson's purpose.

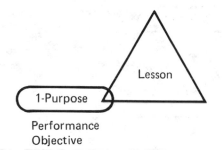

Performance
Objective

A performance objective defines for
the computer the desired student
performance at the end of the lesson.

Chapter 5 will cover the designing and writing of objective-referenced tests to measure a performance objective.

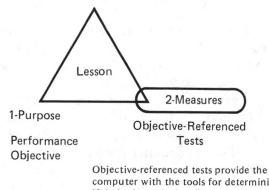

1-Purpose

Performance
Objective

Objective-Referenced
Tests

Objective-referenced tests provide the
computer with the tools for determining
if desired terminal performance has or
has not been achieved.

Chapter 6 will cover the designing and writing of those events of instruction intended to help the student to achieve the performance objective of a lesson.

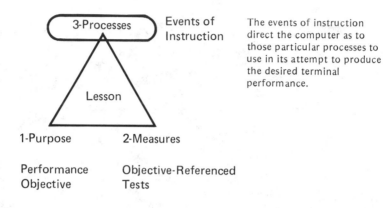

When you have completed Chapters 4 to 6, and learned to perform the procedures involved in each of the three aspects of systematic instructional design, you will then be able to implement them in sequence according to the "simple instructional development model" (see Figure 3.3), in order to produce systematic computer lessons.

The systematic approach to lesson development will be a tool which can serve you well in your relationship with the computer. It will allow you to develop effective instructional materials, or to decide if someone else has done the same.

At this early stage in the use of computers in the classroom, it is important that computer instruction be *quality instruction*. It is important to give students the concept that computer learning is "good learning." A good computer lesson can form a foundation of good attitudes toward the computer. If a computer lesson is a boring, frustrating, or disorganized endeavor, the student may form a negative view of computer learning that will remain for

*Figure 3.3*

*A Simple Instructional Development
Model for the Design of a CAI Lesson*

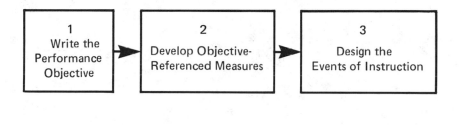

---

some time to come. Good learning means that the lesson "works" and that students learn efficiently on the computer. *Only when computer lessons have been carefully structured and planned will they work effectively and efficiently.*

# Chapter 4

# Defining Lesson Purpose

## Introduction

*Instructional Intent.* The first challenge in training a computer to be a teacher is in deciding what instructional task it is to perform. This chapter will show you how to pursue and accomplish this important step in the design of computer-assisted instruction. As presented in the last chapter, the well-trained computer's teaching framework consists of three major ideas:

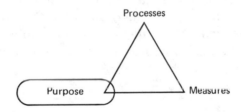

This chapter looks in detail at the purpose aspect of the triangular framework. Its goals and objectives are:

1. Describe briefly the importance of the goal-setting/objective-writing endeavor.
2. Define and relate to each other instructional goals and performance objectives.
3. Relate the development of goal statements to the concept of appropriate target populations.
4. Relate the development of goal statements to the concept of the appropriate use of the computer as an instructional medium.
5. State three components of a precise instructional objective.
6. Identify the characteristics of a complete and well-written computer objective for use in computer lesson design.
7. Describe how to develop a learning map of goals and objectives.

The practice of utilizing goals and objectives in teaching has become quite common, but it is seldom as rigorous as is required for a computer application. Even if you know how to write well-formed performance objectives for a specific goal, and how to create learning maps, we would still recommend your reading this chapter on computer objectives before moving on to the next chapter, dealing with objective-referenced measurement.

*Knowledge Prerequisites.* This chapter starts an in-depth study of the three foundation elements of a well-trained computer, i.e., purpose, measures, and processes. It is important to remember the definitions and relationships of these elements as presented in the previous chapter.

-------------------------------------------------------------------------

## Defining Instructional Intent

### The Need to Define Purpose

A student is attempting to learn how to do a word problem in arithmetic proportion in her fourth-grade math class, and she is having trouble. The teacher senses her problems, and decides that she might better learn this task using the microcomputer. The teacher locates the computer disk on teaching proportion and hands it to the student. The student goes to the computer, turns it on, inserts a disk, starts the program, and is on her way. Here is what the student sees on the screen:

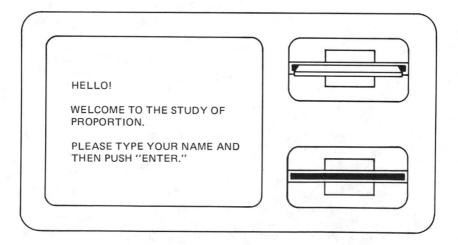

HELLO!

WELCOME TO THE STUDY OF PROPORTION.

PLEASE TYPE YOUR NAME AND THEN PUSH "ENTER."

*Note*: Some computers will have a "RETURN" key rather than "ENTER."

The student types "Betty Martinez" and pushes the ENTER key on the microcomputer keyboard. The computer lesson on proportion starts.

*What should the computer present on its next screen?* The computer cannot behave like a teacher, who, when holding a tutorial, could simply start the student at any point and see how well she did with the topic. A teacher can pick up a math text, select a few word problems, say, "Let's try these and see how you do," and then proceed according to the circumstances encountered in the student's endeavor to work the problems. The computer simply cannot operate in such an intuitive fashion and be the least bit effective. The decisions regarding the screens Betty sees during her proportion lesson must be made long before she pushes the ENTER key. Planning the sequencing of screens in a computer unit or lesson is not a complicated task, but it is one that requires some detailed and systematic thinking.

## Educational Purpose

The general pattern of developing instructional materials is to move from general statements of instructional intent to specific statements of intent. The statements of general intent are commonly called goals, and there may be several layers of goals in an educational setting. For example, the school philosophy may have a goal of "teaching mathematics to all students." A mathematics course implemented to contribute to the reaching of this goal may have a course goal of "teaching students to use proportion in their daily lives," and there may be a unit within the course which has a goal of "teaching students to solve a word proportion problem." Hence, the link between school philosophy and student behavior involves transition from the global purpose toward more precise statements of educational intent.

Notice how, in Figure 4.1, a broad philosophical goal radiates into more specific goals.

The goals of the school philosophy generate course goals, which generate courses, which generate unit goals. A unit goal generates specific lessons, each lesson having a precise statement of instructional intent.

*Figure 4.1*

*Stating Educational Intent*

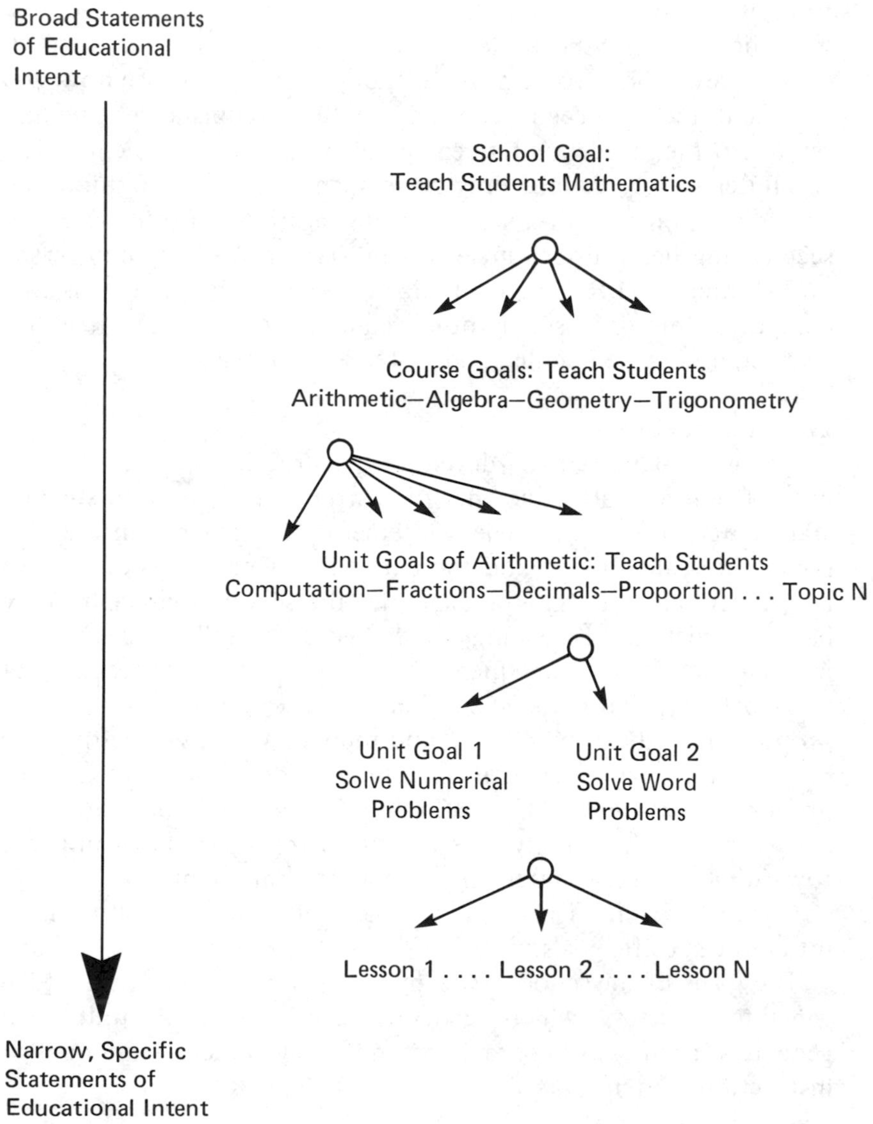

Broad Statements
of Educational
Intent

School Goal:
Teach Students Mathematics

Course Goals: Teach Students
Arithmetic—Algebra—Geometry—Trigonometry

Unit Goals of Arithmetic: Teach Students
Computation—Fractions—Decimals—Proportion . . . Topic N

Unit Goal 1
Solve Numerical
Problems

Unit Goal 2
Solve Word
Problems

Lesson 1 . . . . Lesson 2 . . . . Lesson N

Narrow, Specific
Statements of
Educational Intent

In this chapter, we will provide you with principles to guide the writing of goals for computer units, and performance objectives for computer lessons. Since these two terms—units and lessons—are used in many different ways in educational circles, we want to clarify the way these terms will be utilized here.

> *A computer lesson is instruction designed to reach one specific objective.*
>
> *One or more lessons comprise an instructional unit (or sub-unit). All of the lessons in a unit have a common goal.*
>
> *One or more units comprise a course. All of the units in a course are directed toward achieving the course's goal.*

Rarely, if ever, will an individual teacher attempt to develop a full course on a computer. This is an undertaking which requires many thousands of person-hours of work. Hence, in this book, we will restrict ourselves to discussing the design of a unit of instruction, having a few lessons in each unit. Once the principles and procedures for the design of units have been mastered, it is an easy task to expand them to course design.

## Developing Unit Goals

The first step in designing systematic instruction for the computer is to determine and state the broad goal for the computer unit you wish to develop. Examples of unit goal statements might be: At the completion of this biology unit, the student will understand the concept of a food chain; or, at the completion of this geography unit, the student will understand some of the factors which cause the settlement of towns and villages at specific environmental locations, such as on rivers and harbors. Instructional goals are valuable because they define the domain within which more explicit statements of educational intent can be defined.

When you write a goal for a unit, you must make sure the goal is appropriate to the learners whom it is intended to instruct. Some goals may be exactly the same for a wide range of learners. For example, the goal—"the student will learn to correctly pronounce Spanish"—might be used with any learner from the first grade through adults. The goal—"the student will learn to apply the First Law of Thermodynamics"—would not be reasonable for individuals not having the appropriate background for the unit.

In addition to insuring that the goal is appropriate for the students, you should make sure that the goal is appropriate for use on a computer. If the unit goal were in creative writing, the computer probably might not be the appropriate medium. If, however, the computer medium did seem appropriate, you must then make sure the instructional power of the computer matches the goal. If the goal were to teach first graders primary colors, you would need to make sure a computer with color capability was available. If the unit had a map-reading goal, you would need to make sure the computer handled graphics appropriately. Here are sample goals for two proportion units which have a target population of fourth-grade students. The goals are quite appropriate for using the computer as the instructional medium.

> The student will understand how to do proportion problems in mathematical form.

> The student will know how to solve proportion problems in the form of a word problem.

As you can see, these goals are not stated in a definitive fashion, and they are not measurable. How can the computer tell if an individual "understands" how to do a proportion problem? When does a student "know" how to solve a proportion word problem? It is not possible to look into the mind of a student and discover if he or she knows or understands a topic. The question of whether a student knows something need not be answered at the goals level. The fact that neither goal is directly measurable does not make the goals of lesser value. Goals are road signs which point to the pathway you will follow in designing computer instruction. Performance objectives are the markers along that pathway. They state exactly which turns you are to make and when to make them.

## Deciding Exactly What to Teach

Once you have identified an instructional goal for a unit, statements of educational intent that are much more specific must be stated. Good computer instruction requires very specific statements of educational intent. Following the development of a unit goal, the key question that must be asked is:

> When a student using the computer finishes this computer unit, what will he or she be able to do that he or she was not able to do when walking up to the computer to begin the unit?

A student sits down at a computer and starts to study a unit. He or she studies for two hours. If the student walks away from the computer being able to do exactly what he or she was able to do when first sitting down at the computer, it is clear that no learning has taken place. If the student is unchanged by his or her interaction with the computer unit, he or she has not learned anything. If the student can do something after the unit that he or she could not do before, then the student has learned something. If the student can do something new after the lesson, but you do not know about the new behavior, you do not know that learning took place.

From a systematic perspective, learning consists of observed changes in behavior. There are many reasons for accepting this definition of learning when developing instruction for computers. Most important among these is the fact that there is no way for the computer to determine if something is or is not inside a student's mind. Yet, the computer must be able to determine if a student has or has not learned. Some acceptable standard for learning must be adopted. The computer needs a standard for learning which it can observe and measure. Therefore, at the present time, the easiest and most accurate method of determining learning is to determine changes in student behavior.

**Lesson Objectives**

Goals provide direction to instructional units. Lesson direction is controlled through the use of precise statements which can guide both the development of computer lessons and the progress of students through the lessons. Specific statements of instructional intent are called objectives. Objectives are the benchmarks against which the entire lesson development effort is measured. Actually, there is no systematic manner to determine if a lesson is good or bad if there are no objectives against which to compare the instructional aspects of the lesson.

There are many different names for objectives in educational literature. There are performance objectives, behavioral objectives, criterion objectives, terminal objectives, enabling objectives, instructional objectives, and so forth. In almost all cases, these names refer to specific statements of educational intent. Their general characteristic is that they attempt to state in measurable terms some capability or task that a teacher wishes to teach. When well-written, they state this capability with such precision and in such words that anyone reading the objective (teacher, student, principal, parent, evaluator, or board member) will have the same idea about the objective and the learning outcome it describes. That is, everyone concerned with the lesson will know exactly what performance is expected of the learner when a lesson on the objective is finished. There is no doubt as to what a learner will be able to do as a result of successfully completing the lesson.

*Characteristics of Precise Objectives.* To minimize ambiguity and achieve precision, objectives are generally written so that they include the following three characteristics:

    (1) a statement of the intended student behavior;
    (2) a statement of the conditions under which a behavior is expected; and
    (3) a statement of how well the student should perform the expected behavior.

In order to be appropriate for instructional purposes, objectives should stipulate observable behaviors. So the first feature of a good objective is:

1. Objectives are stated in terms of observable behaviors. They define what a student does to prove he or she has learned something (or already knows it before the lesson starts).

An example of an observable behavior is:

The student correctly spells words out loud . . .

The statement describes a student performance which can be easily observed and evaluated. The performance represents the condition that the student "knows" the spelling words.

The second feature of a good objective concerns the idea that the behavior called for in the objective could possibly be performed under a number of different circumstances, and that these circumstances could affect that performance. That is, a student could demonstrate a capability such as spelling in a variety of environmental circumstances. Spelling words out loud, for example, is a behavior that could be demonstrated: (1) in front of the class, (2) in private with the teacher, or (3) in front of an audience at a spelling bee. The environmental conditions under which the student is expected to demonstrate that he or she has learned something is a very important factor in his or her ability to perform the objective.

Therefore, the second major feature of a good objective is:

2. Objectives state the conditions under which a student will demonstrate that he or she knows something.

An example of this feature is:

While standing in front of the class, and given words spoken by the teacher from Spelling List A-5, . . .

The third feature of a well-written objective states how well a student will perform a given behavior in a given environment. Let's use the previous example again. How many spelling words is the student supposed to learn and be able to spell at one time? Is the student expected to get all the spelling words correct (mastery-level learning), get 90 percent correct, or get half correct?

3. Objectives state the criteria for a successful demonstration of student performance.

For example:

> Will correctly spell 80 percent of 25 words presented. . .

Putting together the three features of a well-written objective, using our previous example, produces the following objective:

> While standing in front of the class, and given words spoken by the teacher from Spelling List A-5, the student will correctly spell 80 percent of 25 words presented.

*Distinguishing Between Clarity and Value.* The example of a spelling objective was chosen to demonstrate that writing an objective and writing a valuable objective may be two different tasks. This example objective may or may not be a good way to have the student demonstrate that he or she knows his or her spelling words, but regardless of its value, it is a correctly written objective. That is, it does contain the three elements which define a good objective, and it is sufficiently precise to fit our requirement that everyone in the learning setting can easily agree on what is expected of the learner.

The strength of an objective lies in the clarity of meaning that the objective imparts. If we were to present our sample objective to a group of ten teachers, we might get a good discussion going as to whether or not the conditions are good for students, whether the criterion of success (80 percent) is too high or too low, and whether Spelling List A-5 has words which are appropriate for this age group. The one thing we do not get is an argument over "what the objective means."

One weakness of objectives can be that although they look rigorous and imposing, with all their features clearly spelled out, an objective can define meaningless learning tasks. Thus, "Spelling List A-5" may be a list of words which are of little or no value to the student. A well-written objective never guarantees a valuable learning experience. But, regardless of its value in an instructional program, an objective simply may not be appropriate to the computer medium and will need tailoring if it is to serve as the basis for design of a computer lesson.

### Stating an Objective for a Computer

There are few logical reasons to attempt to pursue the development of a computer lesson to teach some behavior which is not demonstrable and measurable using a computer. For a computer lesson, you must develop an objective which asks the student to perform a behavior that he or she can demonstrate to the computer, and for which the computer can provide the particular conditions. For example, it is not feasible to have the previous spelling objective as the objective of a computer lesson. The typical classroom computer can neither say the words in the teacher's place, listen to the student, nor evaluate the performance of a student spelling words out loud before a class. However, teaching correct spelling is certainly within the computer's classroom capabilities.

To design a computer lesson to teach students to spell the words in Spelling List A-5, the teacher must decide how a student's spelling performance could be elicited by and made observable to the typical microcomputer. How can the computer ask the student to spell, and how can the student demonstrate to the computer that he or she knows the correct spelling of the words?

The variety of conditions a computer can set up for a student is severely limited by the computer's communication modes. As we have said before, the typical classroom computer will communicate via its screen, which places strict limits on the circumstances it can present to a student.

Similarly, the student's ability to respond to the conditions imposed by the computer will be limited. Student responses to the computer normally are limited to typing words, selecting letters and numbers, and placing marks in various places on the screen.

Finally, the computer is restricted in its ability to judge how well a student performs an objective. The computer must use objective measures of performance.

### The "Computer Objective"

Computer professionals have an acronym which, although overused, is accurate. They characterize a bad program as GIGO.

This acronym stands for "garbage in, garbage out." It means when the computer produces a tangled-up mess of information, it is the result of a tangled-up mess of information being fed into the computer initially. The way to get GIGO in computer-assisted instruction is to skip or skimp on the writing of good objectives for computer lessons.

Although it is highly doubtful that educational literature needs any additional designations for objectives, we feel compelled by necessity to introduce you to the concept of a "computer objective." A computer objective is one which performs the same task as all the other objectives, i.e., making an unambiguous statement of educational intent, but it is a statement which is tailored to the teacher's task of writing objectives for a computer. The computer objective is used to define in measurable terms expectations for what a computer lesson will teach.

Computer objectives are special cases of traditional performance objectives. They have the same three components, but they are severely restricted in their scope by the limitations of the computer. For all practical purposes, the computer screen sets the limits on the conditions under which a student can perform. Text presentation, graphic illustrations, and objective testing characterize the field upon which the student will demonstrate that he or she has learned something.

The assumption made when using a computer objective is that a student has learned the lesson when he or she can pass a test on the lesson. We will describe the computer testing situation as one in which the computer presents to the student "a set of items to respond to," and then evaluates the student's responses to the items presented.

Figure 4.2 illustrates aspects of the testing situation in which the computer elicits student performance. Typically, the computer screen presents to the student one item at a time to respond to, and normally that item is only one of many items that could have been presented to cause the student to attempt to execute the behavior the teacher wants the student to be able to perform successfully at the end of the lesson—the lesson purpose. A test item for a computer lesson can be seen, therefore, as one

*Figure 4.2*

*The Computer Presents a Single Test Item*

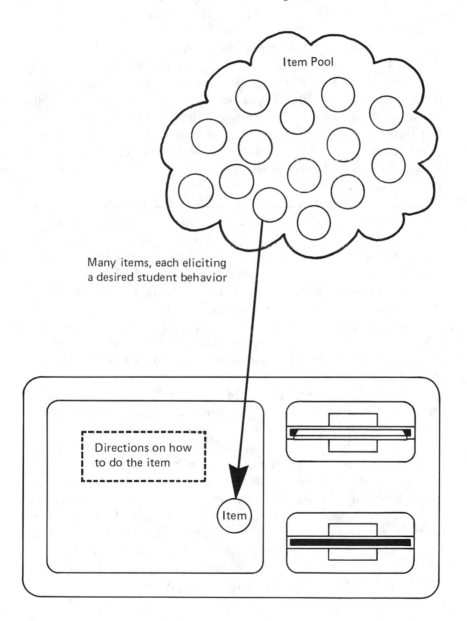

representative of a *class* of test items, with all members of the class representing that behavior which the teacher has in mind as the desired terminal behavior. *The computer objective explicitly describes the class of items the computer can present.*

Suppose that the teacher wants a lesson to teach the student to identify various regular two-dimensional shapes. The teacher decides that the desired terminal behavior for the student is being able to point to the shape in a set of mixed shapes when given the name of any shape. The desired performance and conditions thus known, you can see that there could exist a rather large number of test items, each of which would involve the student in selecting a shape from a set of shapes. Obviously, the teacher's precise instructional intent for this lesson involves limiting this domain of possible items to a specific *class* of items.

One possible class of test items would be defined if the teacher intended the student only to learn to identify triangles, squares, and circles by name. If that were the precise purpose of the lesson, then only triangles, squares, and circles would be candidates for presentation in items. A somewhat more difficult terminal objective would include ellipses, parallelograms, and trapezoids, in addition to the three shapes already mentioned within the item class. In essence, it is possible for the teacher to define the precise intent of the lesson by being specific about the actual class of items that would be candidates for inclusion on a test of the lesson.

Of course, whatever the item class, each test item would attempt to engage the student in the same basic behavior (here, identifying shapes by name) under basically the same conditions (in this case, when given the shape in a mix of shapes).

A test item for a computer lesson can be thought of as a single representative of a class of test items, any one of which could have been presented to obtain a sample of the student's ability to perform the behavior that the lesson is intended to teach. The class of test items that represents the objective of the lesson should be describable by the teacher. For example, here are two classes of items for two different lessons, each lesson having as its intent teaching students to identify shapes by name:

Lesson A:  five two-dimensional shapes (circle, triangle, rectangle, diamond, and ellipse)

Lesson B:  seven two-dimensional shapes (circle, triangle, rectangle, diamond, ellipse, trapezoid, and square) and
four three-dimensional shapes (pyramid, cone, paral-
lelepiped, and sphere)

You can see that two item classes describe two different lesson
objectives. Although in both cases the student's behavior would be
identical (pointing out a shape when it was named), the teacher's
instructional intent (and, therefore, the student skill measured)
would definitely be different. The specific class of test items
described by the teacher defines the performance domain that the
student is to master.

In order to write a good computer objective, you will need to
clearly define the class of items which will be used to determine if
and when a student has completed the lesson. Below are some
examples of items that represent larger classes of items. Each item
is one of a class of items defined by the teacher to represent the
intent of a lesson. Take careful notice of how the teacher has
defined the class of items, and therefore the objective.

Multiply these numbers:
23 X 135 = < ? >

The larger class is defined in this case as all two-number
multiplication problems in which no number has more than three
digits.

Mark the word that is spelled correctly:
<   > receive <   > recieve

Here the larger class is defined as all words with the letters i and
e in adjacent positions.

Name the river marked with the arrow on this map.
THE <                          > RIVER

The larger class is defined as all rivers in a list of North American rivers.

The name of the President who had the nickname "Old Hickory" is:
A. Andrew Jackson
B. George Washington
C. Richard Nixon
Letter of your answer: <    >

The larger class is defined as all known Presidential nicknames.

Complete this sentence: Bob and Joyce <  > both from Chicago.

Here the teacher has defined the larger class as sentences of ten or fewer words which use "is" and "are" as singular and plural verbs.

As you can see from each example above, the conditions under which the student is to execute performance of the desired behavior, and the behavior itself, are clear from examination of a single item. The class description accompanying the test item provides the additional information needed to clearly indicate the teacher's objective for the lesson in each case. Without much difficulty, you can probably imagine several different item classes (and, therefore, different objectives) for each of the above examples.

Let's take a look now at what you know thus far about what is involved in framing a performance objective for a computer. By now, you should have a good idea of two aspects of a computer objective. You know that every item presented on the computer screen will be from the general class of items to be defined by you as the intent of the lesson. You also know that each item will elicit a behavior from the student in which he or she attempts to demonstrate the terminal performance that you desire students to achieve in the computer lesson.

Think about the limitations of the testing situation as it is pictured in Figure 4.2. It is the screen that you will use either to present the items from the general class of items, or to indicate receipt of the student's response. Since space on the computer screen is limited, it will generally only contain directions to the student, an item to elicit student performance, and a place for the student to respond.

Now let's look at what happens inside the computer when the student does respond to the screen's presentation. The student's response to an elicited item is corrected, and a decision is made whether to present more items or declare the student as "passed" or "not-passed-yet." In order to have the computer perform this decision, you will need to stipulate how many items will be presented, and what level of performance is acceptable as a "pass" for the lesson (percent correct of the items presented).

To write a complete computer objective, therefore, you need to be able to state for the computer all of the information shown in Figure 4.3.

### Writing a Computer Objective
The essential task in developing a computer objective is stating exactly what class of items the computer should show the student in order to get the student to demonstrate that he or she can do the performance that is the intent of the lesson. You must decide how you will elicit an appropriate response from the student. For example, in the case of the spelling objective we used previously (where any class of items, whatever their form, would be defined by the spelling words on Spelling List A-5), a decision must be

*Figure 4.3*

*Writing a Computer Objective for a Lesson*

1. State how the computer will get a student to respond to the presentation of a class of items. (Clearly describe the item class!)

2. State how the student is expected to respond to the computer (to show he or she can perform the desired behavior).

3. State the number of items to present and the percent correct the computer should use to judge the student's performance as acceptable.

---

made as to what the teacher wants the student to do in order to demonstrate that he or she can spell correctly those words that the lesson is intended to teach. Some possible, appropriate conditions are: (1) asking the student to identify correctly spelled words, (2) asking the student to identify incorrectly spelled words, (3) requesting that the student type a correctly spelled word into a blank in a sentence, (4) having the student type a word spoken on a cassette tape, (5) asking the student to retype incorrectly spelled words, and (6) having the student type from memory a short list of words.

To convert our example of a classroom spelling objective into a computer objective, the conditions have to be changed to something the computer can handle, such as:

> When the computer presents to the student a word from Spelling List A-5, spelled correctly or misspelled but recognizable, . . .

To elicit a response to the presentation of information, the computer will also have to provide a question or directive statement on the screen to which the student will be asked to respond in some fashion. If the student can satisfactorily perform what the computer asks him or her to do, the teacher will have one sample of the student's ability to perform the desired behavior.

You must be careful to structure the computer's elicitation direction or question in a manner appropriate to the task. For example, if your goal is to have students spell words correctly in written composition, a computer objective could be written to have the students respond to the computer by writing, and the objective would be appropriate to the task. If the students in the class are preparing for a spelling bee, the original performance objective of having the students spell words in front of the class in response to the teacher saying the words would be appropriate and the computer would not. You must always think about what the student is actually doing on a computer, and constantly ask the question: Is the student's behavior appropriate and valuable?

Continuing the spelling example:

> When the computer presents to the student a word spelled correctly or incorrectly, the student will identify a correctly spelled word by placing an "X" beside it.

You have just stated how the student should respond to the conditions set up by the computer. This step corresponds to the statement of intended student behavior in the traditional objective. The objective must also state exactly how the computer will decide if the student has successfully attained the terminal performance the lesson intends to teach. The computer objective should tell how many items to present from the class of items (in our example, the class is defined by the words from Spelling List A-5), and what percent of correct responses is acceptable to show that the student has completed the lesson. If there is a time factor involved in the objective (e.g., "the student must complete the procedure within three minutes"), it should also be stated in the objective. Note the appropriate form to convey the information on the number of items and percent correct:

> When the computer presents to the student a word spelled correctly or incorrectly, the student will identify those spelled correctly by placing an "X" beside it. (25 items, 80%)

The importance, meaning, and methods of setting the appropriate number of items to present and the acceptable level of performance will be topics of discussion in the next chapter.

Here are some other computer objectives which include all three aspects of a well-written computer objective, although in some cases, a description of the class of items has been drastically abbreviated over what would actually be written in order to adequately convey the teacher's intent to the computer.

1. When presented with a map of the United States, having a major river illustrated, but not named (largest rivers of the U.S.), the student will type in the name of the river. (10 items, 75%)

2. When presented with an illustration of a right triangle, with all angles and the length of two sides defined, the student will type in the length of the third side. (7 items, 100%)

3. When presented the directions to find the topic sentence of a paragraph (paragraph no higher than seventh-grade reading level; topic sentence can be in any position, but must be clear), the student will place a marker on the sentence. (5 items, 75%)

4. When presented with an illustration of a cell having a line leading to each of five cell parts, the student will type in the name of each cell part. (4 items, 100%)

5. When presented with a graph of data, the student will interpret the general trend of the graph, choosing the correct description of the graph from five trend choices for each graph. (5 items, 80%)

6. When presented with the simulation that the student is the president of a large chemical manufacturing plant that places toxic wastes into a stream, and presented with data concerning his or her profits and the degree of pollution caused by the materials produced to generate the profits, the student will calculate the rate of production that will produce an acceptable level of both profit and pollution. (5 items, 60%)

## Learning Maps

Normally, a teacher does not teach objectives (lessons) in isolation. More often, the teacher is teaching a course, with one or more units, each composed of several lessons. The organization and planning of a series of lessons is an important aspect of computer instruction.

**Analysis of Learning**

When designing a segment of computer instruction, you should analyze the goals and objectives of the instruction, placing them in an appropriate sequence for optimal learning. The resulting sequence is called a *learning map*. In many cases, the learning map can be presented to the student to help him or her make decisions about and/or organize his or her own learning.

You develop a learning map by starting at the broadest statement of educational intent, and work your way down until the entire sequence of learning events has been described. Although the complete procedure will not be employed each time you want to design a specific lesson, the theoretical progression is: *program goals* to *course goals* to *unit goals* to *sub-unit goals* to *terminal lesson objectives* to *enabling lesson objectives.*

In this book, we will limit ourselves to considering educational intent that is sufficiently narrow in scope to be feasible for the development of computer instruction. This means that we will not examine the analysis of learning (development of learning maps) for educational goals that are broader than unit or sub-unit goals.

*Learning Maps for Goals.* The key to the development of a unit learning map is this: Beginning with the general statement of instructional intent of the unit—a clear and unambiguous statement of what you expect your students to understand or be able to do at the end of the unit—you ask the question: "What should a student know in order to be able to reach this goal?" Then you record your answer to this question as one or more sub-unit goals. Each "answer goal" will, of course, be narrower in scope than was the initial goal statement, but, taken together, the sub-goals are often a rough equivalent of the broader goal with which you began. On a learning map, these prerequisite goals are recorded beneath the goal being analyzed, as a means of indicating that their achievement is necessary to achievement of the broader goal.

Treating each sub-unit goal that was generated in the same manner as you did your main unit goal (i.e., inquiring what a student must know or be able to do to achieve the goal), you are able to generate one or more even narrower prerequisite goals to the particular target goal being analyzed. You keep asking the analysis question of each goal statement until you reach a point in analysis where you can safely assume that most students beginning the unit would already have achieved the goals being generated in the analysis process. The more complex any goal being analyzed, the more statements of prerequisite goals will likely be necessary.

When you have generated the set of goal statements that represent what your students will learn in the unit (above what they already know), writing each set of narrower "answer goals" underneath the "question goal" being analyzed, you will have the graphic representation of the unit's goals already written in the form of a learning map for the unit.

Figure 4.4 shows the top portion of one such learning map for a unit on reading comprehension. In asking the question, "What should the students be able to do to better analyze what they read?," a teacher has identified three sub-goals. To achieve the main goal, the teacher has decided the students will need to be able to weigh importance of ideas, to evaluate appropriateness and objectivity, and to analyze their reading for content relationships.

For each sub-goal identified, then, the teacher can again ask the question of what students need to be able to do before achieving it. As an example of how the questioning process continues with each goal that is generated, Figure 4.4 shows goals identified by the teacher when he asked himself what the students need if they are to achieve his content analysis goal.

Questions of the first sub-goal generated (weighing importance), although not shown in Figure 4.4, might have such answers as ability to identify the main ideas in a passage, or to locate details in a passage. Questions of the sub-goal on appropriateness and objectivity might yield answer goals such as identifying bias or spotting the use of persuasion techniques. Further questioning could lead to even more basic prerequisites. It can be seen that as the analysis proceeds, the goals may become more and more precise in their meaning and easier to picture as candidates for translation into performance objectives.

As we have stated before, points will be reached in this analytical process when subordinate goals generated will already be within the students' repertoire. Further analysis need not

*Figure 4.4*

*A Learning Map for a Reading-Comprehension Unit*

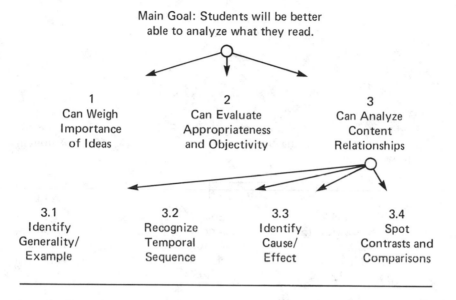

Main Goal: Students will be better
able to analyze what they read.

| 1 | 2 | 3 |
|---|---|---|
| Can Weigh Importance of Ideas | Can Evaluate Appropriateness and Objectivity | Can Analyze Content Relationships |

| 3.1 | 3.2 | 3.3 | 3.4 |
|---|---|---|---|
| Identify Generality/ Example | Recognize Temporal Sequence | Identify Cause/ Effect | Spot Contrasts and Comparisons |

continue whenever such an event occurs during the questioning. There will probably be considerable variability among Goals 1, 2, and 3, above, in the number of prerequisite goals generated beneath them in the learning map.

Once an entire set of goals has been generated, you will be able to decide how to plan for units of instruction. Often, each goal will stand alone as an instructional unit. You can then readily plan a learning sequence, beginning with a goal at the bottom of the map, and plan to "teach your way upward."

Figure 4.5 is an example of just such a situation. Here the unit goal is sufficiently narrow that the sub-goals are more appropriate as segments of a main unit, or perhaps translated into the form of performance objectives for lessons. The teacher's main intent, as seen from this learning map, is that the students learn to use

*Figure 4.5*

*A Learning Map for a Dictionary Unit*

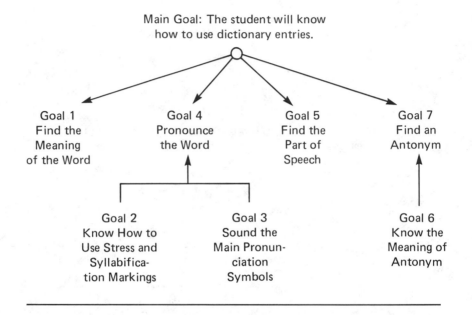

features of a dictionary entry. By examining the four sub-goals that the teacher has deemed prerequisite to the main unit goal (written immediately beneath it), you can see more clearly what the teacher intends the students to know about dictionary entries.

In some cases, a unit learning map presents a simple linear sequence of goals (such as when the teacher determined, upon analysis, that only Goal 6 was needed for inclusion in the unit as prerequisite to Goal 7). More often, the map will be represented in more of a downwardly branching hierarchical fashion, in which two or more goals seem to be required for the learning of a higher-level goal. These prerequisite goals may not be prerequisite to each other, however, as can be seen with Goals 1, 4, 5, and 7 in Figure 4.5. In order to learn the use of a dictionary entry, it is not necessary to learn any specific part first.

The goal at the bottom of a learning map represents knowledge which is determined by the person doing the analysis to be prerequisite to the goal above it, and so on upward through the map. The typical student entering the unit should definitely not have achieved the goal at the top of the map but should definitely possess all the prerequisites for those goals at the bottom of the map. (Some students may, in fact, have already achieved a goal or two at the bottom of the map.) Thus, the learning map defines for most students the sequence of learning tasks that they will accomplish during the unit of instruction.

*Learning Maps for Objectives.* The discussion of learning maps thus far has dealt only with the concept of deriving an appropriate patterning of instructional goals for optimal learning. The same concepts apply to the arrangement of computer objectives into learning maps.

The objective at the top of a map represents the terminal computer objective, and when it is achieved, it is assumed that the student has learned the goal for the unit. Other objectives below the terminal objective are prerequisite to the objective. The number and arrangement of objectives on a learning map are dictated by the complexity of the learning event. A learning map of spelling objectives would be a very simple progression from one set of words to the next. The map of learning to do mathematical word problems in proportion would be much more complex.

Just as with goals, you develop a learning map of objectives by starting at the top, asking the question of what the student must know (be able to do) in order to perform the top objective. The answer to this question identifies the performance which is prerequisite to the terminal objective. This procedure continues until you are sure that most of the students in your class can perform the lowest objectives in the map.

Figure 4.6 is an illustration of a learning map for objectives using a goal taken from a goals learning map.

In this learning map, each objective represents one lesson, with the student progressing from the bottom to the top of the map. The first objective, just above the assumed entry-level skill, defines the starting point of the learning sequence. This objective should

*Figure 4.6*

*A Learning Map of Objectives*

---

Goal: The student will identify the
main idea in a paragraph.

---

↑

---

Terminal Computer Objective

Given on the computer screen a fourth-
grade level reading passage (not more
than three paragraphs of not more
than five sentences each), the student
will mark the sentence having the
main idea. (5 items, 85%)

---

↑

---

Given a reading passage (fourth-grade
level, one paragraph of five sentences),
the student will mark the topic sentence.
(10 items, 90%)

---

↑

---

Given a reading passage (fourth-grade
level, one paragraph of three sentences),
the student will mark the topic sentence.
(10 items, 90%)

---

↑

---

Given two sentences, one with a major
idea and one with a supporting idea,
the student will type an "M"
beside the sentence having the major idea.
(15 items, 90%)

---

⌂

---

Entry-level skill: Being able to read at
fourth-grade level.

---

represent a student performance which most students entering the lesson could either already perform, or be expected to learn to perform rather easily.

## Functions of Objectives

Objectives have three major roles to play in instruction.

1. The use of objectives provides a method whereby you can develop an unambiguous statement of instructional intent. You can make exact plans as to where each student is going on his or her computer. Objectives allow you to make planning decisions, such as whether your objectives are valuable, or are in the correct order for effective instruction.

2. Objectives can be used to tell students what they are expected to learn. After you have utilized the goals and objectives for planning purposes, they may be incorporated into the lesson, providing direction for both the student and yourself in the teaching/learning endeavor.

3. Objectives provide the explicit statements of educational intent which allow valid and reliable measurements of student progress to be made. Objectives are the statements which are utilized to develop computer tests of progress. When objectives are written in terms of observable (by the computer) student performance, the computer has no problem evaluating student learning in terms of the objectives, as you will see in the next chapter.

## Summary

On the basis of this chapter, how should a microcomputer be trained to behave in order to be a well-trained instructional computer? A number of rules are clear. The well-trained computer will always:

- present units and lessons prepared on the basis of explicit written goals and computer objectives;
- present lessons based on computer objectives that are arranged in a systematic manner, according to a learning map;
- present lessons which are based on computer objectives

that are written in such a way as to define the class of
questions the computer will present, the response that a
student should demonstrate, and the criteria for successful
performance; and

- present the goals and objectives for a given lesson to a
  student to guide his or her studies.

This chapter began with a student sitting down at the computer
to study a unit on proportion. A question was posed: "What
should the computer present on its next screen?" This chapter has
provided some answers to that question. You now know that all
screens that will be presented subsequently to the student will be
derived from an underlying structure of goals and objectives,
arranged in a map representing an appropriate sequence for
learning.

In the next chapter, we will explore the question of how the
computer can be trained systematically to measure whether a
student has or has not reached the objective for a lesson. Then, in
subsequent chapters, we will develop the systematic processes used
to actually design the screen presentations that will teach a
student how to achieve the objective.

# Chapter 5
# Developing Performance Measures

### Introduction
*Instructional Intent.* This chapter presents the characteristics of a computer that is well-trained to assess student performance and progress during computer-assisted instruction. This chapter focuses on the second aspect of computer instructional design—the design of computer measures (tests).

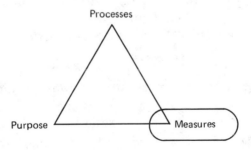

By developing appropriate performance measures, you provide the computer with the information it needs in order to make decisions concerning student learning.

The goals and objectives of the chapter are:
1. Compare and contrast the traditional norm-referenced test with the kind of test employed in CAI.
2. Define an objective-referenced test.
3. State the major decisions a computer makes using objective-referenced tests.
4. Identify the characteristics of a well-written objective-referenced test item.

*95*

5. Compare and contrast an objective-referenced pretest and posttest.
6. Define the characteristics of computer-generated test items and tests.
7. Define validity and reliability in objective-referenced tests.
8. State how to set the level of performance for an objective-referenced test.

*Knowledge Prerequisites.* It is assumed that you have professional knowledge and skills on the writing of objective test items, such as multiple-choice, true/false, matching, and completion items. Because good computer instructional measurement rests on the foundation of performance objectives, it is extremely important that you have the performance objective concept firmly established. There are many works available for teachers on the topic of objectives (see Appendix A).

-------------------------------------------------------------------------

## Varieties of Testing

The type of testing discussed in this chapter is objective-referenced measurement, with which you may or may not be familiar. The information presented here may seem simple and logical, or radical and foreign. The measurement tools employed for use with computers are extremely systematic and learning-oriented. Thus, the concepts in the chapter may challenge some cherished traditional ideas about the purposes of classroom measurement.

### A Brief History

Computers are new to classrooms—while testing and measurement seem "old hat." In reality, testing is not all that ancient. It is within this century that teachers have utilized measurement tools which allow them to compare a student's work to some sort of standards.

Originally, standards were established within the classroom, and classes were small enough in the one-room schoolhouse for a teacher to make individual judgments on how Johnny or Suzie was progressing. Later, as the one-room schools were combined into larger and larger units, and as student mobility from community to community grew, the need developed for tests which would make broader comparisons among students. Thus developed the classroom, district, and subsequently nationwide standardized tests of student performance.

Standardized tests of student performance were founded almost universally on the concept of comparing students with students. There are many reasons for the evolution of this point of view in the educational community, but for whatever reason, the concept that the purpose of a test is to compare a given student with his or her peer population became the standard. Today, many national tests of academic performance reflect this philosophy.

The most outstanding examples of this comparison concept are the national college entrance exams, such as the Scholastic Aptitude Test (SAT) or the American College Testing program (ACT), and achievement tests in all subject areas. All of the college entrance tests and many achievement tests measure and report student performance strictly in terms of accomplishments which are compared to peer performance. The result of this procedure is a ranking of students from high performance to low performance, in a classic "normal distribution" of scores. Often, this procedure yields some sort of grade equivalent statement that places a student at a specific grade level.

Traditional measures are admirable for their ability to rank students according to their knowledge of a given content domain. Traditional testing is not admirable in that the procedures tell nothing about what a given student does or does not know that is useful for planning study or instructional experiences (in any sort of specific manner). After administrating an achievement test in mathematics that establishes grade-level performances for students, there is no way for a teacher to determine what specific knowledge any student had or lacked that caused him or her to achieve a given score.

For example, assume student X wishes to go to college. He takes the SAT and receives a low score in comparison with the other students who took the test. The student decides to study hard and improve his performance the next year. Can he use the information he gets back from the SAT (score, ranking, and, if requested, the set of questions and answers, with his answers) to help him study for the next exam? The answer is an unqualified NO. The purpose of most national tests is to rank students (or groups of students), not to provide data for teaching and learning.

A similar situation can occur at the elementary level. A

third-grade teacher gives his students a mathematics achievement test, which results in his receiving a listing of students and their grade-level performance. Based only on the test results, what should the teacher do to help the students who are below grade level? There is nothing the teacher can do, based on test results, to plan instruction, since the test only provides information on each student's place in a spectrum of student performance at various grade levels. The teacher will need to look elsewhere to define what it is that a student is doing or not doing that causes the student to score below grade level on the math achievement test.

The purpose of many teacher-made classroom tests is also to rank students—nothing more. Many aspects of public education are established in such a manner as to encourage, and, in fact, demand of teachers the use of procedures that will rank students and provide some sort of distribution of grades. Many teachers are unaware of alternatives in testing, such as tests that can be used with computer instruction.

### An Alternative to Traditional Methods

There are some current achievement tests that provide the type of information necessary to diagnose specific strengths and weaknesses in student performance. Oftentimes, these achievement tests are objective-referenced in nature. Their questions are designed in such a fashion as to provide specific performance information on defined objectives.

A computer can be utilized to implement either type of classroom testing, i.e., norm-referenced (comparing one student with other students) or objective-referenced (comparing one student's performance with one objective statement). In some instances, norm-referenced testing is valuable. But, in essentially all instances where the testing is related to instruction, objective-referenced testing is a much more appropriate type of test to use to support and further student learning.

Since this book is concerned with the implementation of the computer to assist learning through effective instruction, the terms "testing" and "measurement" will always, unless otherwise noted, refer to objective-referenced measurement, rather than norm-referenced measurement.

## Computer Testing

The major difference between computer testing and other forms of classroom testing arises out of the basic form and function of the computer. A microcomputer typically serves one student at a time. It is most effective when providing instruction for an individual. In many ways, the computer allows the return to the "one-room school" concept, in which an individual's learning is judged on the basis of "how well Johnny is doing on his lessons" rather than the more customary basis of "how well Johnny is doing compared to other students."

The computer, however, can in some ways improve on the "one-room school" concept! In the one-room school, the teacher generally formed intuitive feelings about how well his or her students were performing in their studies and provided guidance based on these judgments. The computer can provide information to the classroom teacher as to whether a student can or cannot perform a given learning task. In essence, the computer can tell the teacher: "Yes, Johnny can perform this objective," or "No, Johnny cannot perform this objective." The computer, by its systematic nature, makes decisions on the students' learning performances by making objective measurements. The basis and standards for these measurements derive from the statement of intent for any given lesson, i.e., the computer objective for the lesson.

At the heart of computer-assisted instruction is the concept that the computer has the capability of making decisions about student learning. It can decide when the student is "on track" and learning efficiently or when the student is "off track" and in need of additional guidance. Every computer decision must be made on the basis of some sort of student performance, because the computer can only measure performance and has no capability for making intuitive decisions on how well or poorly a student is doing in a computer lesson. The only way the well-trained computer will make such decisions is by using appropriate measurement tools: objective-referenced tests.

While most traditional testing procedures compare the performance of a student with his or her peers, the computer compares the performance of a student with a criterion of success on a learning task. This criterion is established by the computer objective of the lesson. When judging student performance and making instructional decisions, the computer asks the question, "Has the student learned the objective?," rather than the question, "How does this student perform compared to other students?" This is a powerful concept which is probably implemented more easily on a classroom microcomputer than in any other way.

## Testing Decisions in a Computer Lesson

There are two basic kinds of instructional decisions the well-trained computer will be certain to make when teaching. The computer will:

- Decide, BEFORE providing any instruction, whether a student already knows how to do an objective.
- Decide, DURING instruction, whether a student has studied enough and knows the objective.

A well-trained instructional computer will know when a student has finished a lesson, and not continue presenting instruction on the topic. The well-trained computer will also know when not to teach a lesson.

For example, by giving a pretest, the computer may discover that a student has finished a lesson before he or she starts it! To be more exact, the computer may find that a student can perform an objective called for by a lesson, before he or she begins study of the lesson. The student who already knows the objective of a lesson does not need that lesson!

This is an extremely common situation in a classroom. The Kindergarten teacher provides a lesson on "naming the colors" using blocks or water colors. He or she teaches the students to discriminate various colors and apply specific names to each—red, blue, etc. Of course, many of the students in the class have learned the colors at home, before ever coming to class. A certain proportion of students in any class will already know what the computer-teacher is going to teach. The fact is that in any class from Kindergarten through graduate school, the students therein possess different entry-level skills.

Pretesting of skills and knowledge allows the computer to make decisions about who should study a lesson and who should skip to the next lesson. In this book, we will refer to objective-referenced testing with the view that the computer pretest is exactly the same in form and function as the computer posttest. The decision which a computer makes will always be: "Can the student perform the objective?," and the answer will always be "yes" or "not yet."

The computer's decision will require information on both the performance to expect from the student and the criteria of successful performance. In order to decide when a student has adequately demonstrated a performance of a learning objective, the computer will look to the objective for the information it needs.

### Developing Objective-Referenced Tests

Here is an example of a well-written computer objective:

> Given on the computer screen any two two-digit whole numbers, and directions to multiply the two numbers, the student will perform the task correctly. (10 items, 90%)

This objective describes what the computer will present (any two two-digit numbers on the computer), the expected student performance (multiply the two numbers), and the criterion for a successful performance (90 percent correct on a minimum of ten problems). The computer objective describes a class of problems, and the computer will need to generate a set of specific test items from the general class of problems for its objective-referenced test.

*Objective-Referenced Test Validity.* In generating each test item, the computer must set up the exact conditions called for by the objective, and then ask the student to perform the behavior. Every test item it uses must measure exactly the performance called for in an objective—no more, and no less. Notice how the test item below exactly tests the content of the multiplication objective.

MULTIPLY THESE TWO NUMBERS:

$24 \times 33 = <?>$

TYPE YOUR ANSWER < >.

Any two numbers from the class of two-digit whole numbers could be used in the test item, so a large number (actually 99 x 99) of test items could be prepared, each of which would satisfy the performance demands of the objective. Each of these items would be valid measures of the student performance as defined by the objective.

In objective-referenced tests, validity refers to the consistency of the test items to the specific conditions and student performance defined by the objective. If all test items exactly match what is called for by the objective, the test is valid. The extent to which the items do not match the objective is the degree that the test's validity is lessened.

You must be careful to avoid the all too easy mistake of making test items that do not match the objective. For the example of multiplying two two-digit numbers, a test item should not ask the student to multiply a problem of the form <5 x 72>. It is a simpler behavior, and one a student studying the multiplication of two two-digit numbers should already be able to perform. The item represents a different objective, one such as "Given a one-digit and a two-digit whole number,. . ." Another item outside of the class of reference for this objective is a problem of the form <103 x 65>. The following test item would also not be valid: <Sue goes to the store to buy nails for a project to build a push-car. The nails come 25 to a package. Sue buys 11 packages. How many nails did she buy?> The original objective does not stipulate that the student will be required to perform the multiplication task given a word problem. This example item fails to match the performance called for by the objective. Test items of the type <What number times 23 = 46?> also would not be valid. They, too, do not measure the behavior called for by the objective.

When deciding on the form of the test items the computer will present to measure an objective, you must be extremely sensitive to making a careful match of student test behaviors and those called for by the objective. It is at the objectives level that you should make your decisions as to which student performances are appropriate. Once the objective is written and a behavior is decided upon, you must design your objective-referenced test to be a valid tool for the measurement of the objective.

*Objective-Referenced Test Reliability.* Referring again to the two-digit multiplication objective, let's explore the concept of reliability. The objective, you will recall, reads:

> Given on the computer screen any two two-digit whole numbers, and directions to multiply the two numbers, the student will perform the task correctly. (10 items, 90%)
>
> ⌂
> Reliability is concerned with the statement "10 items."

How can you know reliably if a student can or cannot perform the task called for by an objective? The question of reliability arises out of the consideration of the number of problems that are a sufficient number of items to "prove" that a given student has learned the behavior described by the objective.

If the computer presents the student with three multiplication problems and the student gets all of them right, what are the chances that he or she "knows how to multiply two two-digit numbers"? Given another problem, will he or she be able to get it right, too? The computer must present to the student enough items from the total class of items so you can be satisfied that the student's performance on the test accurately reflects his or her capability in the larger class of items.

The reliability of any computer decision on student performance can be increased by augmenting the number of test items presented for the objective. Short of using statistical formulas to determine test reliability, you must use your judgment as to the number of items to present in a test on any given objective.

In some cases, the nature of the objective is such that one and only one test item can be written. If the performance asked for by the objective is, "Type the first ten lines of 'The Ancient Mariner' without error," there is only one possible criterion test item ("Type the first ten lines of 'The Ancient Mariner' without error"). In this case, the class of items holds only one valid item. To assure a more reliable measure of the objective, the computer could repeat its request the number of times the teacher judged appropriate.

Most objectives demand that the objective-referenced test items be sampled from a domain of possible items. For example, the objective, "Given two three-digit whole numbers, multiply the numbers," has up to 999 x 999 or 998,001 possible test items that could theoretically be presented to the student.

> Test item 1: 233 X 567 =
> Test item 2: 444 X 985 =
> Test item 3: 132 X 967 =
> Test item n: etc., until all combinations are exhausted.

Since reliability begins to decrease as a student becomes tired, the number of test items should be the minimum number necessary to establish with reasonable certainty that the student has indeed learned the desired multiplication skill.

Whatever the domain from which the item can be drawn, the properties we are looking for in a good objective-referenced test are that each item directly and accurately corresponds to the conditions and student performance stated in the objective, and that the test has a sufficient (but not excessive) number of items to represent the larger class of items described by the objective. In this way, and only in this way, will the computer be able to present to the student a test that will validly and reliably ascertain the student's ability to demonstrate the performance called for by the objective.

*Performance Levels.* A well-written computer objective includes a statement of how well the student is expected to perform the objective in order to pass the lesson. Here, in this case of a high school computer lesson on engineering bridge design, the performance level is as high as possible:

> Given an illustration of a truss bridge, the length of the span, the materials of the bridge, and the coefficients of stress, compression, and expansion, determine the maximum weight the bridge will support. (3 items, 100%)
>
> ⌂
> The level of performance is 100%.

After the student answers a test question on this objective, the computer provides the answer by having a graphic of a truck, with the student's weight determination posted on its side, move across the bridge. If the student's calculations are correct, the truck completes its journey across the bridge. If they are not, either the bridge collapses or an additional graphic, showing "money wasted," appears on the screen.

This illustration should provide some insight into how to set performance levels. If a student's performance on a lesson is critical to some future performance, the criteria for passing the lesson should be mastery, therefore, 100 percent correct.

Mastery learning is the concept that if an objective is important enough to teach, it is important enough to have students know how to do the objective. (If the objective is not important enough to have students master it, why teach it?) When a person has mastered a skill, it means he or she can always perform the skill (under a normal set of circumstances). A person has not mastered addition if he or she can get 75 percent of a set of addition problems correct. He or she has mastered addition when he or she can get 100 percent correct.

Enter reality. Accepting that mastery means 100 percent performance on the demonstration of some skill, requiring that 100 percent performance may not always be realistic on the part of the teacher. For one thing, no teacher has the time to write test items with such care that they are always unambiguous, and exactly and perfectly match the objective they are supposed to be measuring. Also, students have been known to be a bit careless when doing questions, and after having mastered a topic, they demonstrate their skill with a rather nonchalant attitude. These, and other factors, tend to force a classroom teacher into the position of not requiring the student to demonstrate mastery with a scope of 100 percent on an objective-referenced test.

A suitable compromise, based on classroom experiences with mastery learning, seems to be to allow 90 percent to represent mastery, with the assumption that if all factors were ideal, the student who has mastered the skill could get 100 percent on the test. If students are allowed to pass lessons with performance much lower than 90 percent, the lesson is not a "mastery-learning situation" and should not be called such.

## Summary

When developing an objective-referenced test for a lesson, you must be especially concerned with its validity, reliability, and expected level of performance. These three testing factors are related in an objective in the following manner:

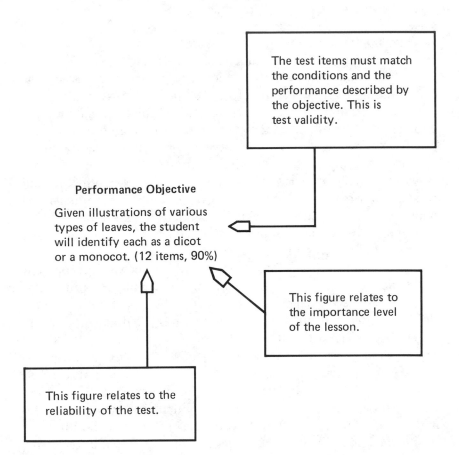

You need to establish test validity by making sure that each test item in the class of items accurately reflects the conditions and student performance requested by the objective. In this way, you will be sure you are testing what the lesson is intended to teach.

You need to establish test reliability by presenting a sufficient number of items to insure yourself that the student could do any set of items in the item class in the same manner.

Finally, you need to establish the level of performance on the test at a point which reflects the importance of the lesson, utilizing mastery for all important lessons.

With the framework of purpose and measures firmly established, you are ready to look at how to design instruction to reach the objective of the lesson. The next chapter moves to the *processes* portion of the development triangle.

# Chapter 6
# The Processes of Instruction

## Introduction

*Instructional Intent.* Presenting a lesson to a student involves much more than simply displaying text on a screen. It involves the patterning of student-computer interactions so as to promote the student's learning of the lesson objective. In a good computer lesson, the interactions will be both efficient and effective in promoting learning. This chapter will help you to do the following:

1. Define the effectiveness of lesson presentation in terms of student performance before and after instruction.
2. Define efficiency of lesson presentation in terms of the duration of student-computer interaction.
3. Identify two key factors in the framework of computer organization.
4. State and describe the nine characteristics of an instructional computer that is well-trained in lesson presentation.

Chapter 3 established the framework of characteristics of a well-trained computer-teacher, Chapter 4 detailed the importance to lesson structure of goals and objectives, and Chapter 5 performed the same task for the appropriate measures of objectives. In this chapter, it is time to examine the "top" angle of the systematic development triangle—the processes of instruction.

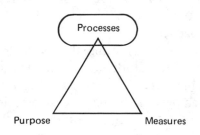

109

*Knowledge Prerequisites.* The "processes" aspect of the framework of computer lesson design involves designating those instructional steps to be used to achieve a lesson's objective. This chapter relates computer lesson presentation to the existing background of a practicing teacher, and we are assuming that you are knowledgeable in traditional classroom lesson presentation techniques.

-------------------------------------------------------------------------

## Lesson Presentation for Computer Instruction

As we have defined it in this book, a *unit* of computer instruction has one goal and represents a set of lessons. The unit goal is reached by having the student study a sequence of *lessons*, each having a specific objective that is measurable by the computer. The number of lessons in a unit is determined by the complexity of the unit goal. Generally, the student will move from one objective to the next in the sequence, achieving the objective taught in each lesson and developing the skills and knowledge required for a given goal. For example, the sample unit below has five lessons, to be studied in sequence.

| Unit 1 | | |
| --- | --- | --- |
| | Lesson 1 → | Objective 1 |
| Unit | Lesson 2 → | Objective 2 |
| Goal | Lesson 3 → | Objective 3 |
| | Lesson 4 → | Objective 4 |
| | Lesson 5 → | Objective 5 |

A single computer lesson consists of the set of teaching steps the computer uses to teach a student how to do *one* objective.

## The Computer-Teacher

The computer, being a systematic beast, must know exactly what to present to the student in order to help the student to reach a given objective. The computer will have to know the processes of teaching it is to use to accomplish its instructional task. Each computer "screen" should lead the student along a pathway of learning—the processes of learning.

WELCOME TO THE WORLD OF
COMPUTER SCREENS.

*Note*: While here we show a complete computer keyboard and screen, in the *remainder of the book* we indicate a screen display simply by enclosing words within rectangles having rounded corners. These "screens" are of various sizes in this book, depending on the amount of wording in each instance, but in actual usage a computer screen does not vary in its overall dimensions.

To develop a systematic computer lesson, you must plan exactly what set of study events will be provided for the student. With a computer, this means planning *exactly* what the student will see on the series of screens that comprise a lesson. If the computer has been trained to be a good teacher, the designated set of study events will prove to be learning events as well.

As noted earlier, the computer is an ideal practice teacher, for far more is known about how to program a computer to teach effectively than is known about how to train a student teacher to teach effectively. Simply put, computers are both simpler and more systematically designed than humans. There are not as many variables associated with a computer as with a person, and these variables have been researched and, to some degree, brought under control. In short, research on computer instruction provides guidelines as to the way computers "should" teach. If you can design or buy a program to make your computer teach in the manner presented in this text, you can assure yourself that your computer has graduated from teacher training with flying colors and has high probability of being effective in its teaching.

### What You Want Your Computer-Teacher to Achieve

The "teaching steps" (processes) of the computer during a computer lesson have the overall purpose of changing a student's behavior. When a student walks up to the computer and cannot do an objective, the computer should be a good enough teacher to have the student, when finished with a lesson, walk away from the computer demonstrating that he or she can do the objective.

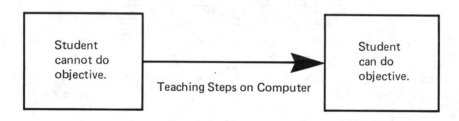

In addition, if the student walks up to the computer and CAN do the objective, the computer should be a good enough teacher to recognize this and not waste the student's (or its own) time.

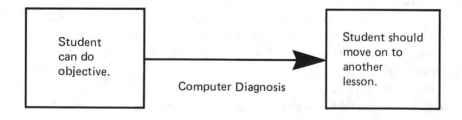

These two concepts are important in the presentation of a

lesson. The first concept relates to the effectiveness of lesson presentation on the computer. Just because a student sits at a computer, is occupied for a period of time, and comes away from the computer "happy," there is no reason to assume that *learning* has taken place. A systematically-designed lesson is one which takes a student from a condition of "not being able to do something" to the condition of "being able to do something," in a planned progression of teaching events.

The second concept relates to instructional efficiency. It is inefficient to have a student sit at a computer which takes the student through a lesson presentation when the student can already do what the lesson is attempting to teach. On almost any lesson that is taught on a computer, a certain proportion of students who walk up to the computer will already have mastered the skill called for by the computer and, hence, will not benefit from further instruction. The lesson presentation should be sophisticated enough to make sure that the computer does not waste its own and the student's time presenting materials that a student has already mastered.

## Structural Elements of Lesson Organization

Any designer of a computer lesson must keep in mind those important aspects of the computer's nature that will bear upon the lesson's organization. Two aspects in particular will need your special attention as you begin the lesson design process: (1) the nature of the computer's presentation mode, and (2) the nature of its memory. Both have implications for lesson organization.

*Thinking Computer "Screens."* Your computer-teacher is limited in the way it can present information to students. Its primary communication mode is through its screen, where it can present verbal information and graphics. A given computer may have other communication modes. It may be able to present color on its screen, and/or sound through a speaker. In very special applications, the computer can be connected to other machines to extend its presentation capabilities. For example, the computer can be hooked to a slide projector, and pictures can be projected when requested by the computer; or it can be hooked to a videodisc player to present random-access video segments. Even with these things taken into consideration, it is still the situation that almost all information presented to students by commercial and teacher-prepared computer instructional materials is presented as verbal and graphic information on the computer screen itself.

This situation is not greatly different from the circumstances of the average classroom teacher. The normal tools of lesson presentation in a classroom are text, graphics, and the spoken word. Clearly, the teacher has a great advantage over the computer in lesson presentation by being able to talk to students and explain verbally various aspects of the lesson. Presenting via the computer screen the same information that a teacher might present verbally is seldom a viable approach. Generally, reading instructions and textual presentations on a computer screen is not nearly as interesting as hearing a teacher present the identical information verbally, but this must be accepted as a present limitation of the computer.

This "limitation," however, may actually be of benefit to some students. Those students who read several times faster than teachers talk may find the computer's textual presentations to be more interesting and challenging than the teacher's oral explanations. Students who need time to internalize explanations may also benefit from the opportunity to read and reread the explanations.

The fact that a computer primarily presents text and graphics means that in general you must learn to "think screens" during the development (or evaluation) of computer instructional materials. This does not necessarily mean you need to learn to think linearly. A computer, in general, should not simply present one screen after another in a predetermined, serial fashion. If this were the case, it would be easier to photograph the screens and print them in order, and place them in a special teaching device called a "book." The power of the computer lies in the fact that it can present screens in a variety of patterns, responding to student demands and accomplishments.

*Thinking Computer "Menus."* Let's assume that you intend to take advantage of the power of the computer to be flexible in its screen presentation. You do not want your computer-teacher to act like a page-turner for text, presenting one screen of text after the other. If you desire that it present screens in such a way as to adapt to the needs and interests of the learner, you will then need to contend with this important fact: except for the single screen in view at any time, a computer lesson is essentially invisible.

Since a computer lesson resides in the computer's memory, with only one "page" of it ever visible at one time, the learning situation can all too easily become a confusing situation for the learner. Good computer lessons, therefore, must not only be well-organized, but also must be designed so that their organization is very obvious to the student—who otherwise will soon become lost in even the best lesson presentation.

A textbook, no matter how poorly written, seldom causes a learner to lose his or her way. The text itself may be confusing, but the pathways through the text are generally quite clear. This derives in part from the fact that the entire text is open and available for inspection. In other words, the book is there and any part can be read at will. Such is not the case with a microcomputer lesson. At any given point in time, 99.99 percent of the lesson to be presented is "hidden" in the computer's memory, and there is no easy way for a student to locate or see this hidden material.

Because the lesson resides in a memory bank which is not accessible to a viewer, the lesson can become disastrously confusing. The organizational plan for a lesson or a series of lessons must be crystal-clear to the user of the lessons. This is normally (but far from universally) accomplished through the use of "menus."

Experience has shown that developing instruction around a menu format leads to greater simplicity in both lesson and unit presentations. A menu is a simple listing of choice options, and it is generally one screen long. An example of a lesson menu screen is shown at the top of the following page.

Often, a lesson menu will lead to another menu. For example, if a student chooses option 3 on the menu illustrated here, he or she might be presented with another menu listing various types of instruction for the objective.

Through the use of appropriate menus of choices, the learner will always have an overview of what is available in memory, and

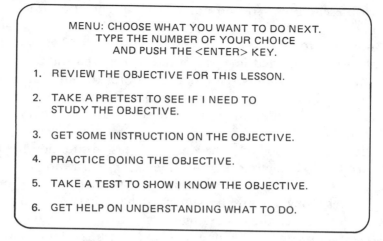

```
MENU: CHOOSE WHAT YOU WANT TO DO NEXT.
      TYPE THE NUMBER OF YOUR CHOICE
         AND PUSH THE <ENTER> KEY.

1. REVIEW THE OBJECTIVE FOR THIS LESSON.

2. TAKE A PRETEST TO SEE IF I NEED TO
   STUDY THE OBJECTIVE.

3. GET SOME INSTRUCTION ON THE OBJECTIVE.

4. PRACTICE DOING THE OBJECTIVE.

5. TAKE A TEST TO SHOW I KNOW THE OBJECTIVE.

6. GET HELP ON UNDERSTANDING WHAT TO DO.
```

will know where he or she can move to and from during his or her studies. In this way, the potential problem of having the student wandering down a maze of hidden computer pathways will be eliminated, and the student will always know, or be able to find out, where he or she is in a lesson.

You will want to organize any lesson that you design in a manner which allows for various student options for learning. Therefore, you will need to design an effective way of allowing the student to choose options. By designing the computer lesson using the menu structure, you can also present menus to the student to help him or her make a choice.

### Features of Effective Presentation

Although presented by the computer, the events in a computer lesson are deliberately arranged by the lesson designer. The lesson events should be designed to have the effect of supporting the student during the processes of learning for a specific objective.

What would be the characteristics of a well-trained computer's lesson presentation? What elements would be present in a well-prepared and systematic computer lesson?

The exact form of the communications to the learner must be designed for each lesson and toward the particular lesson objective. However, there are nine major "instructional events" that have been identified as useful in supporting processes of learning. They are as follows:

1. Provide for motivation/attention.
2. Present the objectives to the learner.
3. Recall prerequisite competencies.
4. Provide the stimulus (problem, topic, concept).
5. Provide learning guidance (how to proceed).
6. Elicit performance.
7. Provide feedback (reinforcement, knowledge of results).
8. Assess performance.
9. Provide for retention and transfer.

(Briggs and Wager, 1981)

The events of instruction are of importance in deciding how the learner can be guided toward any desired capability. Each one of these instructional events, while not to be employed in each and every lesson in a standardized or routine fashion, should be specifically considered by the lesson designer when planning the computer lesson.

The instructional events are described in detail elsewhere (see *Principles of Instructional Design*, Gagné and Briggs, 1979) as functions which need to be carried out in any instruction, whether on the computer or by the teacher in the classroom or by some other means, because they influence and support the processes of learning that enable a learner to proceed from his or her existing performance to the performance desired. Therefore, when designing a lesson for the computer, each of the events of instruction should be considered as a means for activating and supporting the learning process. Additionally, when evaluating a computer lesson that has been developed by another designer, the lesson presentation should be examined to note whether or not needed instructional events are indeed present.

Here is a set of instructional processes that are similar in form to the events of instruction listed above, but that have taken into consideration the specific nature of the computer as a medium of instructional presentation:

### Processes of Instruction
### in a Computer Lesson

1. The computer gets the student's attention and provides motivation.
2. The computer presents the lesson objective.
3. The computer reminds the student of relevant background information.
4. The computer implements the elements of an instructional strategy.
5. The computer provides examples of expected student performance.
6. The computer presents practice on the lesson objective.
7. The computer provides feedback on practice.
8. The computer assesses the student's performance.
9. (Optional, depending on circumstances) The computer implements transfer and retention strategies.

Step nine in the process is optional, since the computer perhaps will not provide for transfer and retention within a single given computer lesson. These two strategies are more often included in a series of lessons, and may be accomplished through careful sequencing of lessons, so that the ninth event of instruction becomes a component of an event in some later lesson. In other words, transfer and retention of a performance learned in one lesson might take place in step three of a subsequent lesson. A special lesson may be designed that has as its unique purpose enhancing the transfer and retention of one or more objectives already taught.

Instructional processes essentially the same as those identified above have been utilized successfully in computer instruction, most notably with the TICCIT system (Merrill *et al.*, 1980).

### Features of an Efficient Presentation

The utilization of the nine processes of instruction in lesson design boost the probability of the computer providing an effective lesson presentation. Effectiveness can be coupled with efficiency to provide maximum teaching power. Efficiency is the process of designing instruction in order to minimize the length of time it takes any individual student to complete a given lesson.

If all students progress through a lesson in a serial fashion, looking at one predesignated screen at a time, the efficiency of the program would, by its nature, be low. Program efficiency means that alternative pathways are available to students—shortcuts through the program when some element of it is not needed by a specific student.

One feature that can be implemented to make lessons more efficient has already been mentioned—that of providing points of exit from a lesson for students as soon as satisfactory performance on an objective can be demonstrated. It is especially important to realize that one point of exit may be as early as at the start of the lesson! Many students will begin a lesson already knowing the lesson. The presentation of a pretest will save much student and computer time. Students should also have the opportunity to call for a test during the lesson at any point at which they feel they can demonstrate satisfactory performance.

Another feature of lesson presentation that makes for an efficient lesson is to vary the number of examples and practice items provided according to the student's needs. The computer can be programmed to monitor student performance on practice, and advise the student when he or she is ready for a test. Some students will be insecure and attempt to exhaust practice items long after they know how to perform the objective. These students should be advised when the computer "thinks" it is time for them to take the lesson posttest.

When a specific instructional strategy is being presented to students, it can be presented in a lean version, at the same time providing optional help for students who request it. In this manner, the mainstream of students can proceed down a sparsely-presented explanation of what they are to learn, while students who need more help with the lesson can get it.

Because of the technical power of the computer to monitor performance and make decisions based on student behavior, you can make deliberate plans for the efficient use of the computer in lesson presentation.

In the next section of this chapter, we combine the nine processes of instruction with the essential elements of efficiency to provide a generalized model of lesson presentation. The model integrates lesson purpose, measurements, and processes for effective and efficient lesson presentation.

## Designing a Lesson Presentation

At this time, do not concern yourself with questions of how a lesson gets programmed into a computer. Let's focus on the question of what the design of a good computer lesson would be like. If the parameters of a good lesson presentation are understood, you will have the capability of designing good presentations and evaluating whether or not someone else has designed a good computer lesson. If, at some later date, you wish to program a computer lesson, you will know that your lesson design is worthy of the time and effort required to put the lesson into action on the microcomputer.

Let us assume that you have a unit you wish to teach via the computer. You have identified all the objectives for the unit, written the objective-referenced tests to measure every objective, organized the objectives into an appropriate sequence and created a lesson map, and are now ready to design the presentation of screens for the first lesson. You will pattern the screens that will teach a student to do the first objective. In order to have an effective and efficient lesson, what should you have the computer present to the student?

### Rules for Lesson Design

For each computer lesson you design, you should take into consideration those features of instruction that make an effective lesson presentation, and those features that make the presentation as efficient as possible with a variety of learners. So, for our purposes in describing what the computer is to present when teaching a lesson objective, we will identify ten rules for you to follow in lesson design. These rules are stated below in a form appropriate to the computer medium, which differs only slightly from the way the processes of computer instruction described earlier in the chapter were listed.

In calling them "rules," we do not mean to imply that strict adherence to them is required. Nor are we saying that all ten absolutely must be included in each and every lesson, or that they be employed only in the specific order in which they are presented here. What we do mean is that all ten rules should be considered when designing or evaluating a lesson on the computer. The rules have been derived from what is known through research about learning processes, and employ what is needed to provide efficient instruction for a variety of learners. Therefore, to ignore them would be to reduce the likelihood of an effective or efficient lesson presentation, whereas accounting for each of them should increase the probability of the computer's instructional processes being successful in teaching the lesson objective with a particular learner.

*Rule 1. The computer should get the student's attention and provide motivation.* Every computer lesson will need some sort of introduction. Generally, it is sound practice to present to the student the name and a brief description of the lesson to make sure the student has put the right disk in the computer. The introduction may ask for the student's name, class, and/or teacher, for record purposes. And, the introduction may provide a brief "pep talk" to convince the student that this lesson is interesting, or valuable, or perhaps even both. The introduction lets the student know a new "piece of instruction" is going to be presented.

---

WELCOME TO THIS LESSON, BOB.

YOU ARE READY TO STUDY HOW TO
MULTIPLY TWO NUMBERS TOGETHER.

THIS SKILL IS IMPORTANT. YOU WILL
BE ABLE TO USE IT OFTEN IN THE
FUTURE TO SOLVE MATH PROBLEMS.

---

*Rule 2. The computer should present the lesson's purpose.* Explain the lesson's purpose to the student. Make sure the student understands the objective of the lesson.

Research clearly demonstrates that if you wish to increase

student performance in your classroom, the most efficient way to achieve this increase is to make sure the student knows exactly what learning behavior is expected of him or her. Often, teachers provide instruction in a very loose manner, and students are required to "figure out" what the teacher wants them to do on a test. (Think back to your own college days, when you were trying to "figure out" what that certain professor wanted you to learn from Chapter 7 of the text.)

A student should in all instances know exactly why he or she is sitting at the computer. Of course, the computer can tell the student this, or you could provide the information yourself from the computer, perhaps as a listing of goals and objectives to achieve in a unit, some to be learned in class and some on the computer. However you do it, one thing is clear: you should be sure that the student knows the precise purpose of his or her study.

In some cases, goals and objectives can be provided to students in exactly the same form as the teacher who uses them in planning. For example, high school and college students benefit greatly by having goals and objectives presented to them in fairly sophisticated form. In other cases, the goals and objectives can be rewritten into a simpler form that is still valuable to students. As shown in the following example, this fourth-grade objective could be rewritten in a simpler form for the computer to present to students.

> Objective: Given various types of numerals, identify those that are fractional numbers. (15 items, 100%)

> Simplified form: I will show you some numerals. You must choose those that are fractions. You must get all the problems right.

In some cases, goals and objectives may be withheld from students. Some children are too young to utilize them effectively, and occasionally, lessons are presented in a fashion to encourage students to supply their own goals or objectives.

As a general rule, however, educational research provides the following advice for you—present students with explicit statements of objectives whenever possible. Attempt to keep the statement as "behavioral" as possible, making sure to tell the student what he or she is expected to do to show the computer he or she has achieved the objective (and therefore the end of the lesson).

*Rule 3. The computer should remind the student of previously-acquired knowledge or skills that relate to the lesson.* Have the student review (and possibly drill on) prerequisite knowledge necessary for the lesson to make sure the student knows everything he or she must know in order to learn the new material. Previous lessons can be integrated at this point, facilitating the transfer of learning from a previous lesson to the present one.

Research has demonstrated that good instructional techniques make sure that the student is entering a new learning experience with all the tools necessary for the task. Often, a student will have forgotten previously-learned material which may be essential for success in a new learning task. The computer should present to the student at least an overview of what skills are essential for success in the lesson. Perhaps the computer could also present a brief review of these materials, with examples and practice items to remind the student what he or she should know.

*Rule 4. The computer should pretest the student to determine if he or she can do the objective.* For the sake of efficiency, the computer should decide whether the student needs any further instruction. This procedure could happen at this stage, or preceding the previous stage of instruction, depending on whether or not you want the student to be reminded of pertinent information.

*Rule 5. The computer should present instructional screens designed to teach how to do the objective.* Now is the time for the computer to teach directly to the objective. Screens can be presented under computer control, or under student control, depending on how you want the computer to teach. The actual instructional presentation depends, of course, on the objective. In some cases, one computer screen will be sufficient to teach the student how to do the objective. In most cases, however, a sequence of presentation is necessary.

Here is an objective for a computer lesson.

> Given a regular noun, the student will change the singular form into the plural form. (5 items, 100%)

Since this is a very simple performance, the singular to plural rule can be presented in just one screen. The single screen below would probably provide sufficient guidance for most students as to how to make plural nouns from singular nouns.

```
LEARN THIS RULE:

TO CHANGE A REGULAR SINGULAR NOUN
TO A PLURAL NOUN, ADD THE LETTER "S."

TO CHANGE THE WORD "COW" TO THE
PLURAL FORM, ADD "S" TO MAKE "COWS."
```

*Rule 6. The computer should present examples of the expected student performance on the objective.* Show the student as many examples of the expected performance as needed to convey the concept of how he or she is to perform on practice items.

```
LOOK AT THESE NOUNS. THEY HAVE BEEN
CHANGED FROM THE SINGULAR TO THE
PLURAL BY ADDING THE LETTER "S."

SINGULAR→("S" ADDED)→PLURAL

COW          + S          COWS
CAT          + S          CATS
PENCIL       + S          PENCILS
```

It is possible that a student would not understand an example provided by the computer. In this case, the well-prepared computer-teacher would be able to help the student. Perhaps the student could simply type "HELP" and receive additional information on the example, or the example could be related back to the previous instructional step.

An instructional HELP might look like this:

```
                REVIEW THESE NOUNS
                AND THEIR PLURAL FORM

        COW ——————————————— COWS
        CAT ——————————————— CATS
        BIRD ————————————— BIRDS
        PENCIL ————————————— PENCILS
        HOUSE ————————————— HOUSES

        NOTICE THAT THEY ALL HAVE "S"
        AT THE END OF THE PLURAL WORD.
```

There should be as many examples available as is necessary to fully support the instruction provided in the previous instructional step. The student should be able to "call for" one example after the other, until the student is satisfied that he or she understands how the example exemplifies the performance designated by the objective. The student should be able to see examples of the same performance that he or she will be expected to display in order to successfully complete the test at the end of the learning sequence.

The student should not be presented with a predefined number of examples, and be forced to look at the examples, whether or not this is necessary. Just as a student should not be directed through a lesson if he or she can already perform the objective, a student should not be forced to look at redundant (to him or her) examples.

*Rule 7. The computer should provide practice items for the student.* The objective told the student what he or she should learn to do, instructional guidance was provided, and examples of how to do the objective were shown to the student. It is time now for the computer to elicit performance from the student. The student should be asked to practice doing the objective.

For the objective on making plurals of regular nouns, a practice screen might look like this:

```
THIS NOUN IS SINGULAR.
CHANGE IT TO A PLURAL FORM.

CAR  <       >

TYPE THE WHOLE WORD AND PUSH <ENTER>.
```

Of course, several practice behaviors can be elicited on the same computer screen, if desired. Here is an example of such a screen:

```
PRACTICE MAKING PLURAL NOUNS BY
CHANGING THE SINGULAR FORM TO
PLURAL:

BIKE              <          >
HAND              <          >
COMPUTER          <          >

TYPE EACH WORD AND PUSH <ENTER>.
```

The computer should, of course, be trained to provide "help" to the student which he or she can request on any practice problem that he or she may not fully understand.

*Rule 8. The computer should provide feedback answers to each practice item.* The computer must decide whether or not the student has satisfactorily performed each practice item.

Each student answer on a practice item would need to be evaluated and feedback provided to the student as to whether or not he or she had done the task correctly. This particular instructional step is a very important one for the learner, since he or she receives information about the correctness of his or her performance.

If a student's practice performance repeatedly indicates successful performance of the task, the computer could be trained to tell the student of his or her readiness for a test. If, on the other hand, the student missed practice problems, feedback and help should be available. When a student misses a practice item, it means that the computer instruction on the objective and/or the examples provided were not sufficient to teach the student how to do the objective. Additional instruction is needed when a practice item is missed.

The computer establishes a practice/feedback/help loop to insure that a student understands why he or she got a practice item wrong in the first place. When the student has sufficiently practiced the skill called for by an objective, he or she is ready to "prove" he or she can do the objective. Then the student can move on to the last step in the instruction—the objective-referenced test.

*Rule 9. The computer should measure the student's performance to decide if the objective has been learned.* The computer must provide an objective-referenced test to determine if the student has reached the previously-designated criteria of success on the performance objective for the lesson.

> YOU ARE READY TO TAKE A
> TEST ON THIS LESSON. YOU WILL
> BE GIVEN REGULAR SINGULAR NOUNS.
> CHANGE EACH NOUN TO PLURAL FORM.
>
> YOU WILL BE GIVEN ALL THE TEST
> QUESTIONS AT ONE TIME, AND YOU
> WILL NOT BE TOLD WHETHER YOUR
> ANSWERS ARE RIGHT OR WRONG.

The student is asked to show, by his or her performance on tasks presented in a test format, that he or she can do the objective for the lesson. The computer presents the student a number of questions as established by the teacher's objective, but does not provide any feedback to the student on how he or she is performing on any items. At the end of the test, the computer decides, based on the teacher's criteria provided by the objective, whether the student has demonstrated that he or she can do the objective.

If achievement of the objective is demonstrated, the student can move on to the lesson closure. If the objective is not achieved, the computer must be trained to make a decision as to whether the student will or will not benefit from going through the lesson again. Other options are to have the computer present more practice screens, or take the student back for more examples, or to recommend more use of "help."

*Rule 10. Whenever feasible and appropriate, the computer should provide help in retention and transfer of learning.* When closing the lesson, it may be possible for the computer to present information that will assist the student in retaining what has just been learned and/or in transferring it to other areas of activity.

A computer could close a lesson by providing examples of the potential usefulness of the new skill or knowledge in various academic areas or in everyday life. It might present a variation on the rationale previously given the student near the beginning of the lesson. We recommend, however, that any enlargement of the lesson beyond the specific instruction needed for efficient and effective learning of the lesson objective be kept to a minimum. Expanding a computer lesson by adding additional information can tend to dilute the lesson in which new learning has just been accomplished. Succinctness in each microcomputer lesson and maintenance of its quite discrete purpose is to be valued in microcomputer lesson design.

In most computer learning situations, serious efforts to promote retention and transfer are probably best reserved for subsequent lessons. By carefully structuring the lesson sequence, the designer of instruction can handle these important aspects of teaching. When designing your own computer instruction, you will want to strive to provide students with opportunities for applying new learning subsequently. You will also want to be sure that review lessons or other means whereby students can integrate new skills and knowledge are provided at appropriate intervals.

By aiming your lesson design toward the sort of lesson presentation set forth above, you will have a good start toward structuring a sound computer lesson for any objective. The next chapter provides an example of the application of the entire sequence of steps to such a design endeavor.

You now know how to pattern an excellent general approach to lesson presentation on the computer, but, of course, even if the computer used all ten rules, it would not yet be fully trained. There are various kinds of objectives, and each requires that slightly different instructional processes be employed during lesson presentation. In Chapter 8, we will show how you can depart somewhat from the general steps above to design various lesson presentations based on the type of objective being taught.

## References

Briggs, L.J., and Wager, W.W. *Handbook of Procedures for the Design of Instruction* (Second Edition). Englewood Cliffs, NJ: Educational Technology Publications, 1981.

Gagné, R.M., and Briggs, L.J. *Principles of Instructional Design* (Second Edition). New York: Holt, Rinehart, and Winston, 1979.

Merrill, M.D. *et al. TICCIT.* Englewood Cliffs, NJ: Educational Technology Publications, 1980.

# Chapter 7
# An Example Computer Tutorial Lesson

## Introduction
*Instructional Intent.* This chapter utilizes the ten rules of computer lesson design set forth in the previous chapter to present a tutorial lesson in simple verbal learning. It also illustrates an example of lesson development and computer instructional power. Its objectives are:
1. Identify the major characteristics of a tutorial lesson.
2. State some student learning options which should be provided in tutorial computer instruction.
3. Describe a basic tutorial interaction pattern for expository presentations.
4. Describe a typical response pattern design for practice items.
5. State a method the computer can use to expedite student transition from practice to performance assessment.

*Knowledge Prerequisites.* You should attempt to imagine yourself watching a student who is engaged in a lesson at the computer. This chapter attempts to simulate that condition, although a text is a poor medium in which to try to demonstrate the power of the computer to jump from one part of a lesson to other parts.

-------------------------------------------------------------------

## A Sample Lesson

You have been introduced to the well-trained instructional computer. Just as the rules of etiquette demand that a person act in appropriate ways in a given social setting, the rules for a well-trained computer demand that the computer act in appropriate ways when in a classroom. Computers do not necessarily act appropriately in classrooms, for many have been programmed to be boorish and unenlightened in an educational setting. The teacher should not allow an unmannerly computer to converse with his or her students, at least not in the name of good instruction.

In this chapter, we will provide an instance of a well-trained computer presenting a lesson from a larger unit of instruction. This example of good training will allow you to form a concrete impression of what actually happens on the computer's screen when a lesson is presented as a series of screens.

The unit we chose to present is one in simple verbal learning. This unit was chosen in order to keep the number of instructional variables to a minimum, since the teaching of simple verbal information is a rather straightforward instructional task. Had we chosen to illustrate the teaching of problem-solving, the computer's task in presenting instruction would have been much more complex.

We will continue to confine our use of the term "lesson" to mean the series of instructional events leading to the learning of a single objective.

### The Context of the Lesson

The unit we are considering, and within which our sample lesson resides, is one of two political geography units that are part of a semester curriculum in an elementary classroom:

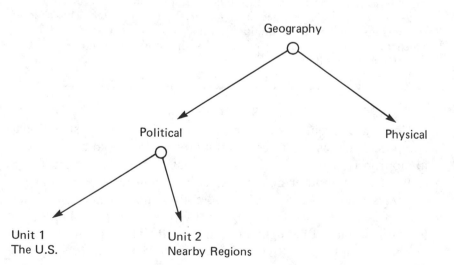

The teacher has available for student use six computer lessons for political geography, two of which are in the unit that focuses on the U.S.A., three of which focus on the home state and nearby states, and one which is a review lesson. Before we examine one of these computer lessons (our sample lesson), let's first examine briefly the instructional context of the lesson. This way we will be able to see how it and the other computer lessons function within the teacher's instructional program.

The teacher's overall goal for the students is that they know those political geographic divisions and locations that are relevant to such things as television broadcast news or everyday conversation. The teacher has identified two main goal areas—study of the United States at large and a study of the region nearby—and so has established two units with goals as follows:

Unit 1— Learn the names and locations of the major political divisions of the United States, including the shape and location of each state.

Unit 2— Learn the names of the state capitals for the student's own and surrounding states, and the location of the capital and major cities within his or her own state.

The goal for each unit generates a number of lesson objectives. The objectives are presented here in what the teacher has determined to be a logical teaching order based on his or her learning maps for the units. The maps are also shown below, with the objectives for the two units in abbreviated form.

### Unit 1 (The U.S.)

Objective 1.1—Given a list of all 50 state names, pronounce the names of the states correctly to the satisfaction of the teacher.

Objective 1.2—From memory, state in writing and in alphabetical order the names of the 50 states of the U.S., not missing more than five state names.

Objective 1.3—Given an outline map of the U.S. and its major regions, name each region outlined on the map, missing no more than one.

Objective 1.4—Given a puzzle frame and mixed puzzle pieces in the shape of states (named), arrange the states within the boundaries of the U.S. to 100 percent accuracy.

Objective 1.5—Given an outline map of the U.S. and its states, write on the map the names of 90 percent of the states.

## Unit 2 (Nearby Regions)

Objective 2.1—Given a list of all important cities in the home state and the capital cities in bordering states, pronounce the names correctly to the satisfaction of the teacher.

Objective 2.2—Given a map of his or her own state, with major cities marked with stars, pick and name the star that represents the capital of the state, and identify the other cities by name with 90 percent accuracy.

Objective 2.3—Name every state that borders the student's own with 100 percent accuracy.

Objective 2.4—Given the name of a state that borders the student's own, name the capital of the state with 100 percent accuracy.

Objective 2.5—Given an outline map of the U.S., identify the locations of the student's own state and every named bordering state with 100 percent accuracy.

### Political Geography Learning Maps

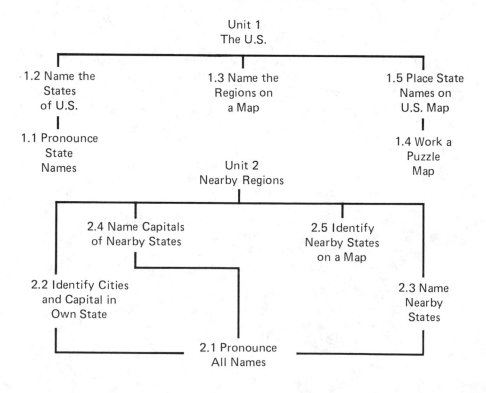

Unit 1
The U.S.

| 1.2 Name the States of U.S. | 1.3 Name the Regions on a Map | 1.5 Place State Names on U.S. Map |

1.1 Pronounce State Names

1.4 Work a Puzzle Map

Unit 2
Nearby Regions

2.4 Name Capitals of Nearby States

2.5 Identify Nearby States on a Map

2.2 Identify Cities and Capital in Own State

2.3 Name Nearby States

2.1 Pronounce All Names

Let's explore the appropriateness of the objectives as candidates to be taught by a computer.

At the bottom of both maps are objectives asking students to pronounce words for evaluation (Objectives 1.1 and 2.1). It is clear that these objectives do not lend themselves to computer instruction. Evaluation to determine whether or not a student is pronouncing correctly a state or city name is not presently a feasible assignment for a classroom microcomputer. Therefore, the teacher would better teach these objectives with other activities, and leave the computer to do those lessons for which it can evaluate student performance.

Objective 1.4, dealing with the shape of the states and where the states fit in a puzzle, could be a candidate for computer instruction, with the computer providing the graphics and the student manipulating the images. But, in general, the choice of the medium should reflect the given instructional task. How much simpler and better it is to present the student with an inexpensive puzzle board and states, and let the student work on the puzzle, than to have the student work with an abstract drawing on the computer screen. Therefore, Objective 1.4 should be taught using an actual puzzle.

For our purposes we will choose, from among the six computer lessons in the unit, Objective 2.4 as our sample lesson. Although we isolate the lesson, it should be understood that the lesson on Objective 2.4 would logically follow the computer lesson on the objective which is below it on the map.

Here is Objective 2.4 in the form of a computer objective:

> Given on the computer screen the name of a state that borders his or her state, the student will type the name of the state's capital city. (6 items, 100%)

**The Lesson as Tutorial Instruction**

The example lesson will be presented with the computer behaving as a tutor who has the ability to respond to student responses. Rather than simply presenting expository material on the states and capitals, like a textbook, the computer can allow the student to interact with each aspect of the lesson. Such an interaction pattern is called tutorial computer instruction, and it is the most powerful application of the computer to lesson presentation.

Although the tutorial is the strongest instructional computer pattern, it is quite difficult to design and program. The reason for this is simply that there are a larger number of ways in which a student may respond to the various aspects of a tutorial lesson, and the computer must be ready to accept and interpret these responses. The number of potential interactions between the computer and the student grows very quickly with the complexity of the lesson.

Since we will be dealing with a well-trained computer, it will be a bit of a "show off" and demonstrate for you all ten of the design rules presented in the previous chapter, as well as demonstrate its capability of sophisticated interaction with the student during its tutorial presentation.

---

### Review of the Characteristics of the
### Well-Trained Computer-Teacher

1. The computer gets the student's attention and provides motivation.

2. The computer presents the lesson's purpose.

3. The computer reminds the student of previously-acquired knowledge or skills that relate to the lesson.

4. The computer pretests the student to determine if he or she can do the objective.

5. The computer presents instructional screens designed to teach how to do the objective.

6. The computer presents examples of the expected student performance on the objective.

7. The computer provides practice items for the student.

8. The computer provides feedback answers to each practice item.

9. The computer measures the student's performance to decide if the objective has been learned.

10. The computer provides help in retention and transfer of learning.

---

### The Lesson Simulation

This lesson will be demonstrated to you via simulated screens of what the student would see when taking the lesson. Of course, this text does not have the capability of responding to student choices the way a computer does, so we will "build in" places where the student chooses one option or another, and at these points will annotate the situation to illustrate what happened or what else might have happened at that point.

In order to maximize your understanding of what is happening during the computer lesson, our simulation screens will not be "fancied up" with graphics. Various graphics, such as moving figures, borders, boxed text, colors (when available), flashing words, etc., could be employed to draw the student's attention to a portion of the screen or to maintain his or her interest in the lesson, but these will not be utilized. This lesson is basically a lesson in verbal learning, and we will present basic verbal material.

Finally, this sample lesson will be purely instructional, and we will not highlight any recordkeeping or CMI. The computer will simply present the lesson in an effective and efficient manner, leading the student toward the lesson's terminal objective.

### The Lesson Begins

The student sits down at the computer and inserts the disk labeled "Learning the States and Their Capitals." She turns on the computer, it whirrs and buzzes, and the first screen lights up.

**Screen 1**

WELCOME TO THIS LESSON.

THIS IS MS. WILSON'S CLASS.

WHAT IS YOUR NAME?

TYPE YOUR FIRST NAME, AND
PUSH THE <ENTER> KEY.

The well-trained computer has the student's attention.

The student types the name "Betty" and pushes <ENTER>. The screen changes to:

**Screen 2**

```
HELLO BETTY. CHOOSE THE
LESSON YOU WANT TO WORK ON.

1. NAMING STATES IN ALPHABETIC ORDER
2. NAMING STATES ON A MAP
3. YOUR STATE AND ITS NEIGHBORS
4. NAMING STATE CAPITALS NEAR YOU
5. NAMING YOUR STATE'S MAIN CITIES
6. REVIEWING THE PREVIOUS FIVE LESSONS

CHOOSE A NUMBER AND PUSH <ENTER>.

TO RETURN TO A MENU AT ANY TIME,
TYPE <MENU>.
```

The menu is important in helping Betty to organize her studies. The computer cannot allow her to get lost when doing the tutorial lesson, if there are many lessons on the disk. The screen tells Betty that any time she wishes to return to this menu all she needs to do is type <MENU>. This same reminder will appear on any subsequent menus Betty might see, permitting her to return to the point of any previous decisions made, and thereby helping her to keep track of where she is in a unit or a lesson.

The tutorial computer has the power to allow the student to choose the lesson on which she would like to work, or it can prescribe the study order. In the case where an objective is prerequisite to another objective, the computer could tell Betty she has to complete the first objective before the second. In our example, although the teacher has a planned sequence of instruction, the objectives are not clearly prerequisite to one another, therefore, the designer has allowed the computer to give the student a choice.

Betty has worked on this disk before. In fact, she has finished computer lessons 1, 2, and 3. Of course, the computer could be programmed to remember this and remind her of what else she has and has not finished. She types the number 4 and pushes <ENTER>.

**Screen 3**

```
HERE IS THE PURPOSE OF THIS
LESSON.

YOU WILL SEE THE NAME OF
A STATE NEAR YOUR STATE. YOU
NAME THE CAPITAL OF THE
STATE. YOU MUST GET 100% OF
YOUR ANSWERS CORRECT TO FINISH
THE LESSON.

CHOOSE:  TYPE <HELP> OR
         TYPE <GO ON> OR
         TYPE <MENU>
```

Betty understands the purpose of the lesson. She types
<GO ON> and moves on. The well-trained computer has provided
the purpose of the lesson. It has also offered the student an
opportunity to receive more explanation before proceeding.

If Betty had typed <HELP>, the computer would have
presented additional information on the objective. The computer
could have provided a restatement of the objective in simpler
terms, presented the objective in smaller steps, placed it in the
context of other objectives to be learned, or done all three.

The well-trained computer gives the student a chance to show
that she can already do the objective. In this lesson, it does not
force a test on to Betty, but rather asks her to decide whether or
not she knows the lesson.

**Screen 4**

```
SUPPOSE YOU READ THE NAMES
OF NEARBY STATES, ONE AT A
TIME. DO YOU THINK YOU CAN
NAME THEIR CAPITALS?

IF YOU THINK YOU CAN, YOU MAY
TAKE A SHORT TEST TO
PROVE IT.

              TYPE <TEST>
CHOOSE: OR
              PUSH <ENTER>
```

Betty decides she is not ready to take the test. She pushes
<ENTER> and goes on. If she had chosen to take the test, the
computer would have provided a final test for the lesson. Then, if
she had not passed the test, the lesson would have proceeded. In
addition, the computer could be programmed to give a diagnostic/
prescriptive test at this point. If Betty had not passed the test, the
computer could have continued in the testing process and made a
decision as to whether she was missing some prerequisite performances for this lesson.

**Screen 5**

```
HERE IS SOMETHING YOU SHOULD
REMIND YOURSELF OF BEFORE YOU GO
ON. IT WILL HELP YOU TO LEARN
THIS LESSON.

REMIND YOURSELF OF THE NAMES
OF ALL THE STATES WHICH ARE
NEAR YOUR STATE.

IF YOU WANT TO SEE A LIST OF THE NAMES
OF THESE STATES, TYPE "LIST."

TYPE <LIST> OR
PUSH <ENTER> AND GO ON
OR TYPE <HELP>
```

Betty decides to view the list of states.

**Screen 6**

```
HERE ARE THE STATES IN ALPHABETICAL
ORDER.

YOUR STATE IS ———— NEW YORK

YOUR NEIGHBORS ARE —————
    CONNECTICUT          NEW JERSEY
    MASSACHUSETTS        VERMONT
    PENNSYLVANIA

CHOOSE:    •—PUSH <ENTER> TO GO ON
           •—TYPE <HELP>
           •—TYPE <MORE> FOR MORE
             EXPLANATION
           •—TYPE <BACK> TO RETURN
             TO PREVIOUS SCREENS
```

If this were a traditional non-computer lecture or textbook presentation, rather than a computer tutorial session, the lecturer would go on to the next topic, and the textbook would present the next paragraph. But since this is a tutorial lesson, the tutor will ask the student if she "really" understands what has just been presented. This is done by allowing the student to choose various learning options, such as <HELP>, <MORE>, or <BACK>. Although we are presenting these options along with the screens of the lesson, the student could be taught all the command options at the start of a unit, and it would not be necessary to repeat them on every screen.

Here is an illustration of the tutorial interaction pattern for the expository material presented on Screen 6:

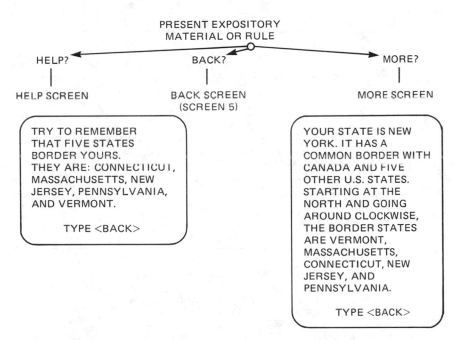

In this fashion, the computer allows three pathways to additional information if the student needs it. Of course, this means that the courseware designer must provide all the paths and additional expository materials! But, without at least one of these options, the presentation becomes not a tutorial lesson, but simply "page-turning" by the computer.

Betty decides she does not need help so she pushes <ENTER> and goes on to the next screen.

**Screen 7**

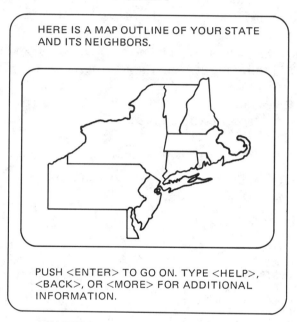

HERE IS A MAP OUTLINE OF YOUR STATE AND ITS NEIGHBORS.

PUSH <ENTER> TO GO ON. TYPE <HELP>, <BACK>, OR <MORE> FOR ADDITIONAL INFORMATION.

She chooses <ENTER>.

**Screen 8**

DO YOU REMEMBER A LESSON YOU HAD WHERE YOU PRONOUNCED THE NAMES OF STATE CAPITALS TO YOUR TEACHER? IT MAY HELP YOU WITH THIS LESSON IF YOU REVIEW THAT LIST OF NAMES.

PUSH <ENTER> TO GO ON OR TYPE <LIST> TO SEE NAMES OF CAPITALS, OR TYPE <HELP>, <MORE>, OR <BACK>

Betty learned the city names previously, and she chooses not to see the list of capitals. She reaches the instructional screens of this lesson. They will guide her in the process of associating the previously-learned names of bordering states with the previously-learned names of bordering state capitals.

There are many ways to make the state-capital association. The instruction might try to make the association using a simple rote method—presenting all the state names and capital names together, and asking the student to memorize the word pairs. Presenting a mnemonic to help in linking the two names is another possible approach. The computer could tell the student to think—"Albany serves ALL NY," "Hartford, Connecticut is HARDt to connect"—and so forth.

This lesson is a rather simple one, however, and since the student studying the lesson has already learned both the state and the capital names, we will have the computer simply link them together.

**Screen 9**

```
OK, BETTY. GET READY TO LEARN
TO LINK THE NAMES OF STATES WITH
THEIR CAPITALS. FIRST, LEARN
YOUR OWN STATE AND CAPITAL.

YOU LIVE IN: NEW YORK
ITS CAPITAL IS: ALBANY

PUSH <ENTER> OR TYPE
<HELP>, <MORE>, OR <BACK>.
```

She chooses <ENTER>.

**Screen 10**

```
NEW JERSEY IS A
NEIGHBORING STATE.

ITS CAPITAL IS: TRENTON

PUSH <ENTER> OR TYPE
<HELP>, <MORE>, OR <BACK>.
```

In the case of this screen, the <MORE> choice could present to the student one of the previously-mentioned strategies for linking the two names. For example, the screen could read:

<MORE> CHOICE

TRY TO THINK OF A WAY TO LINK THE
NAME TRENTON TO NEW JERSEY.

FOR EXAMPLE:   TRENTON (GOT A) NEW
               (FOOTBALL) JERSEY.

          TYPE <BACK>.

Betty sees more screens similar to Screen 10. They provide the association between state capital and state for Vermont, Massachusetts, Connecticut, and Pennsylvania.

The association instruction is summarized on one screen.

**Screen 15**

TO RECAP:

| STATE | AND ITS | CAPITAL |
|-------|---------|---------|
| NEW YORK | | ALBANY |
| CONNECTICUT | | HARTFORD |
| MASSACHUSETTS | | BOSTON |
| NEW JERSEY | | TRENTON |
| PENNSYLVANIA | | HARRISBURG |
| VERMONT | | MONTPELIER |

  PUSH <ENTER> OR TYPE
  <HELP>, <MORE>, OR <BACK>.

The well-trained computer now provides examples of the desired student performance. It does this as follows: first, it presents a state name (selected at random); it then waits three seconds; then it flashes the capital name onto the screen, blinking it on and off.

**Screen 16**

EXAMPLE—YOU NEED TO BE ABLE TO
GIVE THE CAPITAL NAME WHEN I SHOW
YOU THE STATE NAME, LIKE THIS:

PENNSYLVANIA ———— <          >

PUSH <ENTER> TO SEE MORE
EXAMPLES. TYPE <PRACTICE> TO
TYPE CAPITAL NAMES YOURSELF.
OR, TYPE <HELP>, OR <BACK>.

On Screen 16, the name Harrisburg is flashed. Betty can continue to push <ENTER> as many times as she likes, and the computer will continue to mix the order of state presentation, each followed closely by a presentation of the capital name. The interaction pattern for examples is illustrated as follows:

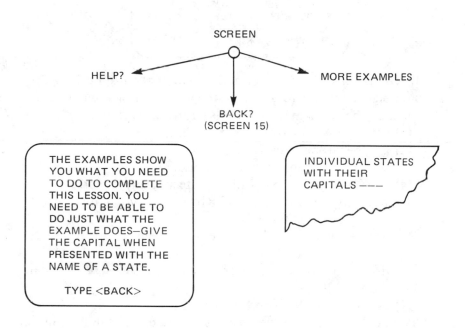

When Betty has seen enough examples, she can type <PRACTICE>, and she will see the same type of screen, except that it asks her to type in the name of the capital for the state name presented. If Betty chooses to move to the practice option before she has seen all the examples, or even before she has learned to associate all the capitals with their states, it is of no great consequence. If Betty does not perform well on the practice items, the computer will sense this, and return her to the examples, or even back to an explanation of the lesson and what she is to learn to do.

**Screen 19**

```
PRACTICE
NOW IT IS YOUR TURN TO TYPE THE
CAPITAL NAME. GIVE THE CAPITAL
FOR THIS STATE —————
NEW JERSEY = <      >

TYPE ANSWER AND PUSH <ENTER>.
IF YOU NEED A LITTLE
HELP, TYPE <HINT>.
OR, TYPE <BACK>, OR <EXAMPLE>.
```

The computer's decisions for action will depend upon how the lesson designer chooses to deal with the variety of possible student responses to the practice item. At this point, Betty could:

    (1) get the answer correct the first time,

    (2) get the wrong answer,

    (3) provide an unanticipated response,

    (4) type in an answer which is technically incorrect but basically correct (e.g., <TRINTEN>, when the correct answer is <TRENTON>),

    (5) decide she cannot do the item and needs to go <BACK> to previous expository materials,

    (6) decide to see the answer flashed on the screen as an <EXAMPLE>, or

    (7) ask for a <HINT> on the item.

Each of these alternative responses could be handled in a number of ways. For example, if Betty gets an answer correct the first time, the computer could:

    (1) simply acknowledge that the response was correct,

    (2) provide positive reinforcement, e.g., "GREAT!," or

    (3) ask a harder question the next time (which is difficult to do on this simple objective).

Alternative feedback for a student getting a wrong answer could have the computer:

    (1) ignore the answer and go on to the next question;

    (2) tell the student the answer is wrong and provide the right answer;

    (3) tell the student the answer is wrong and ask her to try again;

(4) repeat the question;

(5) provide help in the form of an explanation of the item;

(6) display the rule for how to do the practice;

(7) ask the student if she needs help or would like to move backward in the lesson; or

(8) determine exactly what the student's error is and correct it (change her <TRENTEN> to <TRENTON> and tell her she spelled it wrong).

You can see that the number of possible computer responses to likely student actions can be extremely large. For the example given above, a student's simple response to a practice item with the computer scoring it as right or wrong results in many different possible computer responses, not including whether the computer will store the result for future use.

Consequently, rarely will a tutorial session include all of the possible interaction options. Constraints on programming time generally restrain the number of alternative computer replies to a student response. Here is an illustration of a typical response pattern to practice items:

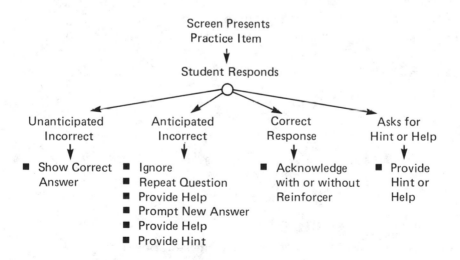

With all the complexity shown above, we have still not tackled questions such as these: "How many practice items should the student see?," "Will the number be fixed or depend on the student's performance?," "Will the items get harder as the student gets more right, or will they all be at the same level?," and so forth.

We decided in this lesson to implement the following responses to Betty's practice answers:

1. Respond to an anticipated correct answer with the word "RIGHT."
2. Respond to an anticipated incorrect answer by correcting the answer to the correct answer, and telling Betty it was spelled wrong.
3. Respond to an incorrect answer by prompting a new answer by stating, "TRY AGAIN, OR TYPE HELP."
4. Respond to <HELP> with the correct answer.

Since the computer can record the student's correct/wrong responses and make decisions based on the response pattern, we also decided that when Betty has correctly performed an association of each state with its capital at least three times correctly in a row, the computer will state it is time to take the final test on the lesson. The computer is programmed to make this decision and to ask Betty if she thinks she is ready for the final test.

After performing the required number of practice items, Betty then sees this screen:

**Screen 33**

```
BETTY, YOU ARE DOING VERY WELL.
YOU ARE READY TO TAKE THE
TEST ON THIS LESSON. HOWEVER,
IF YOU WANT, YOU CAN CONTINUE
TO DO PRACTICE ITEMS.

PUSH <ENTER> FOR TEST.

TYPE <PRACTICE> FOR MORE PRACTICE ITEMS.
```

If Betty decides to do more practice items, the computer will set its "practice counter" back to zero, and when she has completed enough correct practice items for a second time, the computer will re-present Screen 33, until Betty types <TEST>.

The test items are exactly like the practice items, except that no feedback as to how the student is doing is provided. In this example, Betty types <TEST>.

**Screen 34**

```
HERE IS YOUR TEST.

1. TYPE THE CAPITAL FOR

   NEW JERSEY  <      >

THE NAME MUST BE SPELLED CORRECTLY
IN ORDER TO BE COUNTED RIGHT.

      PUSH <ENTER> FOR NEXT ITEM.
```

Following the prescription of the computer objective (six times, 100 percent correct), the computer will present on the test all six of the states being studied. When the test is completed, the student's responses will be analyzed to determine if they are at the criterion level of 100 percent, and Betty will receive feedback on her performance.

**Screen 40**

```
CONGRATULATIONS, BETTY!
YOU HAVE MASTERED THIS LESSON.

YOUR TEACHER WILL BE PROUD YOU
LEARNED THIS LESSON ON YOUR OWN.
TELL YOUR TEACHER YOU'VE FINISHED.

CHOOSE:   TYPE <QUIT> OR
          TYPE <MENU>
          FOR NEXT LESSON.
```

Of course, this computer direction is only one option. The teacher might prefer that the computer store the results in a memory file so that the teacher could review the day's computer work by all students at one time by calling for the file.

If Betty had not received 100 percent on the test, the computer would have directed her back to examples and practice (and the associated help pages for them):

> WHOOPS. YOU MISSED SOME OF THE STATE CAPITALS. STUDY SOME MORE BEFORE TRYING THE TEST AGAIN.
>
> CHOOSE:      TYPE <EXAMPLES> OR
>                      TYPE <PRACTICE>.

To finish this lesson, the computer should provide help in the retention of the newly-acquired knowledge, and provide transfer of knowledge when applicable. In the case of this lesson, to provide additional drill-and-practice for retention would probably not be of much value, since Betty has already just finished that activity. We made the decision that a future lesson will be the retention and transfer lesson. Lesson six on Betty's menu (Screen 2) is a summary lesson. It will provide drill-and-practice on all the information learned in the five previous lessons, and will tie the information together where appropriate.

Thus ends this simple verbal association lesson. It provides an example of a simple computer presentation. The lesson could have been much more complex if a more complex learning task was undertaken, such as teaching conceptual learning or problem-solving. The various types of presentations a well-trained computer could present are discussed in the next chapter.

# Chapter 8
# Fine-Tuning the Processes of Instruction

### Introduction
*Instructional Intent.* The purpose of this chapter is to expand upon the design of lessons for CAI. Its objectives are:
1. State five domains of learning outcomes and give a brief description of each.
2. Identify four categories of learning that comprise the bulk of CAI.
3. State how to appropriately modify the ten rules of lesson presentation to accommodate differences between the major categories of learning.

The chapter builds on the previous chapter and its characterization of a lesson presented by a well-trained computer. Strategies for modifying the ten rules of lesson presentation are identified.

*Knowledge Prerequisites.* We are assuming that you have some background in learning theory, as commonly taught in teacher education programs.

------------------------------------------------------------------

### The "Sort of Well-Trained" Instructional Computer

In Chapter 3, we presented the idea of the well-trained computer and the need for the systematic development of computer instruction according to this simple lesson development model:

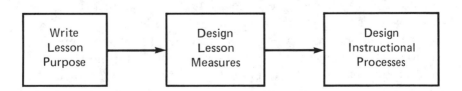

Then Chapter 7 tied together the purpose, measures, and processes into an integrated lesson package, resulting in a description of some of the characteristics of a well-trained classroom computer-teacher. The following features were illustrated in an example lesson.

Processes = Ten Lesson
Presentation
Features

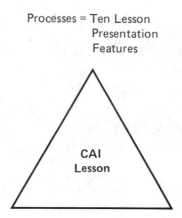

CAI
Lesson

Purpose = Statement of
Computer Objective

Measures = Valid and Reliable
Objective-
Referenced Test

This chapter will attempt to upgrade this "sort of well-trained" computer-teacher by including additional characteristics. We will expand upon the *processes* portion of the triangle and provide a more detailed description of features required for the design and presentation of a good computer lesson.

We have made little mention of the fact that there are various types of performance objectives. No one would argue that the rote memorization of a list of spelling words is the same type of learning as analyzing a literature passage. It is not. As you work with objectives, you will begin to see that they can be categorized into logical groups that define various types of learning.

As learning experts have delved more deeply into the question of how learning occurs, various theories concerning the processes of learning have been developed. All theories recognize the concept that there are different types of learning and that the external (instructional) conditions for one type may well be different from those needed to promote another type.

The result of such research and theorizing is that to be a genuinely well-trained instructional computer, the computer's presentations should reflect the fact that there are different types of objectives, and that these different types of learning objectives ought to have different types of lesson presentations.

### The "Really Well-Trained" Instructional Computer

Suppose the goal of a lesson in a typing class is to have the student learn the finger position on the keyboard for typing the letters "a,s,d, and f." It would only be logical to teach this as a motor skill, rather than as verbal information. That is, rather than having the student memorize and state verbally that the letters a,s,d, and f are letters in order on the second row of the typewriter keyboard, a more logical learning outcome of a typing lesson is that the student should know how to type those letters, without looking at the keyboard. Either way, the student learns the position of those letters on the keyboard, but the type of learning is different. This difference should be reflected in the lesson's performance objective and should result in different methods of instruction.

In order to make systematic decisions concerning the type of instruction to present for a given objective, you need to examine the types of learning that might take place during a computer lesson. It would be most valuable to you to have a pattern by which any lesson objective could be classified and a determination made as to what process of instruction would be most effective to promote learning.

### Some Learning Theory

A broad demarcation of instructional categories can be made on the basis of the type of behavior the student is expected to perform to show he or she has learned an objective.

Based on analysis and experimentation, Gagné and Briggs (1979) described five domains of learning outcomes. The domains of learning they identified are:

- verbal information,
- intellectual skills,
- cognitive strategies,
- motor skills, and
- attitudes.

The first three domains are roughly equivalent to Bloom's taxonomy of the cognitive domain (1956), the domain dealing with knowledge or knowing. The motor skills domain corresponds to what has also been called the psychomotor domain, and the attitudes domain is somewhat equivalent to the affective domain described by Krathwohl, Bloom, and Masia (1964). These five domains identify and categorize the learning which commonly takes place in educational programs, whether or not on the computer.

*Verbal Information.* Verbal information learning is extremely important in the classroom, and it includes student behaviors such as defining words, labeling things, and memorizing passages. In the first grade, the teacher will have students learning their own address and phone number, the days of the week, and the names of the numerals from one to ten. Thus begun, the school's effort to promote the acquisition of verbal information proceeds methodically until the student graduates or leaves school.

*Intellectual Skills.* A second category of learning is concerned with the development of intellectual skills, including the learning of discrimination skills, the development of concrete and abstract concepts, and the formation of rule-using and problem-solving behaviors. Intellectual skills development forms the foundation upon which most elementary and secondary education is built. Learning an intellectual skill often involves symbolic activities, called intellectual operations, on the part of the learner.

*Cognitive Strategies.* Another class of human learning is associated with the way a student responds to an intellectual challenge. Students have different cognitive strategies for solving problems. Cognitive strategies are skills that govern an individual's learning, remembering, and thinking behaviors. They are like a set of behind-the-scenes rules, which direct and govern how a student approaches the solving of a unique problem.

*Motor Skills.* There are classroom situations in which the

student must demonstrate the learning of motor skills. A computerized typing class would certainly incorporate such motor skill training, as would many objectives for industrial arts, physical education, and the performing arts. Although not usually emphasized in school, the learning of motor skills does take place during schooling. For example, teaching young children to hold a pencil and produce letters and numerals is as much motor skills learning as it is cognitive learning.

*Attitudes.* Some lessons may be designed strictly to influence the student's attitude. An objective of this type would be called an affective objective, or an attitude objective. For instance, a computer lesson using computer-generated music could be designed in order to develop student appreciation of the variety of ways that music may be produced, but the student may not be asked to "know" any verbal information about the music.

Most teachers feel that the development of student attitudes is an important phase of school. Teachers hope that they can arrange their classrooms and teach in such a way as to keep students interested in learning, not merely during their school days, but also for the rest of their lives. In effect, what this means is that teachers are interested in having students select learning experiences over non-learning experiences when given the choice.

To help you to better discriminate these five categories of learning, Figure 8.1 provides an example objective for each category.

### Relative Importance of the Categories of Learning to Classroom Computer Instruction

To the average classroom teacher, the five domains of learning are not equivalent in importance. Certain categories of learning are more easily achieved on the computer than others. For example, at the present time it is very difficult to define objectives for attitude development and then carry out instruction specifically to reach the objectives (whether or not on the computer). For the most part, attitude learning does not fit the pattern of our ten rules for effective computer instruction.

Figure 8.1

Example Objectives for the Five Categories of Learning

| Category | Performance Objective |
| --- | --- |
| *Verbal Information* | From memory, the student RECITES the names of all States in the United States, in alphabetic order, omitting no more than five states. (1 item, 100%) |
| *Intellectual Skills* | 1. Given a set of objects in which one object is smaller than the others by ten percent, the student will DISCRIMINATE the smaller object from the larger ones. (20 items, 100%)<br><br>2. Given outline drawings of plants typically found in a forest, the student will correctly IDENTIFY the plant as a tree, shrub, grass, or fungus. (8 items, 80%)<br><br>3. Given any two two-digit numbers, the student will DEMONSTRATE the multiplication of the numbers. (10 items, 90%) |
| *Cognitive Strategies* | Given a problem concerning how to reduce air pollution, the student will ORIGINATE two different approaches to solving the problem. (1 item, 100%) |
| *Motor Skills* | Given a typewriter and a list of nonsense words having the letters a, s, d, and f, the student will EXECUTE the typing of these words correctly. (40 items, 85%) |
| *Attitudes* | Given the option to watch TV or read, the student will CHOOSE to read. (5 items, 80%) |

Although cognitive strategies seem to play a large role in how students approach learning in general, it is not clear at this time how to teach for changes in an individual's cognitive strategies. This area of learning is an area for research rather than instruction.

Motor skills constitute a special category of computer learning. Most skill training occurs at very early grade levels, or at later levels with handicapped students. Seldom does the typical classroom teacher actually teach motor skills. Most classroom motor skills have already been learned by the student by grade one or two. Those that do need to be learned most generally are not of a nature appropriate to being taught using a computer.

The bulk of the learning objectives appropriate to computer-assisted instruction can be readily classified as either verbal information learning or intellectual skills development.

Both the verbal information learning and intellectual skills development categories have been subdivided by theorists. Briggs and Wager (1981) identify three sub-categories of verbal information learning and five sub-categories of intellectual skills development. For our purpose here of illustrating the varieties of learning in the context of the classroom computer, we need not consider the varieties in such great detail. We will treat the learning of verbal information as one category of objectives, and utilize three *sub-categories* of intellectual skills learning—discrimination, concept, and rule-using—as three additional full categories.

The four categories of learning, then, of most interest to the designers of classroom computer instruction are:
- verbal information learning,
- discrimination learning,
- concept learning, and
- rule-using learning.

## Computer Objectives for Our Four Categories of Learning

In order to help you discriminate our four categories of learning, we will present an example objective for each category from some lessons on triangles. To illustrate each objective, we will provide a sample test item from the class of items that would be used to measure the objective. Various aspects of "triangles" are taught from the first grade through high school geometry, and our examples will span that range.

*Verbal Information Learning.* The learning of verbal information is evidenced when a student is able to state the information in some manner, perhaps orally, or by writing or typing it. The student need not use the information (which is an intellectual skill), only be able to produce it. Verbal information can be seen as differing in amount and form of organization. Such information "units" as facts, principles, and names and labels are common in school verbal learning.

Our computer objective and test item for this category are:

> Given a prompt to state six facts about triangles, the student will type statements that include these ideas: (1) a triangle is a plane figure, (2) it is a closed figure, (3) it has three sides, (4) each side is a straight line, (5) it has three angles, and (6) the sum of its angles is 180 degrees. (1 item, 100%)

**Test Item: Verbal Information Learning**

> JACOB, HERE IS YOUR TEST.
> TYPE IN ANY ONE FACT YOU
> KNOW ABOUT TRIANGLES. I
> WILL CORRECT YOUR ANSWER
> AND ASK FOR ANOTHER FACT.
> YOU NEED TO KNOW SIX FACTS
> TO COMPLETELY DEFINE WHAT
> A TRIANGLE IS.
>
> FACT 1 <        >

*Discrimination Learning.* In discrimination, the student is engaged in learning to sense differences in objects and events, or qualities of objects and events. The student will be doing tasks like pointing, sorting, underlining, or matching. Discrimination learning is most important in the early primary grades, where it forms a foundation for the learning of concepts. Our computer objective and test item for this category are:

> Given a triangle among triangle-like shapes and a model triangle, the student will match the model to the triangle shape. (10 items, 100%)

**Test Item: Discrimination Learning**

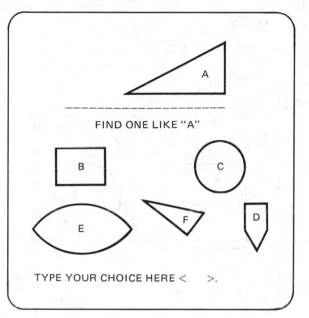

FIND ONE LIKE "A"

TYPE YOUR CHOICE HERE < >.

*Concept Learning.* Concepts can be concrete or defined, but in all cases, the behavior we are attempting to teach is to have the student classify statements or objects into groups based on either a verbal definition or on characteristics possessed by the group.

When a student learns a concrete concept, he or she normally learns to identify an object category, distinguishing the object category from others and giving its common name. A concept is demonstrated when a student can identify an object as a member (or non-member) of a group of objects having the concept name.

Defined concepts, like concrete concepts, call for an assignment of something to a class based on whether or not it possesses the set of attributes considered unique to the class. But, defined concepts do not possess physical attributes. Concepts such as "family," "democracy," and "propaganda" are groupings, but there is nothing in the physical attributes of the members of the class which places them into the class. Our computer objective and test item for concept learning are:

Given on the screen several plane geometric figures, one a triangle and the others not, the student will identify the figure which is a triangle by marking it with an "X." (15 items, 100%)

**Test Item: Concept Learning**

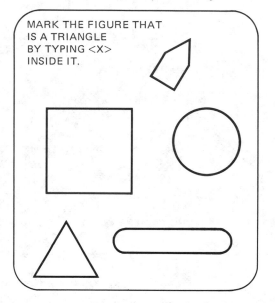

MARK THE FIGURE THAT
IS A TRIANGLE
BY TYPING <X>
INSIDE IT.

*Rule-Using Learning.* Rules are statements which govern the manipulation of information, symbols, or concepts in certain patterns. Along with the teaching of factual verbal information and concepts, it is the most common type of instruction which takes place in classroom instruction, examples being the rules of spelling, all mathematics rules governing how to manipulate numbers, and rules governing the use of grammar and language. The sophisticated use of rules by a student is commonly referred to as problem-solving. For the triangle example, our computer objective and test item are:

Given an illustration of a triangle and the number of degrees in each of two angles of the triangle, the student will determine the number of degrees in the third angle. (15 items, 90%)

**Test Item: Rule-Using Learning**

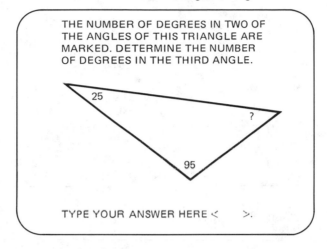

THE NUMBER OF DEGREES IN TWO OF
THE ANGLES OF THIS TRIANGLE ARE
MARKED. DETERMINE THE NUMBER
OF DEGREES IN THE THIRD ANGLE.

25

?

95

TYPE YOUR ANSWER HERE < >.

### Relationships Among These Four Categories of Learning

The categories of intellectual skill learning can and most often do exhibit a hierarchical relationship (Briggs and Wager, 1981). In the case of our triangle examples, the rule-using objective requires the prerequisite development of certain concepts, each of which will, in turn, have its own prerequisites. For example, a student cannot develop the concept of a triangle if he or she cannot discriminate the features which allow him or her to identify a triangle as different from other kinds of geometric figures. The rule-using objective we used as an example will serve as a prerequisite to other higher-order rules.

Discrimination learning, concept learning, and rule-using learning are intellectual skills which demonstrate a hierarchical relationship. The general pattern of this relationship is shown in Figure 8.2.

Each of the three classes of intellectual skills represents a type of skill which is required for the successful accomplishment of the next higher-level type of skill. Successfully completing discriminations permits the student to go on to learn more sophisticated concepts, which allow him or her to use certain rules, which allow him or her to solve problems.

Verbal information learning may or may not be linked to a

*Figure 8.2*

*Intellectual Skills Hierarchy*

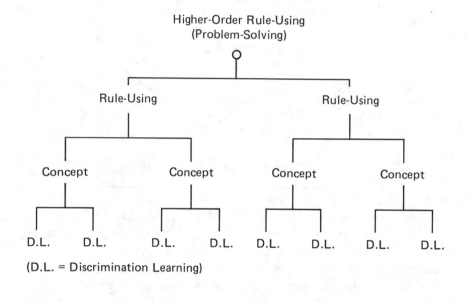

(D.L. = Discrimination Learning)

---

given category of intellectual skill. For example, a problem-solving situation (complex rule use) in mathematics may have very little in the way of a verbal information component, while a problem-solving situation in social studies would be highly loaded on a student's verbal skills.

## Modifying the Ten Presentation Rules

Some aspects of our ten rules of lesson presentation should be modified for the type of learning being taught on the computer, while other rules require little or no modification. The ten rules of lesson presentation are listed in Figure 8.3. Those marked with an asterisk are the most obvious candidates for modification during lesson presentation to accommodate the instruction to the category of learning being taught.

*Figure 8.3*

*Rules of Lesson Presentation*

1. Get the student's attention.
*2. Present the purpose of the lesson.
*3. Review prerequisite knowledge.
4. Pretest skills.
*5. Present instruction designed to teach the objective.
6. Provide examples and helps.
7. Provide practice and helps.
8. Provide practice feedback.
9. Test for performance.
10. Provide for retention and transfer.

*Candidate for modification to accommodate kind of lesson being taught.

## Lesson Purpose

One major aspect of lesson development related to our four categories of learning occurs during the defining of lesson purpose when the computer objective is clearly and accurately stated. That purpose is imparted to the student early in the lesson presentation, and it needs to be unambiguous and easily understood by the student when presented on the computer's screen.

The key to clearly writing objective statements to the student is generally linked to the verb of the objective. Verbs such as state, recite, and summarize almost always designate verbal learning tasks. If the purpose of the lesson is in the verbal information domain, it is important to make sure the student knows this fact, so he or she can focus his or her attention on learning the correct behavior. The same holds true for the categories of discrimination, concept, and rule-using learning. Figure 8.4 identifies the key verbs which most often represent a specific type of learning.

## Reviewing Prerequisite Knowledge

For any given objective, you must ask yourself the question, "What prerequisite learning should have taken place before I present this lesson?" The four categories of learning we have presented will help you to formulate an answer. The categories and the general prerequisite domains that should be addressed for each are shown in Figure 8.5.

*Figure 8.4*

*Key Verbs for Categories of Learning*

| Category of Learning | Key Verb Used in Computer Objectives |
|---|---|
| Rule-Using | Demonstrate, apply, solve, generate |
| Concept | Identify, sort, classify |
| Discrimination | Discriminate (same or different) |
| Verbal Information | List, state, summarize |

*Figure 8.5*

*Prerequisites for Objectives*

| If the Objective Is of This Type | Look for This Type of Learning as a Prerequisite |
|---|---|
| Rule-Using | Other rules, concepts, discriminations, and verbal information |
| Concept | Other concepts, discriminations, and verbal information |
| Discrimination | Other discriminations, possibly verbal information |
| Verbal Information | Other verbal information |

## Presenting Instruction

The presentation of instruction for each of the categories of learning is quite different. The instruction for teaching a student to list a set of facts (verbal information) would be far different from the instruction to teach a student to use a set of mathematics rules to solve a problem regarding triangles.

The key to the development of appropriate instruction for each of the categories of learning is to make sure that the instructional presentation is linked exactly to the objective of the lesson. If the lesson presentation screens are designed in such a manner as to attempt to move the student toward the instructional goal of "doing the verb in the objective," the presentation has a good chance of being appropriate and effective.

*Teaching for Verbal Information Learning.* Verbal information can be divided into three large categories: (1) memorizing verbatim information, (2) learning of facts, and (3) learning of larger bodies of information.

For the memorization of verbatim information on the computer, you should try to employ the following instructional techniques.

1. Provide mnemonic devices or memory bridges which are useful in remembering the verbal information.
2. Call attention to the meaning of the passage being memorized.
3. If the passage is long, break it into parts to be presented and rehearsed in sections.

For the learning of facts, you should utilize the technique of making associations with previous information.

For learning larger bodies of information, the following techniques should be applied:

1. Present questions to be answered after reading the passage.
2. Ask the learner to read, recite, and then review.
3. Have the learner look for major ideas rather than details.
4. Guide the learner to identify concepts in the passage, rather than focusing on rotely memorizing the information.

*Teaching for Discrimination Learning.* The computer does a

good job of teaching young students to discriminate the features of objects in their environment. The task is to teach them to tell if two stimuli on the screen are the same or different. With the computer, the stimuli will always be verbal or visual, unless the computer has the capability of producing sound or tactile stimulation.

The basic procedure for teaching discrimination is to make sure you point out the distinctive features of the shapes to be discriminated.

For example, if you are designing screens to teach a student to discriminate triangles from all other geometric figures, you might use the following screens to point out the distinctive features.

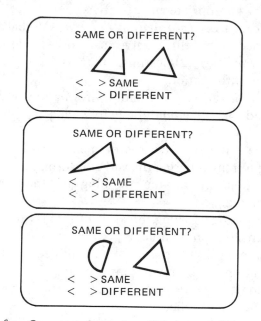

*Teaching for Concept Learning.* When a student is learning to identify or name an object, and therefore to place it into a class of objects, it is important to point out the relevant attributes so that they will be linked to the class. For example, suppose you are interested in teaching the concept of "triangle." The student has already learned to discriminate angles from curves, straight lines from curved ones, and closed figures from open figures. As you present your screens, be sure to point out the relevant features of triangles.

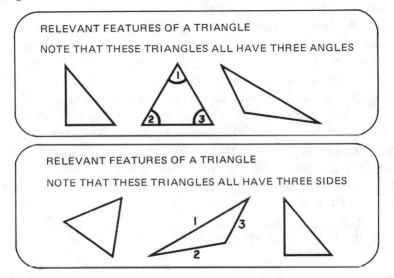

With the other screens, provide those situations where the relevant features stand out as defining characteristics; therefore, those features are to be depended on to separate the members of the class from objects that are similar on other characteristics, but are not members of the concept group. For example, look at this screen:

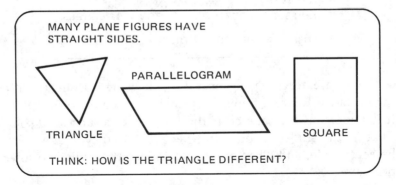

If presenting a defined, rather than concrete, concept, you should make sure you give a clear definition, and show relevant instances of those concepts which compose the definition and their relation to one another. To help a student understand the concept of "plane figure" as it is defined (geometric elements in a particular shape or form, all of which lie in a plane), requires more than the presentation of the definition. The computer should provide relevant instances of the concepts (plane, elements, form) underlying the definition and should show how they relate to one another in order to enable the student to classify objects as belonging or not belonging to the class of plane figures.

*Teaching for Rule-Using Learning.* The using of rules is an extremely important intellectual skill. When the student learns to use the rules that govern the multiplication of two whole numbers, for example, he or she can then apply what he or she has learned with any set of two whole numbers. Rule-using is an intellectual skill that provides the student a method for solving a whole class of problems.

In teaching for rule-using learning, make sure to clearly state the rule. An example is:

```
HERE IS ONE RULE FOR FINDING THE
SIZE OF AN ANGLE IN A TRIANGLE,
WHEN YOU KNOW THE
SIZE OF ANY TWO ANGLES.

TO FIND THE NUMBER OF DEGREES
IN AN ANGLE, ADD THE NUMBER OF
DEGREES IN THE TWO KNOWN ANGLES,
AND SUBTRACT THAT SUM FROM 180 DEGREES.

PUSH <ENTER> TO CONTINUE.
```

If you are teaching higher-order rule-using learning, such as in this instance where a number of rules are used to solve a problem, it is important to make clear the features of a successful solution. That is, the student should know exactly what type of answer will be acceptable, and what other rules might be applied to solve the problem.

## Considerations of Other Lesson Presentation Rules

Although specific modifications for other aspects of lesson presentation will not be explicitly stated here, you should understand that the type of learning being taught should be taken into consideration when you are designing any aspect of a lesson. For example, your instructional examples should exhibit exactly the same characteristics that you have defined in the objective. The example should provide the student with an exact model of the performance he or she is expected to successfully do.

With this principle in mind, it is clear that some categories of learning rely more heavily on examples than do others. Suppose the objective of the lesson is to have the student learn to recite a poem (verbal learning). It is of little value to have the computer simulate this endeavor by presenting examples. It is better if the computer presents the poem and clearly tells the student to learn the poem, and then presents it for learning in small chunks so that the student can master the performance.

If the objective of the lesson is learning a concept, it is essential that students see examples and non-examples of a variety of cases of the concept. If the objective of the lesson is to learn to classify leaves on the basis of their vein structure and to place them into one of three categories, examples of assorted types of leaves having and not having the appropriate characteristics must be presented in sufficient number to establish the classes, and hence, the category concepts.

In general, design the instruction presentation in such a manner that the examples provide an exact picture of what the student is "supposed to do" when he or she has successfully learned the lesson.

Practice items are of exactly the same nature as examples, except that the student performs a test rather than seeing an example task performed for him or her by the computer. Since the examples are exactly congruent with the task described in the objective, and since the practice items are congruent with the examples, you will have no trouble in deciding the type of practice items appropriate for a given learning category.

There are no conceptual differences in the testing procedures between the various categories of learning. The major concept is that the test be exactly parallel with the objective of the lesson, with the examples presented, and with the practice items on which the student has worked.

## Summary

This chapter has not provided explicit directions for the creation of any given lesson. That venture will be left to you. But your creative endeavor should take place within a framework of knowledge about learning and teaching. This chapter has provided that framework and shown you some of the aspects of learning that should influence the direction the development process of instructional materials for the computer will take.

## References

Bloom, B.S. *et al.* (Eds.) *A Taxonomy of Educational Objectives, Handbook I: Cognitive Domain.* New York: Longman, Inc., 1956.

Briggs, L.J., and Wager, W.W. *Handbook of Procedures for the Design of Instruction* (Second Edition). Englewood Cliffs, NJ: Educational Technology Publications, 1981.

Gagné, R.M., and Briggs, L.J. *Principles of Instructional Design* (Second Edition). New York: Holt, Rinehart, and Winston, 1979.

Krathwohl, D.R., Bloom, B.S., and Masia, B.B. *Taxonomy of Educational Objectives, Handbook II: Affective Domain.* New York: Longman, Inc., 1964.

# PART III
# MANAGING LEARNING

Chapter 9: The Well-Trained Computer-Manager

Chapter 10: Preparing a CMI System

# Chapter 9
# The Well-Trained Computer-Manager

## Introduction

*Instructional Intent.* In Chapter 2, we introduced the concept of computer-managed instruction (CMI). Now that the characteristics of a well-trained computer-teacher have been presented, let's look again at CMI, this time in much greater depth. When examining a CMI system, we can ask of it a question similar to that we asked of CAI: "What are the characteristics of a well-trained computer-manager?"

The objectives of this chapter are:

1. State the three basic ways CMI can assist the teacher in the management of student learning.
2. Describe a simple CMI system which performs classroom testing for the teacher.
3. Describe a CMI system which performs all basic CMI functions.
4. Describe some of the types of records that a CMI system can produce for the teacher.
5. List seven structural components possessed by a sophisticated CMI system.
6. Relate the concepts of CAI and CMI.

The microcomputer's repertoire of technical capabilities is such that it can easily handle the giving of tests, recording of student performance, and prescribing of instructional activities. As will be presented in this chapter on CMI, these tasks and others can be integrated in such a way as to take sound advantage of the computer's capabilities, thereby permitting it to take on a significant role in the management of student learning and the tracking of student progress.

*Knowledge Prerequisites.* Knowing traditional classroom procedures for testing, recordkeeping, and prescribing of learning activities will allow you to compare typical classroom practices with those that can be implemented when the computer is employed as a manager.

-------------------------------------------------------------------

171

## The Computer as Manager of Learning

One of the major roles of a classroom teacher, aside from direct instruction, is being a manager of instruction. The teacher makes both instructional and non-instructional plans for the activities in his or her classroom, and oversees and monitors these activities. Management includes the concepts of testing, monitoring student learning performance, keeping records of that performance, assigning learning activities, and ultimately making some sort of judgment concerning student progress in learning. The computer can play an important part in these instructional management activities.

Computer-managed instruction (CMI) is a set of computer functions, created by a program, in which the computer assists the teacher in his or her role as learning manager. Just as CAI has certain features that enable the computer to be effective as a teacher, CMI has certain characteristics that enable the computer to serve in a role as an effective manager and monitor of learning.

Perhaps this is a good time to reiterate an important point. You must clearly distinguish CMI from CAI, and this may be difficult because both of these computer roles have similar elements.

In fact, performance objectives and objective-referenced tests are essential components of both good CAI and good CMI. In CAI, these two elements enable the computer to teach something, i.e., to change a student's behavior. In CMI, however, they function to enable the computer to monitor the student's learning progress—providing information to the teacher as to how well, how quickly, or whether a student is making progress in a learning sequence—and enabling the computer to even recommend appropriate study activities through which the student can progress in his or her classwork. To the well-trained computer, performance objectives and objective-referenced tests are indispensable tools for functioning in either a management or a teaching role.

A program designer can create an effective CMI system that does not teach anything. Similarly, a program designer can create a well-trained CAI system that does not monitor a student's progress as he or she is learning. Often, a computer uses both a CAI system to teach and a CMI system to monitor the teaching. (These systems may be found in conjunction with one another on a single disk.) Although a CMI system does not directly teach, it can, like the teacher who manages the classroom effectively, certainly help to create an overall learning environment that strongly influences learning.

## Functional Elements of CMI

There are three basic ways in which the computer can be asked to contribute to the management of student learning: (1) giving tests, (2) keeping records, and (3) diagnosing performance and prescribing instruction. As we have pointed out in Chapter 2, any of these three functions can be performed by the classroom computer with relative ease. However, a computer that performs one, two, or even all three functions for a teacher in the classroom is not necessarily doing computer-managed instruction.

The whole thrust of CMI is to manage students' learning progress within a specified learning sequence. A system without a clearly-defined curricular structure is not a CMI system, and the computer cannot be a well-trained computer-manager without performance objectives defining that curriculum structure. With quality CMI, the computer's instructional management role becomes that of the monitoring of student performance within an objectives-based learning framework and the guiding of students in their progression through a set of learning tasks.

Goals and objectives play an integral part in effective CMI just as they do in effective CAI. The goals of the CMI learning framework provide the CMI system with direction as to what is "desired" for the learners. The performance objectives operationalize the goals in terms that a computer can "understand." The objectives give the computer the means for "knowing" what is to be monitored.

Within a defined framework of learning objectives, the computer is able to perform its testing, recordkeeping, and/or diagnostic/prescriptive functions in ways that dramatically increase its classroom contribution to the monitoring and guiding of student learning. When placed in the context of performance objectives, these three functions become more clear. As a manager of student progress in learning a sequence of performance objectives, the computer can contribute by:

(1) giving valid and reliable tests to measure student performance on the objectives;

(2) keeping records of student progress through the objectives; and

(3) diagnosing student performance and prescribing study to promote the learning of the objectives.

In the following section, we will illustrate how the contribution of the classroom computer as manager of student learning can grow as it takes on each of these functions in sequence.

### Simple CMI System

Here in this chapter we want to look at CMI from the standpoint of classroom use. The next chapter covers in detail how a teacher prepares a computer disk for his or her students, so here we will focus on application and refer only in general terms to the preparation aspects.

What directly follows is an example of a very simple CMI system which could easily be used in any classroom where students are working individually or in small groups. This example CMI system is so simple that it performs only the testing function of classroom management. It does not even keep any records for the teacher.

Imagine that a teacher in an elementary school class is teaching the division of fractions. The unit has five objectives (provided for him in his school's syllabus of studies). Following very simple directions provided on his CMI computer disk, he places onto the disk ten math questions for Objective 1 of the lesson, 15 questions for Objective 2, and so forth for the five objectives in the unit. He has made a decision as to how many test items he wants for each objective, and he has decided what a "pass" is for each objective. This information he has also placed on the disk. He copies his work onto a student disk, labels the disk, "MATH UNIT THREE: DIVIDING FRACTIONS," and puts the disk aside until it is time for math work.

At lesson time, the teacher puts the students to work on learning the division of fractions, using their textbooks. As soon as the first student completes his or her work, he or she is given the disk and sent to the computer.

Putting the disk in the computer and turning it on, the student sees the first screen:

```
THIS IS A QUIZ ON DIVIDING
FRACTIONS—OBJECTIVE 1

I WILL GIVE YOU ONE FRACTION
TO DIVIDE BY A SECOND FRACTION.

DO THE PROBLEM ON PAPER, AND
TYPE YOUR ANSWER INTO THE
COMPUTER. USE THIS FORM
FOR YOUR ANSWER <1/2>.

PUSH <ENTER> TO SEE
THE FIRST PROBLEM.
```

The student pushes <ENTER>, and the next screen appears:

```
PROBLEM 1:

DIVIDE 1/2 by 1/4.

YOUR ANSWER IS <       >

TYPE ANSWER AND THEN PUSH <ENTER>.
```

The student types < 2 >, and the computer goes on to the next problem. The computer presents five problems to the student, all of which the student gets right. The computer screen then shows:

```
CONGRATULATIONS,
YOU PASSED THE TEST ON
OBJECTIVE 1. SHOW YOUR TEACHER
THIS SCREEN SO HE WILL KNOW
YOU HAVE BEEN SUCCESSFUL.

PUSH <ENTER> WHEN FINISHED.
```

The student calls the teacher's attention to the screen, and then pushes <ENTER>. The screen is then left waiting for the next student.

Figure 9.1 summarizes this simple CMI program.

*Figure 9.1*

*A Simple CMI Program*

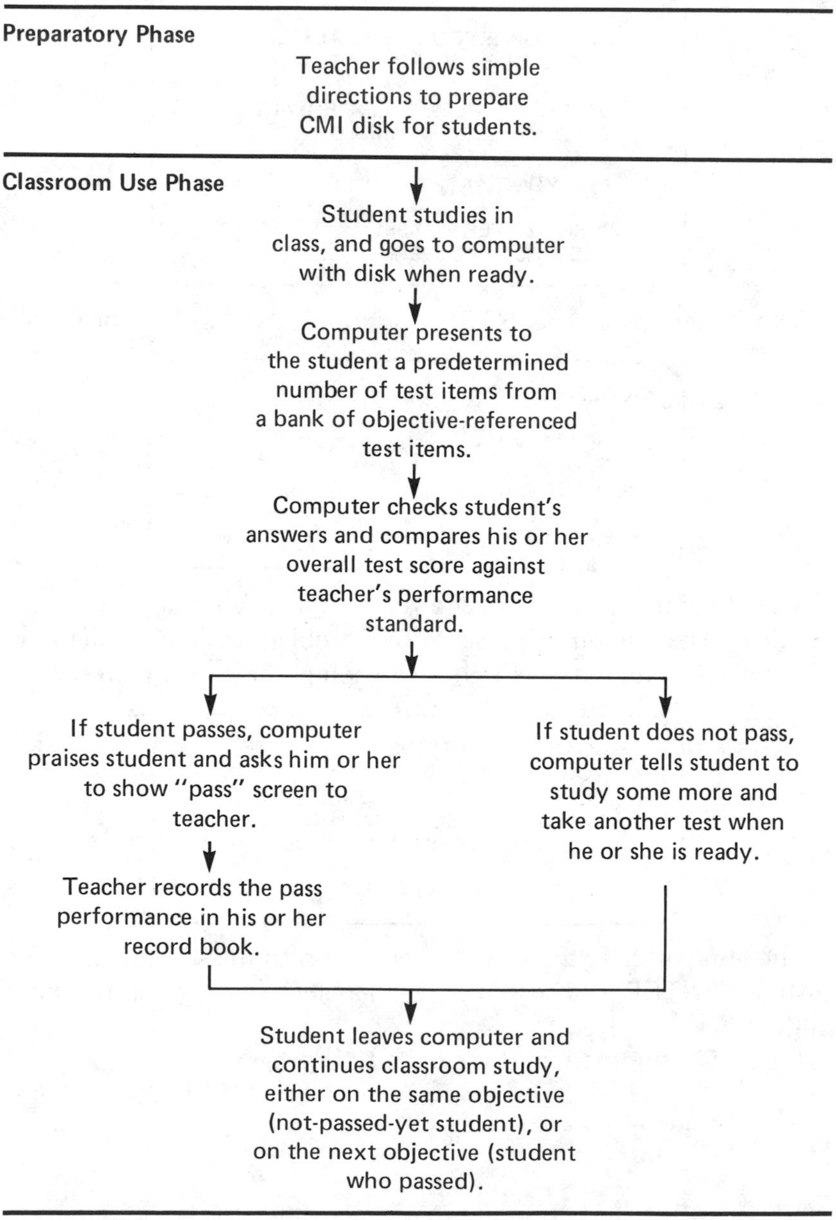

---

**Preparatory Phase**

Teacher follows simple
directions to prepare
CMI disk for students.

---

**Classroom Use Phase**

Student studies in
class, and goes to computer
with disk when ready.

Computer presents to
the student a predetermined
number of test items from
a bank of objective-referenced
test items.

Computer checks student's
answers and compares his or her
overall test score against
teacher's performance
standard.

If student passes, computer                          If student does not pass,
praises student and asks him or her              computer tells student to
to show "pass" screen to                                study some more and
teacher.                                                        take another test when
                                                                    he or she is ready.

Teacher records the pass
performance in his or her
record book.

Student leaves computer and
continues classroom study,
either on the same objective
(not-passed-yet student), or
on the next objective (student
who passed).

---

This system, although simple, provides a teacher with the ability to test any student at any time, as many times as necessary. Your students would probably find such quizzing less threatening than taking a paper-and-pencil sit-down test.

This simple system also enables the implementation of mastery learning/teaching techniques. The test and retest capability of the computer would allow you to teach, while the computer makes the decision about whether any student has or has not yet mastered a given objective. If a student receives a not-passed-yet assessment by the computer, you can approach the topic from another direction, teach the topic again, and have the student retake the test. In this manner, you can make sure that students are mastering topics that are important and required in a sequential program of studies.

Some of the things you teach cannot be appropriately measured using the computer. These things you could continue to test using traditional procedures, while you turn the other areas over to the objective-test-giving computer.

The very elementary, but effective, CMI system we have described works especially well with small groups of students. With larger groups, a more sophisticated system would probably be in order. Think how useful it would be for the computer to store the records of each student's performance, so that the student would not need to call you over after each test to check his or her progress by looking at the screen, and you would not need to record the performance in the record book. Taking over the recordkeeping function in addition to doing the testing is a snap for the appropriately trained CMI computer.

### CMI Recordkeeping

An essential feature of most CMI systems is the ability to monitor a student's progress and keep records on that progress for the teacher. If appropriately trained to do so, the computer will keep records, such as the order of the goals studied, when each goal was started and completed, student performance on each objective under each goal, how many tests a student took while attempting to pass a given objective, and the date of completion of each objective and goal.

Here we will describe a few examples of the types of records commonly used in CMI programs.

An individual student's unit record could include a complete record for one student on one or more units. The record might state the date the student last attempted an objective, whether it was passed or not passed, and whether the test on an objective has or has not been attempted. Let's look at Robert Shaw's record (see Figure 9.2 for a computer printout of this record).

Robert has passed the first two objectives on Unit 3, and then did not pass Objectives 3 and 4. He has not yet started Objective 5. By examining these data, the teacher could decide whether Robert is or is not progressing satisfactorily. You may notice from the dates that Robert took about two weeks after not passing Objective 3 before he tried Objective 4, which he did not pass. It is probable that Robert should be directed back to work on Objective 3, to study until that objective is passed, at which time he would then be guided to Objective 4.

Class records of the performance of all the students in a class or group on an objective provide useful data for the teacher. The chart (see Figure 9.3) shows that McGuire has not yet attempted the objective, that Mendoza passed it on the first try and Thalberg on the third, and that Wang did not pass the objective on his first try. McGuire may be a candidate for some encouragement to get started, and Wang may need help.

A summary of class performance on a unit places the test performance data into a pattern which makes it easy to see how the students are progressing in their studies (see Figure 9.4). As you can observe in the record in Figure 9.4, all of the students in this class have completed Objective 1, all but one have completed Objective 2, and none have completed Objective 5. By looking at the class record for Objective 2 of Unit 3, you could identify the name of the student who had not completed this objective and remind him to work on it. Objective 3 seems to be giving two students trouble. Of the three that took the test on Objective 3, only one passed. You could look at this objective and ask how effective the instruction was in helping the students to reach the objective.

*Figure 9.2*

A Sample Record of a Student's Performance

RECORD OF ROBERT SHAW AS OF FEBRUARY 5
MATH UNIT 3—DIVIDING FRACTIONS

| DATE | PASSED | NOT-PASSED-YET | NOT ATTEMPTED | LESSON |
|------|--------|----------------|---------------|--------|
| 1/17 | X | | | OBJECTIVE 1 |
| 1/19 | X | | | OBJECTIVE 2 |
| 1/21 | | X | | OBJECTIVE 3 |
| 2/03 | | X | | OBJECTIVE 4 |
| | | | X | OBJECTIVE 5 |

*Figure 9.3*

A Sample Record of Class Performance

CLASS PERFORMANCE OF GROUP 1 ON UNIT 3. OBJECTIVE 1—
DIVIDING FRACTIONS (CATEGORY 1/X DIVIDED BY 1/Y)

| STUDENT NAME | PASSED | NOT-PASSED-YET | NUMBER OF TEST ATTEMPTS | DATE OF MOST RECENT ATTEMPT |
|--------------|--------|----------------|-------------------------|------------------------------|
| MCGUIRE | | X | 0 | —/— |
| MENDOZA | X | | 1 | 5/30 |
| THALBERG | X | | 3 | 6/18 |
| WANG | | X | 1 | 6/23 |

*Figure 9.4*

*A Sample Record Summarizing Class Performance*

DATE: SEPTEMBER 29

GROUP 4 HAS FOUR STUDENTS
UNIT 3, OBJECTIVES 1 THROUGH 5

| OBJECTIVE # | NUMBER OF STUDENTS WHO HAVE | | |
| --- | --- | --- | --- |
| | TAKEN TEST | PASSED | NOT-PASSED-YET |
| 1 | 4 | 4 | 0 |
| 2 | 4 | 3 | 1 |
| 3 | 3 | 1 | 2 |
| 4 | 1 | 1 | 0 |
| 5 | 0 | 0 | 0 |

CMI can also be used to produce a variety of other reports, including such reports as parent reports of student progress (see Figure 9.5). With a printer, the teacher can even use the computer to generate printed tests for distribution in class, as well as print out a paper copy of any report which the CMI system can show on the screen.

The sample records we have shown in these charts require class lists and content organization by units and lessons. The teacher follows simple directions to "tell the CMI disk" how many classes he or she wishes to record, how many students are in each class and study group, and the students' names and other information. The more sophisticated the CMI program, the more preparatory activities on the part of the teacher are required to provide appropriate information to the computer.

With the provision by the teacher of class lists, test items, objectives, goals, and criteria for passing lessons in a unit, a CMI

*Figure 9.5*

*A Sample Record of a Report to Parents*

---

REPORT TO PARENTS OF MARY BROWN
SUBJECT AREA: LANGUAGE ARTS


SCHOOL:   CENTRAL MIDDLE SCHOOL
DATE:       MARCH, 1984
TEACHER:  DON NORETSKI


THIS REPORT SHOWS HOW WELL YOUR CHILD HAS DONE ON SKILLS
SHE HAS BEEN STUDYING IN SCHOOL.

---

CONGRATULATIONS: MARY HAS LEARNED THE FOLLOWING SKILLS:

   FINDING THE MAIN IDEA OF A PARAGRAPH.
   FORMING COMPOUND WORDS FROM FAMILIAR WORDS.
   FORMING WORDS WITH POSSESSIVE FORMS.

MARY NEEDS HELP ON THE FOLLOWING SKILL:

   UNDERSTANDING THE WORD ENDINGS -ER AND -EST.

THE RECOMMENDED HOME STUDY ASSIGNMENT ON THIS SKILL
IS ON PAGES 45-49 IN HER LANGUAGE WORKBOOK.

---

IF YOU WISH INFORMATION, CALL THE HOME STUDY
COORDINATOR AT 354-4478.

---

---

system can exhibit good management skills. It is ready to be used
in a more sophisticated manner.

## A Basic CMI System

Suppose that a CMI system is monitoring reading comprehension. The teacher has established objectives for the CMI using the
school's curriculum goals for reading comprehension. He or she
has entered onto the CMI disk the appropriate number of unit
goals and lesson objective numbers directly from the curriculum

guide. He or she has entered an appropriate bank of test items for each objective and the number of items and performance level standards for each objective.

The teacher would then teach the first lesson, using whatever method he or she chose: such as small-group instruction, independent study using a reading test, or some reading program. As soon as a student had finished the first lesson, the teacher would have him or her go to the computer.

> WELCOME. PLEASE TYPE YOUR
> NAME. <                    >
>
> PUSH <ENTER> WHEN DONE.

The student types <JANICE SMITH>, and the computer checks the record to make sure she is a member of the class. The computer says:

> THANK YOU, JANICE.
>
> YOU ARE SCHEDULED TO TAKE
> A TEST ON UNIT 1,
> LESSON 1. HAVE YOU
> STUDIED THIS OBJECTIVE
> COMPLETELY?
>
> PLEASE TYPE YES OR NO.
>
>     <        >
>
> PUSH <ENTER> TO GO ON.

The computer had checked Janice's record and found that she had not yet tried any tests on any objective, therefore it started her on Unit 1, Lesson 1. For future reference, the computer will keep a complete record of which objectives Janice attempts, which she completes, and when she completes them. The computer will automatically present Janice with the correct objective to be evaluated. Janice types "YES" and pushes <ENTER>.

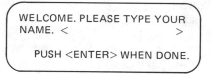

> HERE IS YOUR TASK.
>
> THE SCREEN WILL PRESENT A PASSAGE

> AND THEN ASK YOU TO ANSWER FIVE
> QUESTIONS ABOUT THE PASSAGE. YOU
> MUST GET FOUR OF THE QUESTIONS
> RIGHT TO PASS THIS OBJECTIVE. THE
> READING IS NOT TIMED. PUSH <ENTER>
> TO MOVE AHEAD THROUGH THE READING,
> PUSH <B> TO MOVE BACK TO PREVIOUS
> PARTS OF THE READING.
>
> PUSH <ENTER> TO SEE THE READING.

Janice pushes <ENTER>, reads the passage, and then is presented with five comprehension questions. The computer will check her answers, score the test, determine if she has achieved the teacher-designated performance level, and record her as passed or not-passed-yet. After the test, the screen will display either of the following:

> CONGRATULATIONS, JANICE. YOU PASSED
> OBJECTIVE 1. CONTINUE YOUR
> STUDIES ON UNIT 1, LESSON 2.
> RETURN WHEN
> YOU ARE READY TO TAKE
> THE TEST ON OBJECTIVE 2.
>
> PUSH <ENTER> TO STOP.

or

> SORRY, YOU DID NOT PASS
> OBJECTIVE 1. CONTINUE YOUR
> STUDIES ON THIS OBJECTIVE.
> ASK YOUR TEACHER TO GIVE YOU
> HELP. I WILL SEE YOU WHEN YOU
> ARE READY TO TRY THE OBJECTIVE
> AGAIN.
>
> PUSH <ENTER> TO STOP.

The flowchart in Figure 9.6 illustrates the steps in this relatively simple CMI system.

The computer will record the performance of all members of the class, and at some future time, such as at an end-of-week update or when it is time to prepare reports, the teacher can review the class records of student performance.

*Figure 9.6*

*Steps in a Basic CMI System*

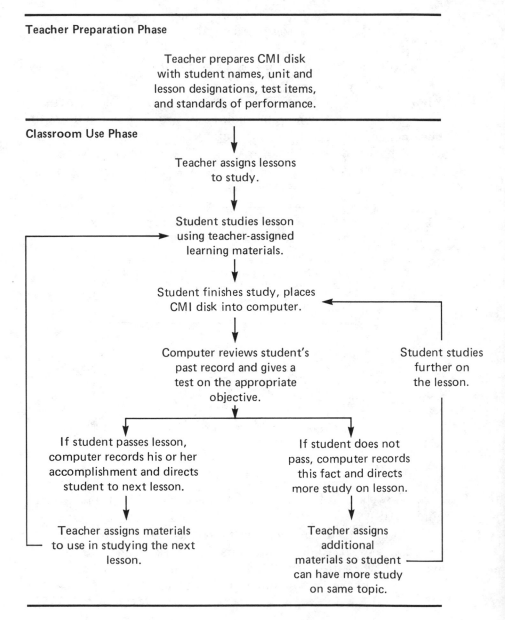

**Teacher Preparation Phase**

Teacher prepares CMI disk
with student names, unit and
lesson designations, test items,
and standards of performance.

**Classroom Use Phase**

Teacher assigns lessons
to study.

Student studies lesson
using teacher-assigned
learning materials.

Student finishes study, places
CMI disk into computer.

Computer reviews student's
past record and gives a
test on the appropriate
objective.

Student studies
further on
the lesson.

If student passes lesson,
computer records his or her
accomplishment and directs
student to next lesson.

If student does not
pass, computer records
this fact and directs
more study on lesson.

Teacher assigns materials
to use in studying the next
lesson.

Teacher assigns
additional
materials so student
can have more study
on same topic.

## A Powerful CMI System

More sophisticated CMI systems will train the computer in a third function, that of diagnosing and prescribing new study for the students who pass a given test, and prescribing additional study for those whose performance on the test is not-passed-yet. In such a system when the computer diagnoses a given student's performance on a specific test, the computer will present the student with a learning prescription for subsequent study. The expectation is that the student will turn off the computer, study the material prescribed by the computer, and then return at a later date to be evaluated. The computer would evaluate the student who had passed and gone on to study new material on the objective of that new study. It would evaluate other students on the topic they had not yet passed, using a second set of test items to measure their performance. The testing/diagnosis/prescription/ study/retest cycle would continue as long as necessary, until each student demonstrated he or she had learned everything expected of him or her by the teacher.

In this way, the teacher would not even need to spend class time telling a student what to study. This task would be in the computer's "hands." The first time a student used the program, the CMI system would test the student to determine his or her entry behavior for the lessons, starting his or her study on the first lesson on which he or she did not reach the lesson standards. The computer would then present on the screen a study assignment for the lesson.

Here is a series of screens which illustrates this sort of CMI system.

```
HELLO, MARK. WE NEED
TO WORK TOGETHER TO HELP
YOU LEARN ALGEBRA. FIRST,
YOU WILL NEED TO TAKE A SERIES
OF QUIZZES TO DETERMINE WHERE
YOU SHOULD START YOUR STUDIES.

    PUSH <ENTER> TO CONTINUE.
```

FOR EACH OF THE FOLLOWING QUESTIONS, FIND THE
CORRECT ANSWER.

1.  3X + 17 = 23                          X = <?>
    A.  23
    B.   6
    C.   2
    D.   0

TYPE THE LETTER OF YOUR ANSWER TO #1: <      >

The computer presents a series of items, and then presents this
sequence of screens to Mark:

CONGRATULATIONS, MARK.

YOU PASSED THE FIRST THREE OBJECTIVES FOR UNIT 1.

PUSH <ENTER>.

YOU SHOULD START YOUR STUDIES ON OBJECTIVE 4
OF UNIT 1.

                         YOU CAN SOLVE SIMPLE EQUATIONS
---OBJECTIVE 4---  IN ONE UNKNOWN OF THE FORM 3X + 34 = 43.
                         YOU FIND THE VALUE OF X, GETTING AT
                         LEAST 8 OUT OF 10 QUESTIONS CORRECT.

PUSH <ENTER>.

YOU CAN USE THESE MATERIALS IN THE CLASSROOM TO
STUDY THE OBJECTIVE.

■ STUDY YOUR ALGEBRA TEXT, PAGES 17-23.
■ DO PROBLEMS 1-25 ON PAGES 24 AND 25 OF YOUR
  TEXT.
■ REVIEW THE SLIDE-TAPE PRESENTATION #5
  (IN BOX ON OUR LIBRARY SHELF).
■ OPTIONAL: DO DRILL AND PRACTICE ON S.R.A. MATH
  CARDS, BOX 3, CARD 4.
  PUSH <ENTER> TO PRINT THE OBJECTIVE AND STUDY
  ASSIGNMENTS ON THE PRINTER.

```
YOU CAN START YOUR STUDIES NOW, MARK.
WHEN YOU FINISH, COME BACK AND
TAKE THE TEST ON UNIT 1, LESSON 4.

PUSH <BREAK>.
```

Figure 9.7 shows the pattern of a powerful CMI system.

Just as the student will not see the same test items on a retest as were encountered on the first test, neither will the computer prescribe the same study assignment to the student for whom the prescribed study materials proved insufficient as instruction. A CMI system can be programmed to offer a series of restudy assignments.

The pattern of CMI shown in Figure 9.7 is quite comprehensive and a sophisticated learning system, but that does not mean it is necessarily complicated to set up and use. The utilization of a "pre-written" computer program to prepare this pattern makes life much simpler for the teacher. Many elements of this pattern for instruction are present in good teaching. Many school districts have moved to "objectives-based" teaching and testing, and coupling these elements with appropriate instructional materials is well worth the effort required.

## The Structural Elements of CMI

In order to perform the functions we have illustrated in this chapter, a good CMI computer needs the following structural elements:

- It has the organization of the teacher's groups or classes (how many and how many students in each, and who they are).
- It has the plan of units and lessons (goals and objectives) the teacher is teaching.
- It has a bank of valid test items for each instructional objective in the system.
- It has instructions for the number of items to present to students to insure a reliable test.
- It has the level of performance the teacher expects of his or her students on each objective.

*Figure 9.7*

*Pattern of Powerful CMI System*

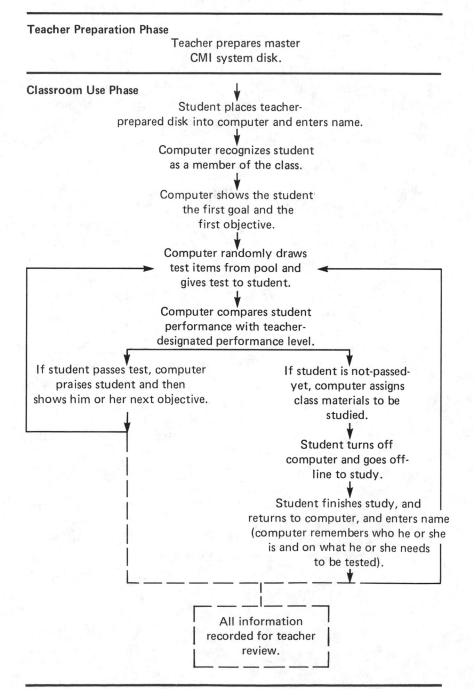

**Teacher Preparation Phase**

Teacher prepares master
CMI system disk.

**Classroom Use Phase**

Student places teacher-
prepared disk into computer and enters name.

Computer recognizes student
as a member of the class.

Computer shows the student
the first goal and the
first objective.

Computer randomly draws
test items from pool and
gives test to student.

Computer compares student
performance with teacher-
designated performance level.

If student passes test, computer
praises student and then
shows him or her next objective.

If student is not-passed-
yet, computer assigns
class materials to be
studied.

Student turns off
computer and goes off-
line to study.

Student finishes study, and
returns to computer, and enters name
(computer remembers who he or she
is and on what he or she needs
to be tested).

All information
recorded for teacher
review.

- It has a sufficiently large bank of test items to enable retesting of each objective.
- It has lists of classroom learning resources keyed to specific objectives.

With these structural elements, the computer has not only the capability to effectively guide and monitor student progress in learning, but it also has the capability of keeping extensive student records showing how each student is progressing in his or her studies.

### Integrating the Ideas of CMI and CAI

In Chapter 7, we presented an example tutorial lesson in which a student progressed through a CAI lesson. That lesson was a simple CAI presentation independent of any CMI. At the end of the lesson, the student, Betty, was asked by the computer to call over her teacher to demonstrate to the teacher that she had finished her lesson. In the case of this lesson that procedure was all right, since the teacher could present a brief oral quiz to make sure that the student was pronouncing all the names of the states and capitals correctly, but in many cases, the efficiency of a CAI lesson can be increased dramatically by tying CAI to CMI.

Figure 9.8 illustrates how a CMI component can be integrated in two different ways with the triangle that represents a well-trained computer-teacher.

When *within* a CAI lesson, CMI becomes the monitor program for the CAI, tracking the student's progress through the lesson. It can be used with the purpose of providing the teacher with a record of important aspects of the student's interaction with the learning system. It can, however, play a larger role. By monitoring the student's use of examples and helps, and by noting the degree of success with practice items, the CMI component can use the information to adjust the instruction the student receives. It can, for example, use the information to prescribe practice of a different difficulty level, or to automatically branch the student to particular explanations or hints.

As was described in this chapter, CMI can also monitor student progress *across* a series of objectives, some of which may be taught

*Figure 9.8*

*Integrating the CMI Component*
*into the Total System*

**Within-Lesson CMI**

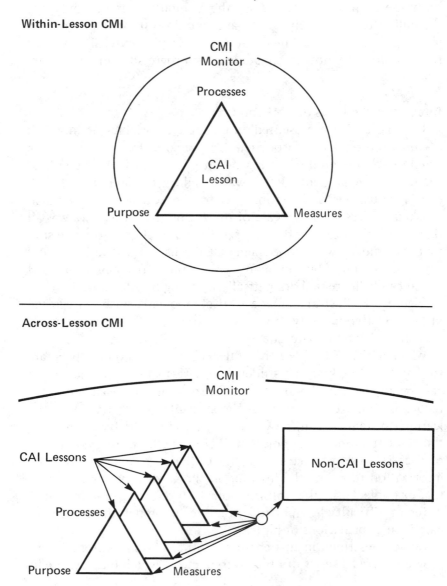

via CAI lessons, and some of which may be taught by other means. While the purpose may again be simply to report the student's progress to the teacher, the CMI system can also play the more powerful role pictured in Figure 9.7 on page 188.

In a strict CMI system (with no CAI component), if a student has not yet passed a lesson:

If student is not-passed-
yet, computer assigns
class materials to be studied.

↓

Student turns off
computer and goes off-
line to study.

↓

Student finishes study, and
returns to computer, which
remembers who he or she is and
on what he or she needs to be tested.

In a CMI/CAI system, these actions may be replaced by the following:

↓

If student is not-passed-yet, an
appropriate tutorial lesson
is provided on the computer.

↓

Student finishes CAI lesson,
and CMI takes over again to
determine next lesson.

With this pattern, the student never leaves the computer, but rather is presented the appropriate CAI lesson to teach the objective that the computer has diagnosed the student needs to learn. The pretesting/study/testing/restudy/retesting/recordkeeping cycle continues on the computer until the student has mastered the assigned lessons.

A well-trained CMI/CAI computer can liberate the teacher from the more mundane tasks of testing, recordkeeping, and prescribing, and some aspects of teaching, leaving more time for the teacher to concentrate on helping individual students in ways that a computer cannot.

# Chapter 10
# Preparing a CMI System

## Introduction

*Instructional Intent.* You now have some knowledge of the capabilities of a classroom computer that is well-trained in CMI. This chapter takes a practical look at how a CMI system is organized and the type of information it requires and produces.

This chapter will help you to reach the following objectives:

1. Compare and contrast an open CMI system and a closed one.
2. State the function of CMI menus.
3. Describe the organization of a good CMI system.
4. List some of the types of information needed in a CMI system.
5. Describe the process a teacher uses to provide information to a CMI system.
6. Describe the process a teacher uses to obtain information from a CMI system.

The teacher must prepare a CMI system prior to using it in the classroom. This chapter outlines the procedure the teacher uses to provide the CMI system with the information it needs to enable the system in turn to produce useful information on student progress.

*Knowledge Prerequisites.* The reader should comprehend the role of CMI as presented in Chapter 2, and have knowledge of the nature of an effective CMI system—its functional and structural elements—as presented in Chapter 9.

-------------------------------------------------------------------------

## Establishing a CMI System

CMI systems come in a multitude of forms. Some are the product of a commercial development effort on a specific topic. These "closed systems" leave no room for the teacher to add any aspect to the system that has been purchased. Some systems are "open" to additions. In fact, there are open systems that are free of all subject matter content and are simply the framework for the teacher to create his or her own monitoring and record system. Other CMI offerings provide a basic framework of objectives and tests on a given topic, and allow teachers to add test items or objectives as required for their specific needs.

Whatever the configuration of the system and no matter who develops it, a well-trained computer's CMI system will have the functional capabilities and structural elements we identified in Chapter 9. Here we will utilize an open CMI framework that is totally void of content to illustrate how a versatile CMI system would be prepared for classroom use. As this chapter progresses, our blank system will be completed by a hypothetical teacher who is using the system for the first time.

The CMI system can be blank because the record management portion of the system is independent of the content portion of the system. A functional CMI system can be thought of as having two parts, the general CMI framework, and the specific content used by the framework to monitor learning. In other words, a basic CMI system could be used to monitor any number of different units and lessons. The different lessons would be the content of the system, and the framework that organizes the content is the CMI system *per se.*

As with any blank CMI system, the sample system illustrated here will make provisions for the entry of the objectives in the learning sequence that the computer is to monitor. Additionally, the teacher will be able to enter those test items he or she wants to use to measure performance on the objectives. For every objective the computer itself is to measure, the teacher will be able to specify the size of the tests (number of test items) and the performance level the computer will use to determine whether or not a student has passed the objective.

As any good CMI system must do, our example system will need to provide for the teacher's entering of the names of his or her students in groups or classes. The teacher should also have the flexibility that will allow him or her to add and delete names as students come and go, and to reorganize the groups as learning progresses. And yet, with all these features, our sample system still must be easy for the teacher to use.

## A Menu-Driven CMI System

No CMI system will be appreciated by a teacher unless it is simple to use. The typical CMI system may be monitoring the progress of a hundred or more students through a number of learning tasks. If the system does not organize this information into an easily accessible pattern, it will be of little or no use to a busy teacher. Because a teacher must add a great deal of information to a blank CMI system, the facility with which the task of getting such a system ready for use becomes an even more critical factor.

Our hypothetical teacher will see this screen when he or she begins readying the CMI system for classroom use.

```
WELCOME TO INSTRUCTIONAL SYSTEMS
      PROGRAM FOR CMI

        COPYRIGHT 1984

PUSH <ENTER> TO CONTINUE.
```

A number of screens would then teach the user how to move forward to the next screen by pushing the <ENTER> key, and to move back to the previous screen by pushing the <←> key. Other directions such as type <HELP> and push <CONTROL-R> to record data would also be taught. We will not include these screens, but you should know that the teacher is using the procedure taught when moving from one screen to the next.

After reading all the instructional screens, the teacher pushes the <ENTER> key and moves to the first menu.

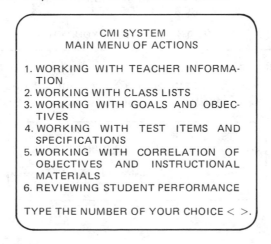

```
              CMI SYSTEM
          MAIN MENU OF ACTIONS

  1. WORKING WITH TEACHER INFORMA-
     TION
  2. WORKING WITH CLASS LISTS
  3. WORKING WITH GOALS AND OBJEC-
     TIVES
  4. WORKING WITH TEST ITEMS AND
     SPECIFICATIONS
  5. WORKING WITH CORRELATION OF
     OBJECTIVES AND INSTRUCTIONAL
     MATERIALS
  6. REVIEWING STUDENT PERFORMANCE

TYPE THE NUMBER OF YOUR CHOICE < >.
```

The teacher's choice of any menu item leads to another menu. In some cases, that menu leads to still another menu. Any series of choices finally leads to one or more action pages. At an action page, the teacher provides information or instructions to the computer.

In the menu-driven format, all of the actions a teacher can make in the CMI system are accessed through a cascade of choices:

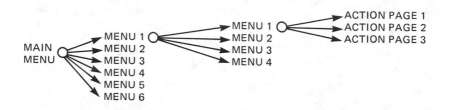

This type of organization is easy to deal with once a teacher has worked with the system and sees how to move forward to a new menu or action page, or backward to the previous menu.

### Setting Up the System

The hypothetical teacher chooses <1> on the MAIN MENU and pushes <ENTER> to arrive at another menu of choices for teacher action.

```
MENU 1: WORKING WITH TEACHER INFORMATION

    1. SETTING UP SYSTEM
    2. REVIEWING INFORMATION
    3. ADDING NEW INFORMATION
    4. DELETING OLD INFORMATION

        TYPE THE NUMBER OF YOUR CHOICE <  >.
```

On this menu, the teacher chooses the number <1> and pushes <ENTER> to arrive at an action page where content can be entered into the computer to establish aspects of the CMI system.

```
SYSTEM SET-UP
ACTION PAGE 1: TEACHER IDENTIFICATION

PLEASE TYPE LAST NAME, FIRST NAME
    <                                >
```

The teacher types <SMITH, SUE>, pushes <ENTER>, and the computer creates a new page.

```
SYSTEM SET-UP
ACTION PAGE 2: TEACHER PASSWORD

DO YOU WANT TO ESTABLISH A PASSWORD SO THAT
ONLY YOU WILL BE ABLE TO USE THIS CMI PROGRAM IN
THE FUTURE? TYPE <YES> OR <NO>.
```

Sue Smith types <YES>, and the computer shows a new screen.

```
–2–
CHOOSE A SINGLE WORD OF EIGHT LETTERS OR LESS
AS YOUR PASSWORD. CHOOSE A WORD YOU CANNOT
FORGET. IF YOU FORGET THIS PASSWORD, THERE IS NO
WAY TO ENTER THIS PROGRAM AGAIN. DO NOT CHOOSE
YOUR NAME OR INITIALS, OR OTHER WORDS SOMEONE
MIGHT GUESS. DO NOT WRITE THE PASSWORD DOWN IN
A PLACE THAT COULD BE SEEN BY A STUDENT. IF YOU
LEAVE THIS ENTRY BLANK, YOUR PASSWORD IS
<BLANK>, AND ANYONE CAN PRESS <ENTER> TO
ACCESS ALL THE RECORDS.

    TYPE YOUR PASSWORD <    >.
```

The teacher types <PANDA> and pushes <ENTER>, and the computer presents a new action page.

```
SYSTEM SET-UP
ACTION PAGE 3: CLASS GROUPING

THIS PROGRAM CAN MONITOR MORE THAN ONE GROUP
OF STUDENTS AT A TIME. NO STUDENT CAN BE IN
MORE THAN ONE GROUP, HOWEVER.

    HOW MANY STUDENT GROUPINGS DO YOU WANT TO
    CREATE? PLEASE TYPE A NUMBER FROM 1 TO 10.

            <    >
```

Ms. Smith wants the program to monitor four different classes of students (first, third, fifth, and sixth period classes). She types <4> and pushes <ENTER>. The computer shows a new screen:

```
-2-
DO YOU WANT TO GIVE THE GROUPS NAMES (SUCH
AS GROUP 1 = BLUEBIRDS, ETC.)? IF SO, TYPE IN
NAMES FOR GROUPS, PUSHING <ENTER> AFTER
EACH NAME. IF NOT, PUSH <ENTER>.

    GROUP 1 <         >
    GROUP 2 <         >
    GROUP 3 <         >
    GROUP 4 <         >
```

Our teacher decides there is no need to name her classes, so she pushes <ENTER>. The computer then summarizes the action pages with this screen:

```
SUMMARY PAGE FOR SYSTEM SET-UP

THIS CMI PROGRAM IS FOR SUE SMITH'S CLASSES

THE PASSWORD FOR THE PROGRAM IS PANDA

FOUR GROUPS OF STUDENTS WILL BE MONITORED
```

### Establishing Class Lists

After setting up the system, the teacher returns to the MAIN MENU (refer back to page 195).

Having completed MAIN MENU choice <1>, Sue Smith is ready to establish her class lists, providing the computer with the names of the students in each group to be monitored. She chooses MAIN MENU option 2, WORKING WITH CLASS LISTS, and sees:

```
MENU 2: WORKING WITH CLASS LISTS

1. MAKING UP CLASS LISTS OF STUDENTS
2. ADDING A STUDENT TO AN EXISTING CLASS
   LIST
3. DELETING A STUDENT FROM AN EXISTING
   CLASS LIST
4. REVIEWING A CLASS LIST

    TYPE THE NUMBER OF YOUR CHOICE <    >.
```

The menu categories listed allow the teacher easy access to the development and maintenance of class lists. New students come and old students go, and it must be easy to update the lists. This menu provides for that function.

If the teacher pushes <BREAK>, she will return to the MAIN MENU of action choices. If the teacher types a number and pushes <ENTER>, she will move forward to either another menu or action, depending on the choice. Ms. Smith chooses <1> on this menu, and arrives at another menu.

```
MENU FOR MAKING UP A CLASS LIST

1. WORK WITH CLASS LIST #1
2. WORK WITH CLASS LIST #2
3. WORK WITH CLASS LIST #3
4. WORK WITH CLASS LIST #4

   TYPE THE NUMBER OF YOUR CHOICE <   >.
```

The number of classes on this menu (4) is a result of our teacher having previously completed the SYSTEM SET-UP pages on class grouping. The computer remembered that Ms. Smith wanted to have four groups. When she types <1>, she sees the following screen:

```
CLASS LIST
ACTION PAGE 1: GROUP 1

DIRECTIONS: LIST THE STUDENTS' NAMES IN
ANY ORDER. TYPE THE LAST NAME AND A COMMA,
FOLLOWED BY THE FIRST NAME. THEN PUSH <ENTER>.
IF TWO STUDENTS' NAMES ARE IDENTICAL, YOU MUST
MAKE THEM DISTINGUISHABLE IN SOME MANNER,
PERHAPS BY ADDING A 1 AND 2 TO THEIR NAMES
(EXAMPLE: JONES1, SAM, AND JONES2, SAM).

STUDENT #1'S NAME IS <          >.

PUSH <ENTER> TWICE WHEN LISTING IS COMPLETE.
```

The teacher continues to enter names until all students to be monitored have been listed for the computer. The computer will count the number of names she enters for each group in order to know the size of each group.

By working with the four choices on the class list menu, Sue Smith tells the CMI system the names of all her students.

**Designating Curriculum Content**

Since this CMI system is completely open, the teacher will next need to enter the objectives that will be monitored by the system. Ms. Smith picks option 3 of the MAIN MENU—WORKING WITH GOALS AND OBJECTIVES (refer to page 195 for the MAIN MENU). This choice moves her to another menu:

MENU 3: WORKING WITH GOALS AND OBJECTIVES

1. SETTING UP UNITS AND LESSONS
2. ADDING AND DELETING UNITS OR LESSONS
3. EDITING STATEMENTS OF GOALS AND OBJECTIVES
4. SETTING PREREQUISITES AND OPTIONS
5. REVIEWING EXISTING GOALS AND OBJECTIVES

TYPE THE NUMBER OF YOUR CHOICE <    >.

The choice of <1> produces:

UNIT/LESSON SET-UP
ACTION PAGE 1: NUMBER OF GOALS

YOU MAY HAVE FROM 1 TO 5 UNITS.

HOW MANY UNITS ARE COVERED IN THIS CMI SYSTEM?

TYPE NUMBER <    >.

The teacher types <2>, and the next action page appears.

UNIT/LESSON SET-UP
ACTION PAGE 2: NUMBER OF OBJECTIVES

YOU MAY TYPE FROM 1 TO 10 OBJECTIVES PER UNIT.

HOW MANY LESSON OBJECTIVES ARE IN UNIT 1? <   >

HOW MANY LESSON OBJECTIVES ARE IN UNIT 2? <   >

Ms. Smith tells the computer that there will be eight lesson objectives for Unit 1, and five objectives for the second unit. The computer will record and remember the teacher's entries, and on the subsequent action pages the computer will present Ms. Smith the appropriate number of entry spaces automatically.

UNIT/LESSON SET-UP
ACTION PAGE 3: GOAL STATEMENTS

DIRECTIONS: STATE THE GOALS FOR THE TWO
UNITS. USE NO MORE THAN 256 LETTERS,
NUMBERS, AND SPACES FOR EACH GOAL. (IF YOU
CHOOSE TO MANAGE RECORDS USING ONLY GOAL
NUMBERS, PUSH <ENTER> TWICE.)

PUSH <ENTER>, AFTER TYPING A GOAL.
IF YOU MAKE AN ERROR IN TYPING BEFORE
YOU PUSH <ENTER>, SIMPLY WRITE OVER THE ERROR.
IF YOU MAKE AN ERROR AFTER PUSHING <ENTER>,
YOU WILL NEED TO PUSH <BREAK> TO RETURN TO
THE UNIT/LESSON SET-UP MENU AND CHOOSE
OPTION <3> TO EDIT THE STATEMENT.

1. GOAL FOR UNIT 1 IS: <                >.

2. GOAL FOR UNIT 2 IS: <                >.

The CMI system would know how many lessons were required for each goal, and so would ask the teacher to type in an objective for each lesson (if she chose to do so). It is not necessary to enter the goals and objectives into the computer in written form. That is, it may be sufficient for the teacher's purpose to keep the goals and objectives in alphanumeric (letters and numbers) form where the numbers and/or letters are correlated with objectives in a book, course outline, curriculum guide, or syllabus of studies.

The next action page is:

UNIT/LESSON SET-UP
ACTION PAGE 4: OBJECTIVE STATEMENTS FOR UNIT 1

DO YOU WANT TO STATE WRITTEN OBJECTIVES? IF NOT,
ON ALL RECORDS THE UNIT NUMBER AND THE OBJECTIVE
NUMBER WILL BE PROVIDED. IF SO, THE WRITTEN OBJECTIVE
WILL BE PROVIDED.

TYPE <YES> OR <NO>.

Ms. Smith chooses to type in objectives.

—2—
OBJECTIVE FOR UNIT 1, LESSON 1.

STATE THE OBJECTIVE. USE NO MORE THAN 256 LETTERS,

```
┌──────────────────────────────────────────────────────┐
│ NUMBERS, AND SPACES FOR EACH OBJECTIVE. IF AN          │
│ OBJECTIVE IS LEFT COMPLETELY BLANK, ITS NUMBER WILL    │
│ BE USED IN ALL RECORDS.                                │
│                                                        │
│ <                                                   >  │
└──────────────────────────────────────────────────────┘
```

### Designating Test Content

In an open CMI system, the teacher will be required to enter the test items. The computer will ask Sue Smith to define how many items will be needed from the pool of items stored by the computer for the reliable testing of the objective. The computer will also need her performance levels for decision-making.

All of the items for any given objective must be referenced to the objective, and by definition, be parallel. These items will be used in a variety of ways, depending on the nature of the CMI system and the actions of a given student. The teacher enters the test items by choosing option 4 on the MAIN MENU (refer to page 195).

```
┌──────────────────────────────────────────────────────┐
│          MENU 4: WORKING WITH TEST ITEMS               │
│                  AND SPECIFICATIONS                    │
│                                                        │
│     1.  SETTING UP TESTS FOR OBJECTIVES                │
│     2.  ADDING AND DELETING ITEMS AND ANSWERS          │
│     3.  EDITING TEST ITEMS AND ANSWERS                 │
│     4.  REVIEWING ITEMS                                │
│                                                        │
│     TYPE THE NUMBER OF YOUR CHOICE <   >.              │
└──────────────────────────────────────────────────────┘
```

The choice of option <1> provides an action page:

```
┌──────────────────────────────────────────────────────┐
│ TEST SET-UP                                            │
│ ACTION PAGE 1: TEST PARAMETERS                         │
│                                                        │
│ YOU NEED TO STATE HOW MANY ITEMS AND THE               │
│ PASS LEVEL FOR EACH OBJECTIVE.                         │
│                                                        │
│ FOR EACH UNIT AND LESSON, TYPE THIS                    │
│ INFORMATION IN THE FORM <XX, YY> AND                   │
│ PUSH <ENTER>. TYPE <00,00> IF YOU PLAN                 │
│ TO TEST AN OBJECTIVE YOURSELF OFF-LINE.                │
│ UNIT 1,   LESSON 1 <      >                            │
│           LESSON 2 <      >                            │
│           LESSON 3 <      >                            │
│           LESSON 4 <      >                            │
│           LESSON 5 <      >                            │
│           LESSON 6 <      >                            │
│           LESSON 7 <      >                            │
│           LESSON 8 <      >                            │
└──────────────────────────────────────────────────────┘
```

Ms. Smith types in the appropriate standards for each objective. She is then presented with:

```
TEST SET-UP
ACTION PAGE 2: TEST ITEMS

DIRECTIONS: YOU WILL BE PRESENTED ONE PAGE
AT A TIME, WITH THE UNIT AND LESSON NUMBER
AT THE TOP. THERE WILL BE A SPACE WHERE YOU
CAN ENTER YOUR TEST ITEM. TYPE THE ITEM INTO
THE SPACE. WHEN YOU ARE SATISFIED WITH YOUR
ITEM, PUSH <ENTER>. YOU WILL THEN BE ABLE TO
PROVIDE THE ANSWER.

IF YOU NEED TO CHANGE AN ITEM OR ANSWER
AFTER IT HAS BEEN ENTERED, USE THE EDIT
FUNCTION ON THE TEST MENU.
```

```
UNIT/LESSON SET-UP
ACTION PAGE 3: ENTERING TEST ITEMS AND ANSWERS
UNIT 1, OBJECTIVE 1, TEST ITEM 1

YOU MUST TYPE YOUR QUESTION WITHIN
THIS SPACE.
_____


_____
ANSWER <                              >

PUSH <ENTER> TO DO NEXT ITEM.
```

Ms. Smith continues to enter test items until the entire set of items on every objective is in the system. To complete her system, she chooses to enter assignments for each objective in the system.

### Designating Prescriptive Content

If Ms. Smith places appropriate information into the system, the computer can *prescribe* instructions for the student as to what to study for any given objective.

In order to accomplish this, the computer must know what instructional materials to present for which objectives. Ms. Smith provides this information to the CMI system via choice # 5 on the MAIN MENU—WORKING WITH CORRELATION OF OBJEC-TIVES AND INSTRUCTIONAL MATERIALS (refer to page 195). She then sees:

```
MENU 5: WORKING WITH CORRELATION OF
OBJECTIVES AND INSTRUCTIONAL MATERIALS

1.  ENTER INSTRUCTION STUDENT IS TO SEE
    THE FIRST TIME HE OR SHE STUDIES AN OBJECTIVE.

2.  ENTER INSTRUCTION STUDENT IS TO SEE IF HE OR
    SHE NEEDS TO RESTUDY AN OBJECTIVE.


3.  EDIT STATEMENTS OF INSTRUCTION.

      TYPE THE NUMBER OF YOUR CHOICE <    >.
```

The choice of <1> causes the computer to present this action page:

```
ASSIGNMENT FOR OBJECTIVES
ACTION PAGE 1: UNIT 1, OBJECTIVE 1


YOU WILL BE PRESENTED WITH THE NUMBER FOR EACH
OBJECTIVE IN ORDER. TYPE IN AN ASSIGNMENT TO SHOW
THE STUDENT WHEN HE OR SHE BEGINS STUDIES.


YOU MAY TYPE IN UP TO
256 LETTERS, NUMBERS, AND SPACES.

<                                           >

PUSH <ENTER> TWICE FOR NEXT OBJECTIVE.
```

The teacher types in the assignment for the first objective, and the computer then presents the same type of page for Objective 2 of Unit 1. It continues in this manner until an assignment is provided to students at times designated by the specific CMI system (refer to the bottom screen on page 186 for an example of one such system).

### Reviewing Student Performance After the CMI System Is in Operation

Once Sue Smith has her system set up and in operation, she can use the system to monitor student performance. The operational program consists of two sections, a student section which has no password, and which students use during their studies, and a teacher section which has a password and is used by the teacher to review student progress. For example, during a work period, Ms. Smith places the class CMI disk in the computer, types the password "PANDA" in order to get into the teacher section of the disk, and the computer presents the MAIN MENU. She chooses option 6 from the menu—REVIEWING STUDENT PERFOR-MANCE (see Figure 9.1 in Chapter 9). She then sees this menu:

```
MENU 6: REVIEWING STUDENT
        PERFORMANCE

1. REVIEWING A STUDENT'S PERFOR-
   MANCE
2. REVIEWING A GROUP'S PERFOR-
   MANCE
3. REVIEWING PERFORMANCE ON SPE-
   CIFIC OBJECTIVES

      TYPE THE NUMBER OF YOUR
      CHOICE <   >.
```

If Ms. Smith chooses #1 on this menu page, she will see an action page giving her the option of calling for the record of one student, or of the whole class, one student at a time.

```
STUDENT PERFORMANCE
ACTION PAGE 1: RECORD SELECTION

TYPE THE NAME OF THE STUDENT'S
RECORD YOU WANT TO SEE. IF YOU
WANT TO SEE THE WHOLE CLASS IN
ALPHABETICAL ORDER, PUSH <ENTER>.

<                    >
```

The teacher can review an individual student's performance on all the objectives on the units and lessons covered by this disk. (You can review such a chart by referring back to Figure 9.2 in Chapter 9.) If Ms. Smith has a printer attached to her computer, she will have the option of printing out any student's record.

Ms. Smith can also review a group's performance on a portion of the curriculum sequence. This information would provide insight into how well the students were progressing. The choice of #2 on the review menu would result in the following screen:

```
GROUP'S PERFORMANCE
ACTION PAGE 1: RECORD SELECTION

CHOOSE THE UNIT AND LESSON SPAN AND GROUP
YOU WANT TO REVIEW.

GROUP      <  >
UNIT       <  >
FROM LESSON    <  >
TO LESSON      <  >
```

(You can review a record such as would be produced by responding to this page in Figure 9.4.)

Choosing the third option on the review menu provides Ms. Smith with the opportunity to review how well a class did on specific objectives. This information is similar to that provided in the previous chart, but it focuses on the objective rather than on the students. (An example of such a chart may be found in Figure 9.3.)

### The Power of CMI

This chapter has allowed you to watch Sue Smith as she developed a CMI system for her students. You should have some idea of the work it takes, and the work it will do for Sue Smith after it is completed.

You now realize that setting up a comprehensive CMI program is no small undertaking. On the other hand, many school districts have been moving toward the utilization of explicit goals and objectives and objective-referenced testing, and with the availability of these items through a group development effort, the work required to establish a CMI system is very much reduced. We hope you also realize that although work is required to set up the CMI system, a good system will reduce work in the long run, through its ability to take many standard non-instructional chores off your hands (such as testing, prescription, and recordkeeping). What you really will be doing if and when you develop your own classroom CMI system is trading one job for another. You will put more work into setting up the system, and you will do less work in the classroom on the tasks performed by the computer. In all likelihood, if you have chosen wisely the work you wish to turn over to the computer, the two will not be equal. Instead, you will find the effort expended to establish a good CMI system considerably less than that typically expended by you daily in management and monitoring functions.

Never before in the history of the educational endeavor has a classroom teacher had the ability to follow student progress in such an "automatic" manner as with computer-managed instruction. We hope many more teachers make appropriate use of this computer tool.

# PART IV
# ACQUIRING EFFECTIVE COURSEWARE

Chapter 11: Programming Courseware

Chapter 12: Evaluating Courseware

# Chapter 11

# Programming Courseware

## Introduction

*Instructional Intent.* Up to now we have been building the foundation knowledge for what constitutes a "good computer lesson." This chapter will engage some of the questions concerning the programming of lessons for classroom use. The chapter will include the following goals:

1. Define the term "computer language."
2. Compare and contrast human language with computer language.
3. Explain the "computer language spectrum" concept and name a few languages along the spectrum.
4. Name three classroom-relevant computer languages and list a few characteristics pertinent to the teacher for each.
5. Compare and contrast an authoring system with a computer language.
6. State six sources of information on how to learn computer languages.

Throughout the book, we have emphasized the importance of programs to the success of the computer in the classroom. We have also tried to make it clear that software can be created by the classroom teacher, or purchased. This chapter explores in some depth the concept of learning a computer language for the purpose of programming classroom lessons.

If you already "speak" a computer language, this chapter may be too basic for your interests.

*Knowledge Prerequisites.* Before beginning this chapter, you should understand the phases of training a computer (see Figure 3.1) and recognize computer programming as the translation of some instructional design for teaching or management (or for any task performance by the computer) into a form that a computer can "understand."

It should be mentioned here that the prerequisites to reading and understanding this chapter, and those to programming computers are two quite different sets of competencies. Hopefully, all who read this chapter will get a better understanding of what a computer language is, and have some knowledge of how one could be learned if so desired. But, not everyone who reads and understands this chapter will be interested in learning a computer

*211*

language. The systematic nature of programming does not appeal to everyone, and some get lost in the rigors of various commands in the world of GOTO and FOR NEXT. Reading this chapter and some hands-on experimentation with a computer while attempting to learn a language will tell you if you have the dispositional prerequisites to learn how to program a classroom computer.

-------------------------------------------------------------------------

## Programming Considerations

The first question that confronts you when securing instructional materials for a microcomputer is the question of whether to learn to program lessons, or to purchase something already programmed by someone else. If materials are available in your area of interest, they can be evaluated using the criteria presented in the next chapter, and, if proven valuable, purchased. One guideline is clear. Whenever possible, buy ready-made lessons off the shelf and get started in classroom computing.

Often, however, an area of interest has no ready-made materials of adequate quality available. The question then becomes one of doing without computer materials or carrying out the development yourself. Should you learn to develop and program your own lessons?

The development and programming of an instructional unit for the computer is a large undertaking. The design and development of goals, objectives, objective-referenced tests, and instruction to match the objectives is difficult in itself. After the lesson (or lessons) is(are) designed, the instructional plan must be programmed for presentation on the computer. This, too, can be a large undertaking. A commercial publisher may invest two or three person-years in a computer program before it is ready for market. Therefore, even a fairly simple program can be extremely costly in terms of development and programming time.

One way of proceeding is to do the instructional design phase, and then make contact with a computer programmer who can translate the design into a computer program for use on your computer. Often, a fellow teacher has programming interests, but no interest in curriculum design, and he or she will gladly match your development effort with his or her programming effort. If you have a good curriculum design, you may be able to find a professional programmer who will do the programming with the expectation of marketing the finished product to a commercial software distributor.

There are factors in favor of your doing your own development and programming. First, if you choose your lesson wisely, you can choose some "charted territory" in which someone has already put work into developing the goals, objectives, and tests. There are many such endeavors waiting for translation to the computer, for example, government programs that have no copyrights, and school-developed programs. Second, you can choose a well-defined lesson, which is not too large to tackle, and start with that. Future programming can grow on a small, initial base. Third, you can program exactly what you want for your students—rather than accept what some company has produced that it thinks you want. So, all in all, you may wish to consider seriously the idea of learning to program your own instructional materials.

Thousands of teachers *have* programmed lessons, so it is not as if it cannot or should not be done. Read this chapter, and if the idea of programming your lessons still interests you, find some of the resources listed in Appendix E and give it a try.

At this point, we will make the assumption that at some time in the future you will want to move to a level of using a computer in your classroom that includes either modifying or writing your own programs. Let's explore what that means.

### Computer Languages

The use of the word "language" as in "computer language" is a good choice of words. Just as people communicate with other people using various human languages, people can communicate with computers using languages. Often, the language of communication between computers and people is something that looks a lot like English. For example, can you guess what this computer program is telling the computer to do?

```
TO DRAW
CLEARSCREEN
SHOW TURTLE
```

*(Continued)*

```
FORWARD 50
RIGHT 90
FORWARD 50
RIGHT 90
FORWARD 50
RIGHT 90
FORWARD 50
RIGHT 90
END
```

Too complicated? Probably not if you have a bit more background. First, understand that this set of 12 commands is a computer program. It is written in a computer language called LOGO. Each time one of these lines is entered into the computer using the keyboard, the computer acts on the line, doing certain things based on the meaning of the line. After this entire message (program) is written into the computer and the computer is told to "RUN" the program, it will do this series of steps, in order. Let's analyze this program.

The first command, "TO DRAW," means that the computer should get ready to put into the memory of the computer a program called "DRAW." The program will draw a figure.

The next command, "CLEARSCREEN," will cause the computer to clear the screen, i.e., make it blank, when the program is run.

The next command, "SHOW TURTLE," means "show a turtle." Yes. The command says to the computer "please show a turtle in the center of the screen." The computer will respond to this command when the program is run by placing in the middle of the screen a turtle-shaped (triangular) figure. The figure will move in response to directions in English, such as move forward, and move right. Perhaps this explanation of "turtle" gives you the clues you need to understand the meaning of the next set of statements.

"FORWARD 50" means "move the turtle forward 50 spaces on the screen, leaving behind a light trail as you go." This will create a line. "RIGHT 90" means "turn right 90 degrees (right angle). The other statements which follow mean exactly what they say.

If a person commands a computer with this program to run the "DRAW" program, it will draw a square in the center of the computer screen.

LOGO was chosen as our example, because it is such a simple language to illustrate, because considerable facility with LOGO can be achieved very quickly, and because LOGO can be a joy to play with and a good avenue to travel in order to learn more about how a computer language works.

Now people are people, and computers are computers. It follows that the language the computer "prefers" is not necessarily the language in which humans prefer to communicate. Understanding computer "preference" requires a bit more background.

### The Nature of Computer Language

Computers are designed in such a fashion that the basic action of the machine is the turning on and off of switches. In the good old days, this meant that physical switches were switched either on or off in patterns which resulted in some specific and predefined action. A current in one wire and no current in a second wire conveyed a specific meaning to the computer operator. Later, vacuum tubes were utilized as electronic switches, and soon they were displaced by transistors, which were displaced by the silicon chip. Although the form of the switches changed radically through time, the function of the switches remained the same. A computer is a sophisticated arrangement of switches, each having two states, on and off, in patterns which convey meaning to the computer operator.

*The Binary Language of Computers.* Since computers do their work via a simple on/off switching pattern, the basic language of communication within a computer is composed of two "letters": "switch on" and "switch off." Everything a computer does can be described in terms of these two letters. The computer shorthand for "switch on" is the number 1; "switch off" is the number 0. Messages are communicated to, from, and within the computer using a series of 1's and 0's. For example, transmitting to the computer in the appropriate fashion for a given machine, the message "1001" conveys the English (Arabic) numeral 9. Any word or number in the English language (or any other) can be communicated to the computer in the form of strings ("words) of 1's and 0's.

What the computer does with the strings of 1's and 0's depends on the type of computer receiving the message. Computers do not all communicate using the same words, which creates the problem that Apple programs cannot be used in TRS-80 machines. But nonetheless, the 1's and 0's "talk" composes the language of all the machines. Hence, it is called *machine language.*

*People and Machine Language.* Now just as computers make poor intuitive teachers (since they operate very systematically), people have problems "speaking" machine language. Of course, there are sophisticated programmers who can read and write machine language, but the average person soon gets lost in a blizzard of 1's and 0's when attempting to converse with a computer in its native language. The solutions to this problem have taken the form of the purposeful invention of various compromise languages.

Man's invention of artificial language to facilitate computer/human communication has resulted in a spectrum of languages. The spectrum ranges from machine language at the computer end to natural human languages at the other end. Between machine language and human language are a large number of computer-human pidgin languages. The pidgins at the computer end of the spectrum favor the computer, i.e., the computer will need to do less "translation" to perform a given job. The pidgins at the human end of the spectrum favor the human at the expense of the computer. That is, for a given message that is convenient for humans, the computer will need to waste time and energy translating the message from the human-related language to a machine-related language.

### The BASIC Computer Language

BASIC (Beginners All-Purpose Symbolic Instruction Code) is a language that was developed to help people learn to use computers in an effective and efficient manner. There are scores of books available on BASIC and how to teach yourself to program in BASIC. There are also a number of instructional computer programs available that teach BASIC. Millions have learned BASIC as their first computer language.

BASIC is a good language because it is relatively simple, and yet it has a great deal of power (the ability to do what you want done with the computer).

Here is a simple five-line program in BASIC:

```
PRINT "HI, I AM YOUR COMPUTER!"
PRINT "MASTER, WHAT IS YOUR NAME?"
INPUT NAME1
PRINT "OH, SO YOUR NAME IS";NAME1
END
```

This program is put into the computer by typing the five commands into the computer using the keyboard. As the five lines are entered, each is given a line number. The lines could be numbered 1,2,3,4, etc., but normally 10,20,30,40, etc., are used in order to leave space if additional lines need to be added to the program later in its development. Here is what the program looks like after it is entered into the computer (this is the picture on the screen):

```
10  PRINT "HI, I AM YOUR COMPUTER!"
20  PRINT "MASTER, WHAT IS YOUR NAME?"
30  INPUT NAME1
40  PRINT "OH, SO YOUR NAME IS"; NAME1
50  END
```

This program is in the computer's memory, but not in this form. Earlier, we stated that a computer is a "switching device" with a machine language consisting of 1's and 0's. As this BASIC program is typed into the computer, a portion of the computer automatically converts the "English" into machine language. Practically every computer available today has this automatic BASIC conversion program built into or available for the machine. Hence, the programmer types BASIC, and the machine uses machine language to operate.

Pushing the <CLEAR> key on the keyboard erases all of the words on the screen of the computer, but these five lines remain in the active portion of the computer, waiting to do their job. That task is initiated by the command "RUN," which is typed into the computer. At that command, what do you think the computer will do? Read the program, first line to last, and see if you know what the computer will do.

The computer does pretty much what the English text states. First, the computer looks at the first line of the program and prints onto the blank screen:

HI, I AM YOUR COMPUTER!

The computer then looks at the next line of the program (line 20) and follows that direction. Since it has no <CLEAR-SCREEN> command, it puts the next line under the first. The words on the screen now are these:

HI, I AM YOUR COMPUTER!
MASTER, WHAT IS YOUR NAME?

Looking at the third line of the program yields:

HI, I AM YOUR COMPUTER!
MASTER, WHAT IS YOUR NAME?
? <                    >

The "?" blinks insistently, waiting for you to answer. When a name (<JONES>, for example) is typed in and the <ENTER> key pushed, the computer states:

HI, I AM YOUR COMPUTER!
MASTER, WHAT IS YOUR NAME?
? <JONES>
OH, SO YOUR NAME IS JONES.

Did you figure out what this BASIC program would do? BASIC language is an example of a fairly simple-to-learn computer language that utilizes English-like words and commands. To use all the power of BASIC requires quite a bit of study, but the task is certainly NOT beyond the average teacher to fully master.

## Other Computer Languages

LOGO and BASIC and machine language are only a few of the many computer languages. The following figure illustrates the spectrum of languages from the human to the computer.

*Figure 11.1*

*The Computer Language Spectrum*

Human End of Spectrum

Natural Human Language
Authoring Language
Disk Operating Systems (CP/M, UNIX, TRSDOS)
Computer Authoring Languages (PILOT)
LOGO
Artificial Intelligence (LISP)
BASIC
APL
ADA
PASCAL
ALGOL
COBOL
FORTRAN
FORTH
Assembly Language
Monitor Language
Machine Language

Computer End of Spectrum

Each of the languages and systems listed above (and many others) has been developed for specific purposes. Some make writing business programs easier and more powerful; others do the same for instructional programs. In many ways, all of the languages are similar, since the "underlying" computer is the same in each case. In other ways, however, the languages bear no resemblance to one another.

### Learning a Computer Language

In order to choose an appropriate language to learn, you must do some homework. The homework can be self-assigned and self-learned. That is, there is no need to necessarily search out courses and programs of formal study. Every language listed in

Figure 11.1 has self-instructional materials which will assist you in learning the language. And the learning of computer languages is not necessarily difficult. After learning an initial computer language, you will find that a second, third, and fourth language can be picked up much more rapidly. Indeed, the fundamentals of a language such as LOGO can be learned in an evening. Children commonly master LOGO fundamentals rapidly.

The key to learning a computer language is to have the computer available to interact with during the learning process. Then, when learning the language, you can speak with the computer, and it will provide the feedback as to whether or not you are correctly communicating. The computer is an ideal teacher for instructing how to use a computer language. With access to a computer on which to try out the newly learned aspects of the language, progress comes rapidly.

**Learning to Communicate at the
Human End of the Spectrum**

Let's consider the question of picking a computer language. Given that you need to communicate with the computer, will it be by using a human-oriented or a computer-oriented language? Why make life difficult? If your goal as a teacher is to use your computer primarily as an instructional tool, our suggestion is that you first investigate those languages that are at the "human end" of the computer/human spectrum, specifically instructional authoring languages.

*An Authoring Language.* An authoring language uses computer commands that the author of an instructional lesson might use. For example, in PILOT, one command is "T" for "TYPE," which means whatever follows the command will be typed onto the screen for the student to read. Authoring languages generally utilize simple English-like commands, often chosen from a menu of possible comments. Such languages are written so as to provide a simple set of commands to do a specific set of tasks. In other words, the computer is preprogrammed by someone else to provide what the author needs. What a teacher needs is a simple and straightforward method of programming instructional sequences.

The inventors of an authoring language look carefully at the set of tasks that the program is going to be developed to perform. In the case of lesson construction, it is clear that text will need to be presented to the student, example items given, practice items presented and answers corrected, and feedback on answers provided. All of the factors concerned with lesson development for the computer are defined, and then computer commands are developed that specifically reflect the needs of the lesson programmer.

The developer of an authoring language produces computer language that is very specific in the type of commands it offers, and is extremely limited in what it can do. For example, an authoring program developed to program instructional lessons, while very capable in the lesson programming task, is totally useless in the programming of computer materials to be used by accountants. As the developer of the authoring language zeroes in on a specific area, various commands outside of the field of interest are dropped or ignored, thus creating a high-level language devoted to essentially one task.

One such language is PILOT, which is available on many types of computers from large to small. PILOT (Programmed Inquiry, Learning Or Teaching) was developed at the University of California specifically for the purpose of aiding the development of computer-assisted instruction. This interactive language enables a person without prior programming experience to develop and utilize programs for instructional purposes. The structure and commands of the program are easy to learn and use.

With PILOT, you can present the student with a reading passage, give him or her time to study it, and then ask questions based on the passage. The program is designed to correct and score the questions. By scanning the student's answers, the computer can provide feedback to the student based on how the student answered the questions. The computer can also provide comments and direct the student to various topics to study based on how well the student performs.

PILOT commands are simple, as you can see from these eight examples of instructions to the computer:

```
T: TYPE
A: ACCEPT
M: MATCH
J: JUMP
U: USE
E: END
C: COMPUTE
R: REMARK
```

Here is an example of a very simple PILOT program for a part of a lesson teaching the state capitals.

```
T:   WHAT IS THE CAPITAL OF NEW YORK?
A:
M:   ALBANY.
TY: RIGHT!!!
TN: THE CORRECT ANSWER IS ALBANY.
E:
```

This language has some severe abbreviations, but once you learn them, the language becomes rather simple. The symbol "T" means "TYPE the following text on the screen." "A" means "wait to ACCEPT the student's answer." The symbol "M" means "MATCH the student's answer using the following answer." "TY" means "TYPE the following feedback on the screen when the answer is correct." "TN" means the same thing, but for a wrong answer.

In summary, this simple PILOT lesson asks the student to name the capital of New York, accepts the student's answer, corrects the answer, and provides feedback for right and wrong answers.

Of course, the complete PILOT language is more complex than that used in this simple lesson, but the example provides an idea of how easy lesson development can be, given a high-level computer language.

When developing PILOT, persons at the University of California interested in computer-assisted instruction had the goal of inventing a computer language that teachers could easily use to write lessons. They wrote a special program (using a program from the computer end of the communication spectrum) that allowed a teacher to talk to the computer using language from the human end of the communication spectrum. What this means to you as a teacher is "ease of learning."

*Authoring Systems.* There is another way to create courseware other than learning a computer language. You can utilize an authoring system. A courseware authoring system is a preprogrammed framework into which you can place instructional materials. An authoring system is much like a courseware authoring language, except the system has already been programmed for many more features than a language.

The CMI system presented in the previous chapter is a good example of an authoring system. Our hypothetical teacher needed no knowledge of a computer language to develop and implement the CMI system.

Authoring systems are developed by projects in which educators and computer programmers work as a team. These individuals develop a pattern of instruction or CMI and then use a lower-level language to implement the pattern on the computer. The predesignated instructional pattern will allow you to enter such things as tests, answers, objectives, instructional screens, rules, examples, and feedback statements directly to the computer with ease. Such systems are generally menu-driven, and the entering of instruction is as easy as calling for a blank screen on which to place your message.

Many authoring systems allow you to develop graphic illustrations with ease and facility. Using a computer language to program graphics, such as illustrations, graphs, and figures is a difficult task. Programming these graphics with an authoring system can be very simple, because someone else has done all the work, and you can utilize the results of his or her efforts with a few simple keystrokes.

Of course, as with any commercial computer instructional materials, you must make sure that a given authoring system provides you with all of the features that you feel are important. Normally, it takes an expert programmer to add a feature to an authoring system. You may want to provide a certain type of feedback to practice items, but if the authoring system does not have this feature, you will have to do without it.

*The Disk Operating System.* There is one other system you should know about—the disk operating system. If and when you get your own computer with disk storage of information, you will need to learn how to use this system.

The disk operating system (DOS) is similar in concept to an authoring system. The management of a disk by a computer is a fairly complicated task. The computer must determine where on a disk to store information, and after it is stored, how it can be retrieved. To use simple terms, the computer must have a system to remember how to store and where it has stored information on the disk. As with an authoring system, others have thought of all the problems associated with the storage and retrieval of information on disks, and have produced ready-made control systems.

A DOS is normally menu-driven, and you will quickly be able to learn the rules and commands whereby the computer stores and retrieves information. Since almost all DOS's do the same job, and since there are many good DOS's available, by reading reports and reviews of these systems in popular magazines and professional journals, you will be able to choose the one that suits your needs.

### Finding a Language That Suits You

With the spectrum of languages and systems that are available, how does one set about finding them, and deciding which to learn and use?

The finding of the language is straightforward. Information on computer languages may be secured from:
- College catalogs
- Commercial schools
- Public Libraries
- Fellow teachers interested in computers
- Computer magazines sold in bookstores
- Commercial computer stores
- Mail order computer stores
- Computer companies
  (write Apple, Radio Shack, etc.)
- Department of Computer Studies at local colleges

Review potential languages, placing special emphases on those designed to be used in the programming of instruction. You will find in computer magazines a number of authoring languages offered by commercial companies. Of course, just like any product offered for sale, the "ads" might far exceed the product's ability to produce results. You must compare the product's capabilities against your goals for a computer language.

## Summary

It is true that any lesson could be created in several different languages or authoring systems. That is, many languages and systems have the power to be used to develop instructional lessons. It definitely is not true that any lesson could be created as easily in one language as in any other language. And that is the key concept in choosing an authoring language or system. The language or system must be easy to learn and use for lesson development.

What has been presented in earlier chapters of this book should provide you with some guidelines for the selection of a means with which to author computer instructional materials. Here are some summary ideas concerning choosing a language or a system.

- Choose a versatile language or system that will carry you as far as you feel you may want to go in learning how to program.
- Choose a language or system that will facilitate the systematic development of lessons in the manner you have learned in this book.
- Make sure the language or system matches your intended function. Some languages favor lesson presentation, while others are more comprehensive and include methods of easily keeping records on student performance.
- Pick a language or system and jump in. Do not be overly concerned about which language you choose. There is a controversy as to whether a teacher should study and utilize a quickly learned, but simpler, authoring language, or a more slowly learned, but more sophisticated, lower-level language. Once you have selected a language, you are

not stuck with it forever. Most of the basic ideas about programming are the same, no matter what language or system you have chosen, and often it is easy to make a transition from one to the other. So do not feel that a first choice is irrevocable.

The first experience with a language should be, above all, productive and satisfying. As you gain experience with programming, you can choose later to learn a second language. The experience of learning the first language will make the second much easier to master. As with any acquired language, whether computer or foreign, growth will come with practice.

# Chapter 12

# Evaluating Courseware

## Introduction

*Instructional Intent.* If you have the capability of developing your own computer courseware, this chapter on evaluating courseware may be applied during and after the development process. If you do not have the capability or intent to develop a specific piece of courseware, it must be secured from other educators or purchased. Shopping for courseware includes the concepts of finding the right courseware and evaluating that courseware to determine if it is instructionally valuable and worth its price.

The goals and objectives of this chapter include:

1. State the criteria for making a decision about a given piece of courseware as to the amount of evaluation it should have.
2. Describe how to implement a formative evaluation plan for courseware you develop.
3. Describe how to implement a summative evaluation plan for courseware you secure from others.
4. Distinguish between design evaluation and tryout evaluation.

*Knowledge Prerequisites.* Evaluation means "making decisions" based on data. In addition to expecting you to know the characteristics of CAI and CMI, this chapter also assumes you to be a content expert for any courseware to be evaluated, and that no specific information on content needs to be provided.

--------------------------------------------------------------------------

## Parameters of Computer Courseware Evaluation

Instructional evaluation involves making professional decisions concerning some instructional product or process. We will present for your use an evaluation plan for making decisions about your own as well as others' instructional materials.

While the evaluation criteria are essentially the same, the plan for assessing your own courseware is quite different from that used for the evaluation of materials developed by others. The main difference is one of access. If you develop your own courseware, you will have it available for modification during every phase of its evolution from an idea through classroom use. You can utilize a *formative* evaluation process which can take place *during development* to help you form an effective and efficient final product.

It is generally impossible to evaluate courseware developed by others in a formative manner. Most of the time this type of courseware cannot be changed. Normally, you can only evaluate such materials using a *summative* evaluation process, which describes the effectiveness and efficiency of a *final product*.

For the purposes of this chapter, we will assume you intend to design and program your own computer lesson, following the model presented in this book. As you design and develop each portion of your courseware, you will want to employ evaluation to make sure the end-product is effective and efficient.

At the same time, the evaluation procedure we provide can be utilized to assess the value of materials prepared by others, such as fellow teachers and commercial sources, and it will help you in deciding whether to accept or reject their products for use with your students. For the rest of this chapter, we shall refer to courseware developed by others, whether by fellow teachers or commercial sources, as commercial materials.

### Deciding Whether to Evaluate

Evaluation can be a time-consuming endeavor, and the amount of time and effort spent on evaluation should reflect the courseware being analyzed. That is, it would be foolish to spend a lot of time evaluating a $25 program which advertises that it will "review French words," when you only want to use it with a few selected students in your class who are taking a special program of French. The amount of time that would be required to do a complete evaluation would cost far more than $25! There are four main aspects that you should take into consideration when deciding whether or not to evaluate any given program:

(1) the number of students who will use the program;
(2) the scope and sequence of the program, i.e., the amount of material covered by the program;

(3) the advertised power of the program, i.e., whether it makes claims for good design and valuable content; and

(4) the manner in which the materials will be used, i.e., whether they will play an adjunct or optional role, or be the sole instructional method.

If it is expected that a large number of students will use a program, it is imperative to evaluate the program regardless of the cost. If the program is inexpensive, the cost may reflect the fact that it was cheaply developed, and it may cause more harm than good.

If a program is broad in scope, it requires evaluation. There are now programs on the market which cover grades K through six (or more), and whether used with large numbers of students or selected groups, the continual impact of the program on the student users commands that the courseware be evaluated prior to use.

Commercial producers of courseware advertise their products in popular magazines, professional journals, and through direct-mail sales. Many of these ads make rather substantial claims concerning the effectiveness of their products, and the cost often is correlated with the claims. If an ad presents you with a product which seems to be powerful and valuable, it deserves to be evaluated and proven so.

Often, computer materials are created as adjunct learning materials to support some other form of instruction. These materials do not need the scrutiny required of computer instruction which will stand alone and provide the main or sole source of instruction on a topic.

And, of course, if the courseware is your own product, it deserves the best, and it should be evaluated.

### Determining Who Evaluates

Evaluating is not a purely objective assessment of merit. It involves subjective decisions. It is wise to involve others in the formative evaluation of your own courseware during its development and also to evaluate commercial courseware using as many individuals as the importance of the courseware warrants. The individuals do not need to be experts in evaluation. If you follow carefully the evaluation model presented in this chapter, and attempt to make objective decisions, you and your fellow teachers will be experts enough.

### Determining What to Evaluate

When assessing your own development product, you will be evaluating a single lesson or a series of interrelated lessons, with each lesson having an objective. Any units will be clusters of lessons, with all lessons geared to reaching the unit goal. All these elements will be arranged on a learning map (at least that is the way we taught you to do it in previous chapters). The map defines the interrelationships and assures appropriate student progression through some learning sequence. The sequential pattern of your units and lessons that results will perhaps look like that in Figure 12.1.

Our evaluation model for computer courseware is built on the assessment of the measurable aspects of computer instruction, therefore, it is built on the objectives in the learning sequence. The instruction for every learning objective (therefore, each lesson) is evaluated on its design and on its effectiveness at helping students achieve the objective.

For your own computer courseware, the evaluation is a two-part endeavor with one component being the evaluation of the CAI part of your work, the second component being the evaluation of the CMI aspect.

You use the process described in the rest of this chapter to evaluate each individual lesson, beginning with evaluating the objective of the lesson, then the tests for the lesson, and the processes of instruction. Good computer instruction should have each corner of the triangle incorporated into its lessons. Of course, evaluation will tell you to what extent a given lesson has the elements of a good lesson. In addition to these elements, the content of lessons needs evaluation, as do the technical characteristics of lesson presentation.

There may or may not be any CMI integrated into your lesson(s). If there is, it will be evaluated separately after you have completed the CAI evaluation.

*Figure 12.1*

*Instructional Sequence Based on a Learning Map*

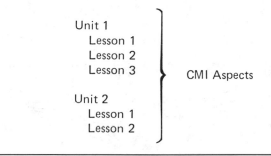

If you are evaluating commercial materials, the pattern may be similar to that presented in Figure 12.1, but more likely it is not. Often, commercial courseware producers have never heard of performance objectives, and they may not think in performance terms. To use the evaluation approach described here for commercial materials, the first step in the evaluation process will be looking at their curriculum structure and attempting to locate and decipher (or infer) their goals and objectives. Once the objectives are identified, then as with your own materials, the characteristics of a well-trained computer form the basis for making evaluation decisions (see Figure 12.2).

### How to Evaluate Courseware

During the process of developing and implementing your own courseware, you will need to conduct evaluation in two ways.

Throughout the design phase of development, you will need to evaluate your materials for internal consistency and adequacy. You will need to determine if your materials have all the components for good computer instruction, and if all those components are integrated with each other to make a consistent presentation. The evaluation criteria presented in this evaluation model can be used as guidelines throughout the development process. If during the design process some component of your materials is evaluated as not acceptable, you can revise the faulty segment.

*Figure 12.2*

*Elements of the Courseware Evaluation Process*

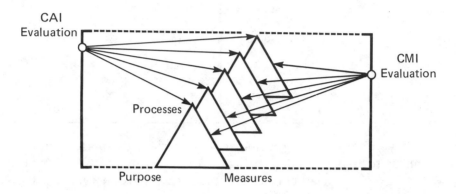

Complete evaluation requires not only examination of each individual lesson (see arrows), but also scrutiny of the lesson sequence.

---

Satisfying consistency and adequacy criteria when a lesson is on the drawing board boosts the likelihood of your producing a quality lesson, but it is certainly not insurance that the lesson will indeed work with students. To evaluate whether the lesson works as designed, you need another form of evaluation—the tryout. As soon as possible in the development effort, any lesson should be tried with students, and evaluated to determine how well it works with them.

If the materials you are evaluating are not your own, you have a different task. Since it is generally impossible to revise someone else's program, you will not be able to improve the materials. You will be faced with an accept or reject situation during the consistency/adequacy evaluation. Any commercial program also should be given a tryout with students, and a determination made as to its effectiveness in doing what it says it will do.

The early and middle portions of this chapter are devoted to presenting to you an evaluation plan which assesses the design consistency and adequacy of your own and others' courseware. Later in the chapter, you are presented the methods for conducting a tryout evaluation with students.

## Evaluating the Design of CAI

### Evaluation of Objectives

Objectives are the heart of a well-developed computer program. If the objectives are weak, all other components of the program will probably be weak.

The evaluation process for objectives is presented in the form of a flow diagram. Look at Flow Diagram 12.1. You may not be familiar with the use of flow diagrams to describe a process, so we will provide a brief explanation of the parts and logical flow of the diagram. The diagram consists basically of numbered rectangles and diamonds, and arrows between those figures. The phrase within a rectangle is a statement of something you must do: it is an action statement. The word or phrase within a diamond is a decision statement: it is something you must decide. Arrows guide the flow of logic from action to action, or action to decision, or decision to action. Outside of each decision box will be the words Yes and No (or Yes and Not Yet). They label the arrow leading away from the diamond, and they represent the flow of logic based on whether the decision was positive or negative. You will understand flow diagrams better after we have worked our way through this first one.

The main idea in the use of the flow diagram is simple: you follow the diagram, doing everything a rectangle says to do and making the decision a diamond asks you to make, using questions which are pertinent to the aspect being evaluated. In short, the flow diagrams and their accompanying evaluation questions will provide you all the information necessary to evaluate each aspect of your computer instructional materials.

To use Flow Diagram 12.1, begin at the word Start. If you are evaluating your own courseware, you will utilize the middle and lower-third of the flow diagram to perform a formative evaluation. That is, you will perform the evaluation while you are developing

*Flow Diagram 12.1*

*Evaluation of Objectives*

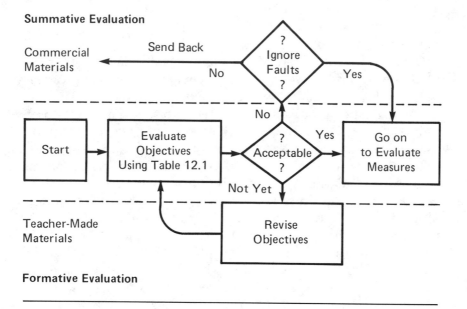

the materials. If you are evaluating someone else's courseware (commercial or another teacher's), you will use the middle and top-third of the flow diagram to perform a summative evaluation, which is the evaluation of a finished product.

Look at the lower-third of the flow diagram and the upper-third. Note that a formative evaluation can result in the revision of instructional materials, while a summative decision on commercial materials results in a decision for acceptance or rejection, since those are your only options on commercial materials.

Let's get started with the evaluation. Move to the rectangle which states you should evaluate the objectives using the evaluation questions found in Table 12.1, which has a series of Yes/No questions.

First, decide which questions are pertinent to the program you are evaluating, and then answer each pertinent question Yes or No.

*Table 12.1*

*Evaluation of Objectives*

| Purpose Considerations | Yes or No |
|---|---|
| • Does the program have goals and objectives stated in either the courseware itself or in a teacher's guide? | .................. |
| • Are the objectives stated in behavioral terms? | .................. |
| • Do the objectives state the conditions under which the students will perform? | .................. |
| • Are the criteria for successful performance stated? | .................. |
| • Are the objectives arranged in a map from simple to complex? | .................. |
| • Do the objectives have educational value? | .................. |
| • Are the objectives appropriate to the students' age, background, and characteristics? | .................. |
| • Are the scope and sequence of objectives reasonable? | .................. |

When you complete this evaluation, you have completed rectangle 2. The arrow moves you to diamond 3, which states you must make a decision whether or not to accept the objectives for the program, as they are written. This decision will not be easy to make—generally, it will not be a simple and clear-cut decision of Yes or No. You must make it a Yes or No by collapsing your answers to the evaluation questions into a single decision. You must decide if the objectives for the program, based on the questions in Table 12.1, are acceptable or not. If they are acceptable, this phase of the evaluation is finished, and you follow the Yes arrow to the next evaluation flow diagram. If they are not acceptable and are your own materials, you follow the Not Yet arrow downward to the revision rectangle box. Note the logic of this series of rectangles and diamonds (see Figure 12.3).

You evaluate the objectives using the questions in the diagram, and if the objectives are judged as not yet acceptable, you must revise them. From the revised objectives rectangle, you go back to the "evaluate objectives using questions" rectangle a second time, and a re-evaluation is made. This cycle continues until the objectives are acceptable.

*Figure 12.3*

*The Formative Evaluation Revision Cycle*

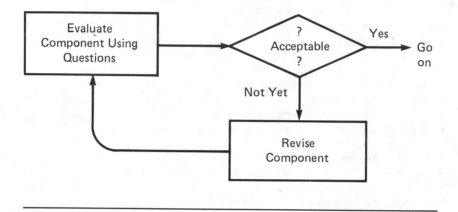

If you are evaluating commercial materials and you deem the purposes of the program not acceptable, you will need to decide (use the diamond in the top-third of Flow Diagram 12.1) whether to reject the program on that basis, or whether other considerations cause you to ignore its faults. The first decision will cause you to send the materials back to the producer; the second will send you further in the evaluation.

If or when the program passes the instructional purpose evaluation for all of its objectives (or lessons, as the case may be), its testing component should be evaluated next.

### Evaluation of Measures

Given the program has valuable and well-stated instructional purposes, a decision must be made whether the tests and measures of the courseware are also adequate. Flow Diagram 12.2 illustrates the evaluation process for this aspect of your courseware.

It should be easier for you to follow the flow of logic in Flow Diagram 12.2, since it is the same as for the first diagram, except for the aspect being evaluated and the specific evaluation questions. This time you are evaluating the testing component of

*Flow Diagram 12.2*

*Evaluation of Measures*

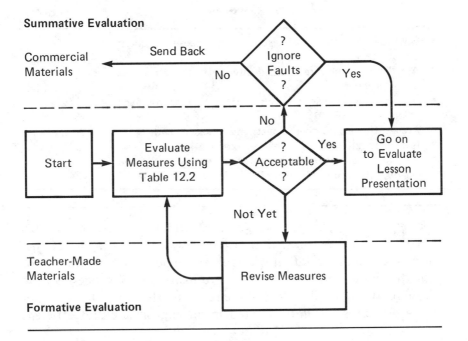

**Summative Evaluation**

Commercial Materials

Teacher-Made Materials

**Formative Evaluation**

---

your courseware, using the questions in Table 12.2. To make a decision on the acceptability of the testing component, answer each question in Table 12.2 Yes or No, and collapse your answers into an overall decision as to whether or not the tests as designed are satisfactory. Then, follow the flow diagram to determine your next action.

Notice in Table 12.2 that some of the questions are directed primarily at commercial materials. For example, the first question asks if the program has test items to measure student performance. We are confident that your program will have them, so we intend this question to be directed at commercially-prepared materials.

**Evaluation of Lesson Presentation**
If the courseware has passed to this point or has been revised to

*Table 12.2*

*Evaluation of Measures*

| Measures Considerations | Yes or No |
|---|---|
| • Does the program have test items to measure student performance? | .................. |
| • Are the test items referenced directly to the objectives of the program? | .................. |
| • Are there a sufficient number of test items for each objective? | .................. |
| • Are a sufficient number of tests and retests provided? | .................. |
| • Is an adequate performance level expected? | .................. |
| • Are the test items technically correct, i.e., written clearly, unambiguously, etc.? | .................. |

a pass condition, it is now evaluated on lesson presentation. Do not confuse lesson presentation with lesson content. The evaluation of lesson presentation will look at the questions of whether or not the ten design rules for effective instructional processes have been followed in the development of the lessons, and whether these processes are implemented in an appropriate and efficient manner.

With commercial materials, it is often possible to evaluate CAI purposes and tests from the teacher's guide provided with the software. It rarely is possible to do this with lesson presentation. The program will probably need to be reviewed on-line using a computer, with you acting "as a student." The questions in Table 12.3 will need to be addressed. These evaluation questions directly relate to the processes of lesson presentation presented in Chapter 6. You will need to evaluate each lesson separately using Flow Diagram 12.3 and the questions in Table 12.3.

**Evaluation of Lesson Content**

There are a number of criteria to be evaluated under the concept of "content." This does not make for an easy task, since you will be faced with the problem of having both good and bad

## Flow Diagram 12.3

## Evaluation of Lesson Presentation

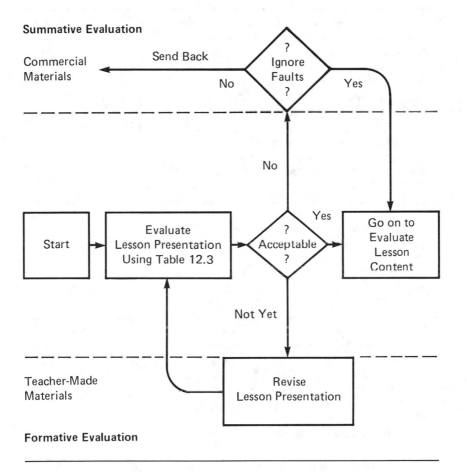

**Summative Evaluation**

Commercial Materials — Send Back — No — ? Ignore Faults ? — Yes

No

Start → Evaluate Lesson Presentation Using Table 12.3 → ? Acceptable ? — Yes → Go on to Evaluate Lesson Content

Not Yet

**Teacher-Made Materials** — Revise Lesson Presentation

**Formative Evaluation**

---

aspects in every program. Any one factor might be sufficient to warrant a reject decision for commercial materials. For example, if a classroom has a high value associated with teaching content free of race, ethnic, sex, or other stereotypes, any stereotyping in a program might be sufficient reason not to purchase it. In another situation, the program might be purchased and labeled "sex stereotypes" present, and then used as a good discussion point.

See Flow Diagram 12.4 on page 242 for evaluation of lesson content.

*Table 12.3*

*Evaluation of Lesson Presentation*

| Instructional Process Considerations | Yes or No |
|---|---|
| • Does the computer get the students' attention? | .................... |
| • Does it present the purpose of the lesson to the students? | .................... |
| • Does the computer pretest the students to determine if they can do the objectives for the lesson? | .................... |
| • Does it remind the students what they have learned in the past and need to know for this lesson? | .................... |
| • Is the lesson presented appropriately for the type of learning, i.e., for discrimination, concept learning, etc.? | .................... |
| • Does it provide examples of the expected student performance for the objective? | .................... |
| • Does it provide example helps? | .................... |
| • Does it provide practice items on the objective? | .................... |
| • Does it provide practice helps? | .................... |
| • Does it provide practice feedback? | .................... |
| • Does it provide a posttest to determine if the students have been successful on the objective? | .................... |
| • Does it provide for retention and transfer? | .................... |

| Presentation Feature Considerations | Yes or No |
|---|---|
| • Is lesson presentation in the form of a tutorial rather than a linear presentation? | .................... |
| • Is the presentation clear and logical? | .................... |
| • Are graphics/color/sound used to support the presentation when needed? | .................... |
| • Does the presentation motivate the students to continue their work? | .................... |
| • Do the students have the option of controlling the rate of presentation of the lesson? | .................... |
| • Do the students have the option of controlling the sequence of presentation of the lesson? | .................... |
| • Will the students learn if they faithfully attempt to complete the instruction as presented? | .................... |
| • Is the instruction efficient, i.e., not redundant, boring, time-consuming? | .................... |

*(Continued)*

*(Table 12.3 Continued)*

- Can the system diagnose student performance and branch the students to appropriate instruction?  ..................
- Does the program use the concept of "not-passed-yet" rather than failure when students have not yet accomplished a task?  ..................

*Flow Diagram 12.4*

*Evaluation of Lesson Content*

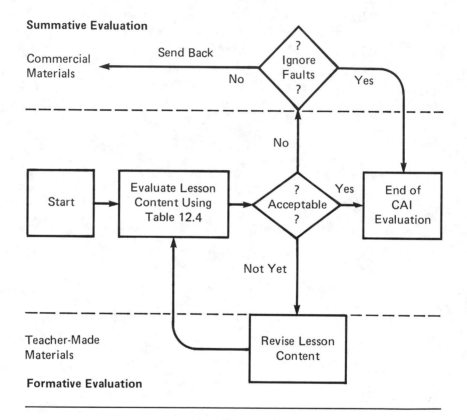

In the evaluation of lesson content, the evaluation questioning proceeds in a different manner than it did for the objectives, tests, and instruction. Look at Table 12.4. Two criteria will be evaluated for each item. First, you must make a decision on the importance of the evaluation question itself. Some of the questions will not be pertinent to a given piece of CAI courseware. For example, you may not think it is important to reach the objective—you may be willing to supplement the CAI instruction yourself.

But, if an evaluation item is deemed "important," then it should be evaluated on the second criterion, that of whether or

*Table 12.4*

*Evaluation of Lesson Content*

| Instructional Content | Importance | | Rating | |
|---|---|---|---|---|
| | High | Low | Good | Bad |
| • Is the content accurate? | ................... | | ................... | |
| • Does the content have educational value? | ................... | | ................... | |
| • Is the content free of race, ethnic, sex, or other stereotypes? | ................... | | ................... | |
| • Is the content sufficient to insure the students can reach the objectives if the lesson is studied? | ................... | | ................... | |
| • Is the content appropriate to the students' background and interests? | ................... | | ................... | |
| • Is the reading at the appropriate level for the students? | ................... | | ................... | |
| • Is the content presented objectively and without bias? | ................... | | ................... | |

not the program in question was effective in utilizing the feature. Failure to effectively develop one aspect of a program may not necessarily rule out its purchase, but it certainly does lower the program's overall instructional value.

Following the guidelines of the flow diagram, you will revise your own materials to remedy content deficiencies, and on commercial materials, you will need to make a decision as to whether the content is good enough to accept, or bad enough to reject.

Although there is no easy way to summarize the information gained from evaluating this set of questions, it certainly can be argued that it is better to have considered the ideas than never to have considered them at all.

## Evaluating the Design of CMI

We will approach the evaluation of CMI somewhat differently. Because the difficulty of the programming task makes it quite rare that a teacher will develop his or her own CMI program, here CMI will be evaluated as a commercial program. If you ever do decide to develop any CMI program, you can use these guidelines for your development effort.

The CMI being evaluated might be an aspect of CAI, or it might stand on its own. Either way, the evaluation of CMI follows the process outlined in Flow Diagram 12.5 and the guidelines set forth in Chapters 9 and 10. The courseware should be assessed on each of the criteria in Table 12.5 using the concept of "importance" first, and of "rating" next. For each evaluation question, first decide whether the concept is important to the materials you are evaluating. If the decision is "yes, they are important," then move on to decide if the application of the idea in the courseware is well done.

You should remember that the CMI program being evaluated might be a completely closed document providing only what the developer has to offer (CMI in a reading program, for example), or it might be an authoring system which is completely open to teacher additions. The nature of the program will have to be taken into consideration on each of the evaluation questions in Table 12.5. Whatever the program's nature, however, any CMI program will need to be tried out on the computer to determine its organization and the ease with which the user can move through the system.

The CMI evaluation examines two major aspects: (1) the preparation of the master disk, and (2) the recordkeeping capabilities of the system.

## Evaluation of Miscellaneous Factors

There are a few factors hanging that do not fit conveniently in the other areas. To any given teacher, they may or may not be important. You may want to consider the questions in Table 12.6 on page 248 before purchasing commercial courseware.

## Tryout Evaluation

One of the powers of developing your own materials lies in the ability to perform formative evaluations of each component while

*Flow Diagram 12.5*

*Evaluation of CMI*

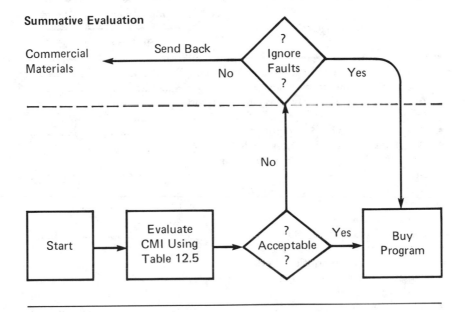

the materials are being developed. But it should be remembered that no matter how well the material is designed and how well it is evaluated, the "proof of the pudding is in the eating." The evidence for effective CAI and CMI is in the teaching, and for a complete evaluation, the following procedure should be implemented. Look at Flow Diagram 12.6.

When you employ this student testing and revision process, you can employ many of the evaluation questions presented in Tables 12.1 through 12.6, and those of the type in Table 12.7. Student tryouts of materials are often performed in the following order:

1. Try the materials with one student, observing the student during the computer sessions. Revise materials based on observations.

2. Try out the "semi-polished" materials with a small group of students (three to ten). Evaluate the materials using relevant questions from Tables 12.1 through 12.6. Revise the materials based on evaluation.

*Table 12.5*

*Evaluation of CMI*

| Preparing the Master Disk | Importance | | Rating | |
|---|---|---|---|---|
| | High | Low | Good | Bad |
| • Is a manual for using the program provided? | ............ | | ............ | |
| • Does the program have menus? | ............ | | ............ | |
| • Are the menus clear and easy to read and follow? | ............ | | ............ | |
| • Does the teacher have a password? | ............ | | ............ | |
| • Can students be assigned passwords? | ............ | | ............ | |
| • Are provisions made for entering enough students? | ............ | | ............ | |
| • Can the teacher enter performance objectives? | ............ | | ............ | |
| • Can the teacher enter test items? | ............ | | ............ | |
| • Can standards be set for performance? | ............ | | ............ | |
| • Can instructional materials be linked to objectives, for prescription purposes? | ............ | | ............ | |
| • Can students be placed in as many groups as needed? | ............ | | ............ | |
| • Can student groups be named? | ............ | | ............ | |
| • Can students be easily added or deleted from a group? | ............ | | ............ | |
| • Can the disk be duplicated as often as needed by the teacher? | ............ | | ............ | |
| **Recordkeeping Capabilities of the System** | **High** | **Low** | **Good** | **Bad** |
| • Is the disk protected so that students cannot see other students' records? | ............ | | ............ | |
| • Are the records of the system easy to locate? | ............ | | ............ | |
| • Are the records easy to read? | ............ | | ............ | |
| • Are the records available by individual students? | ............ | | ............ | |
| • Are the records available by class, for a given objective? | ............ | | ............ | |
| • Are the records available by objective, for a given class? | ............ | | ............ | |

*(Continued)*

*(Table 12.5 Continued)*

- Do the records tell when a student attempted an objective? .................. ..................
- Do the records tell how many times a student has attempted an objective? .................. ..................
- Do the records provide information across a span of units and lessons? .................. ..................
- Does the CMI system have an optional print capability for student records? .................. ..................
- Does the system have an optional print capability for producing printed tests for specific objectives? .................. ..................
- Does the system have an optional print capability of listing the objectives of the program? .................. ..................
- Can the system print parent reports on what the students have learned using the program? .................. ..................

*Table 12.6*

*Other Factors*

| Other Factors | Yes or No |
|---|---|
| • Is there a teacher's guide to the materials? | .................... |
| • Is the guide clearly written and easy to use? | .................... |
| • Is the program itself easy to use? | .................... |
| • Is there support for the teacher from the seller, if a problem arises with the program? | .................... |
| • Can the program be reviewed prior to purchase? | .................... |
| • Can the students use the program without special help from the teachers? | .................... |
| • Did the program run on the computer as promised? | .................... |
| • Was the program stored on high-quality disk or cassette? | .................... |
| • Can the program be easily duplicated? | .................... |

3. Try out the "polished" materials in a normal classroom setting. Evaluate the materials using questions from Tables 12.1 through 12.7. Make final revisions. Then the course-ware is ready for use by anyone (and if you designed it yourself, perhaps it is ready for sale through commercial distributors).

Only the third procedure is applicable to commercial materials, since you will not have the power to modify them. One key to the evaluation process in Flow Diagram 12.6 is to ask the question, "When the students use the materials, do they achieve the objectives?" After all, that is your reason for designing or purchasing the courseware in the first place.

You can also ask other kinds of questions of your trial group of students. You can determine how well they liked any lesson(s) and what suggestions they have for improvement, and how valuable the materials are from their perspective. Table 12.7 does not attempt to present an exhaustive set of questions of these types, since the type of questions you will want to ask of the students will vary greatly according to the program being evaluated and the method you use to ask the questions. You can

*Flow Diagram 12.6*

*Formative Evaluation of CAI or CMI Courseware*

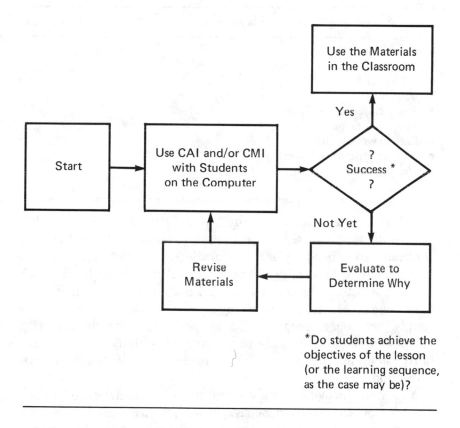

*Do students achieve the objectives of the lesson (or the learning sequence, as the case may be)?

---

ask the questions orally of the students, present them on paper, or present them in a special section at the end of your computer lesson(s).

## Summary

We have presented a set of evaluation criteria which can be applied during a design and development process or used when making a decision regarding whether or not to purchase a program produced by someone else. Generally, you will not want or need

*Table 12.7*

*Student Evaluation of Materials*

| Do the students think the materials are/have: | Yes or No |
|---|---|
| • Interesting? | ................. |
| • Clear? | ................. |
| • Effective? | ................. |
| • Valuable? | ................. |
| • The right amount of material? | ................. |
| • Too many facts? | ................. |
| • Easy to work with? | ................. |
| • Easy-to-understand directions? | ................. |
| • Well-organized? | ................. |

to utilize all the criteria presented in this chapter. More generally, you will want to select and choose those criteria that are applicable to a specific piece of courseware. Our intent has been to provide you with a fairly comprehensive framework from which you can select the questions you need to ask about your materials. Care must be taken not to skip over important criteria simply because a program "looks good" on the surface. If a courseware offering is going to be used in a serious manner with a fairly large number of students, it deserves close professional inspection.

You must provide your computer with well-designed courseware if you expect it to behave effectively as a teacher or as a manager of instruction. Your students deserve no less than a very well-trained computer in their classroom.

## APPENDICES
## RESOURCES FOR USING THE MICROCOMPUTER IN THE CLASSROOM

A.  Readings in Instructional Development

B.  Computer Manufacturers

C.  Computer Magazines

D.  Periodicals of Professional Organizations

E.  Books on Computers

F.  Sources of Information on Educational Software

# Appendix A
# Readings in Instructional Development

Books and articles listed below are generalized works on instructional development. Resource materials specific to the computer are in Appendix E.

There are many very good sources of information on instructional design and development that are not specific to the computer, but are very helpful to anyone interested in gaining more instructional development expertise. In reality, many of the principles presented in this book apply to a variety of educational materials in addition to those for the computer, such as printed texts, audio-visual presentations, and videotape and videodisc programs.

The works designated with an asterisk(*) were identified in a study of instructional design professionals conducted by Roberts A. Braden and Steven G. Sachs (*Educational Technology, 23*(2), February, 1983) as the top ten books recommended for use by persons interested in learning about instructional development.

Baker, R.L., and Schutz, R.E. (Eds.) *Instructional Product Development.* New York: Van Nostrand Reinhold Co., 1971.

Banathy, B.H. *Instructional Systems.* Palo Alto, CA: Fearon Publishers, 1968.

Bass, R.K., Lumsden, D.B., and Dills, C.R. (Eds.) *Instructional Development: The State of the Art.* Columbus, OH: Collegiate Publishing, Inc., 1978.

Bloom, B.S., Madaus, G.F., and Hastings, J.T. *Evaluation to Improve Learning.* New York: McGraw-Hill Book Company, 1981.

Bloom, B.S. *et al.* (Eds.) *A Taxonomy of Educational Objectives, Handbook I: Cognitive Domain.* New York: Longman, Inc., 1956.

Braden, R.A. One Hundred Book Titles: A Twelve-Foot Shelf of Basic References for Instructional Design and Development. *Educational Technology,* 1981, *21*(9), 41-45.

*Briggs, L.J. (Ed.) *Instructional Design: Principles and Applications.* Englewood Cliffs, NJ: Educational Technology Publications, 1977.

*Briggs, L.J., and Wager, W.W. *Handbook of Procedures for the Design of Instruction* (Second Edition). Englewood Cliffs, NJ: Educational Technology Publications, 1981.

*Davies, I.K. *Competency-Based Learning: Technology, Management, and Design.* New York: McGraw-Hill Book Company, 1973.

*Davis, R.H., Alexander, L.T., and Yelon, S.L. *Learning System Design: An Approach to the Improvement of Instruction.* New York: McGraw-Hill Book Company, 1974.

*Diamond, R.M. *et al. Instructional Development for Individualized Learning in Higher Education.* Englewood Cliffs, NJ: Educational Technology Publications, 1975.

*Dick, W., and Carey, L. *The Systematic Design of Instruction.* Glenview, IL: Scott, Foresman and Company, 1978.

Fleming, M.L., and Levie, W.H. *Instructional Message Design.* Englewood Cliffs, NJ: Educational Technology Publications, 1978.

Gagné, R.M. *Essentials of Learning for Instruction.* Hinsdale, IL: The Dryden Press, 1974.

*Gagné, R.M. *The Conditions of Learning* (Third Edition). New York: Holt, Rinehart, and Winston, 1977.

*Gagné, R.M., and Briggs, L.J. *Principles of Instructional Design* (Second Edition). New York: Holt, Rinehart, and Winston, 1979.

Gerlach, V.S., and Ely, D.P. *Teaching and Media: A Systematic Approach.* Englewood Cliffs, NJ: Prentice-Hall, Inc., 1971.

Gilbert, T.F. *Human Competency: Engineering Worthy Performance.* New York: McGraw-Hill Book Company, 1978.

Hartley, I. *Designing Instructional Text.* London: Kogan Page, 1978.

Heinich, R. *Technology and the Management of Instruction: Monograph 4.* Washington, D.C.: Association for Educational Communications and Technology, 1970.

Heinich, R., Molenda, M., and Russell, J.D. *Instructional Media and the New Technologies of Instruction.* New York: John Wiley and Sons, 1982.

Hilgard, E.R., and Bower, G.H. *Theories of Learning* (Fourth Edition). Englewood Cliffs, NJ: Prentice-Hall, Inc., 1975.

Jonassen, D.H. *The Technology of Text: Principles for Structuring, Designing, and Displaying Text.* Englewood Cliffs, NJ: Educational Technology Publications, 1982.

*Kemp, J.E. *Instructional Design: A Plan for Unit and Course Development* (Second Edition). Belmont, CA: Fearon Publishers, 1977.

Krathwohl, D.R., Bloom, B.S., and Masia, B.B. *Taxonomy of Educational Objectives, Handbook II: Affective Domain.* New York: Longman, Inc., 1964.

Mager, R.F. *Goal Analysis.* Belmont, CA: Fearon Pitman, 1972.

*Mager, R.F. *Preparing Instructional Objectives* (Second Edition). Palo Alto, CA: Fearon Publishers, 1975.

Markle, S. *Designs for Instructional Designers.* Champaign, IL: Stipes, 1978.

Merrill, M.D. (Ed.) *Instructional Design: Readings.* Englewood Cliffs, NJ: Prentice-Hall, Inc., 1971.

Merrill, M.D. *et al. TICCIT.* Englewood Cliffs, NJ: Educational Technology Publications, 1980.

Popham, W.J. *Criterion-Referenced Measurement.* Englewood Cliffs, NJ: Prentice-Hall, Inc., 1978.

Postlethwait, S.N., and Associates. *Exploring Teaching Alternatives.* Minneapolis: Burgess Publishing Co., 1977.

Salomon, G. *Interaction of Media, Cognition, and Learning.* San Francisco: Jossey-Bass, Inc., 1979.

Schramm, W. *Big Media, Little Media: Tools and Technologies for Instruction.* Beverly Hills, CA: Sage Publications, Inc., 1977.

Snelbecker, G.E. *Learning Theory, Instructional Theory, and Psychoeducational Design.* New York: McGraw-Hill Book Company, 1974.

Wileman, R.E. *Exercises in Visual Thinking.* New York: Hastings House, 1980.

Wittich, W.A., and Schuller, C.F. *Instructional Technology: Its Nature and Use* (Sixth Edition). New York: Harper and Row, 1979.

# Appendix B
# Computer Manufacturers

Manufacturers of microcomputers are pleased to supply information concerning their products. Any request for information should emphasize an interest in software for their product, as well as in their hardware. Although the manufacturers are, in most cases, in the business of selling hardware, they are well aware that software sells hardware. All will be able to provide either a catalog of software for their machine, or a listing of suppliers of programs for their machine. These are some leading firms.

## Companies

Acorn Computers Corp.
400 Unicorn Park Drive
Woburn, MA 01801

Apple Computer, Inc.
20525 Mariani Avenue
Cupertino, CA 95014

Atari
1265 Borregas Ave.
Sunnyvale, CA 94086

Bell and Howell
7100 North McCormick Road
Chicago, IL 60645

Commodore International
Computer Systems Division
487 Devon Park Drive
Wayne, PA 19087

Compucolor Corp.
P.O. Box 569
Norcross, GA 30071

Data General Corp.
Route 9
Westboro, MA 01581

Digital Equipment Corp. (DEC)
146 Main Street
Maynard, MA 01754

Exidy Systems, Inc.
1234 Elro
Sunnyvale, CA 94086

Franklin Computer Corporation
7030 Colonial Highway
Pennsauken, NJ 08109

Heath/Zenith Company
Benton Harbor, MI 49022

Hewlett Packard Co.
974 E. Arques
Sunnyvale, CA 94086

IBM Corporation
P.O. Box 1328
Boca Raton, FL 33432

Kaypro Corp.
533 Stevens Avenue
Solana Beach, CA 92075

M/A-Com System, Inc.
7 Oak Park
Bedford, MA 07730
(Formerly, Ohio Scientific)

NEC Home Electronics
1401 Estes Avenue
Elk Grove Village, IL 60007

North Star Computers
14440 Catalina Street
San Leandro, CA 94577

Radio Shack/Tandy Corp.
1800 One Tandy Center
Fort Worth, TX 76102

TeleVideo Systems
1170 Morse Avenue
Sunnyvale, CA 94086

Texas Instruments
P.O. Box 53
Lubbock, TX 79408

Xerox Corporation
Long Ridge Road
Stamford, CT 06904

# Appendix C
# Computer Magazines

Computer magazines are proliferating at an ever-increasing rate, and you must make sure the magazines you purchase are slanted toward your interests. Most magazines will send a single issue for examination purposes, and many of these magazines can be found on the bookshelves of computer stores, in bookstores, and wherever magazines are sold. New magazines appear all the time.

BYTE
McGraw-Hill Publishing Company
70 Main Street
Peterborough, NH 03458

CLASSROOM COMPUTER
  LEARNING
(previously CLASSROOM COM-
  PUTER NEWS)
19 Davis Drive
Belmont, CA 94002

COMPUTE MAGAZINE
Circulation Department
P.O. Box 5406
Greensboro, NC 27403

COMPUTER EDUCATOR
International Computer Education
  Center
1540 Halsted Street
Chicago, IL 60411

COMPUTER GRAPHICS WORLD
P.O. Box 122
Tulsa, OK 74101

COMPUTER TIMES
Hayden Publishing Company
1050 Commonwealth Avenue
Boston, MA 02215

COMPUTERS & ELECTRONICS
  (previously POPULAR ELEC-
  TRONICS)
P.O. Box 2774
Boulder, CO 80321

COMPUTERS & PEOPLE
Berkeley Enterprises, Inc.
815 Washington Avenue
Newtonville, MA 02160

COMPUTERWORLD
P.O. Box 880
375 Cochituate Road
Framingham, MA 01701

THE COMPUTING TEACHER
Department of Computer & Information Science

University of Oregon
Eugene, OR 97403

COMPUTRONICS
H & E Computronics, Inc.
50 North Pascack Road
Spring Valley, NY 10977

CREATIVE COMPUTING
15 Dumont Place
P.O. Box 789-M
Morristown, NJ 07960

CURRICULUM PRODUCT RE-
    VIEW
530 University Avenue
Palo Alto, CA 94301

EDUCATIONAL COMPUTER
Edcomp, Inc.
P.O. Box 535
Cupertino, CA 95015

EDUCATIONAL TECHNOLOGY
140 Sylvan Avenue
Englewood Cliffs, NJ 07632

80 MICRO
P.O. Box 981
Farmingdale, NY 11737

ELECTRONIC EDUCATION
1311 Executive Center Drive, Suite
    200
Tallahassee, FL 32301

MICROCOMPUTERS IN EDUCA-
    TION
QUEUE, Inc.
5 Chapel Hill Drive
Fairfield, CT 06432

MICROCOMPUTING
Subscription Service
P.O. Box 997
Farmingdale, NY 11731

PERSONAL COMPUTING
Subscriptions Department
4 Disk Drive
P.O. Box 13916
Philadelphia, PA 19101

POPULAR COMPUTING
P.O. Box 307
Martinsville, NJ 08836

TEACHING-LEARNING-COM-
    PUTING
P.O. Box 9159
Brea, CA 92621

TECHNOLOGICAL HORIZONS
    IN EDUCATION
(T.H.E. JOURNAL)
P.O. Box 992
Acton, MA 01720

# Appendix D
## Periodicals of Professional Organizations

There are a number of educational periodicals that include computer-related topics. Sometimes these will be at a higher technical level and not of great value to a teacher who is searching for good classroom instructional materials. These journals and magazines may warrant checking out, however, especially if your interests lie in the area covered by the publication.

A.D.C.I.S. NEWSLETTER
Association for the Development of
   Computer-Based Instructional
   Systems
Bond Hall
Western Washington University
Computer Center
Bellingham, WA 98225

A.E.D.S. MONITOR and A.E.D.S.
   JOURNAL
Association for Educational Data
   Systems
1201 16th Street, N.W.
Washington, DC 20036

COMMUNICATIONS
   OF THE ACM (Newsletter)
Association for Computing Ma-
   chinery
P.O. Box 12114
Church Street Station
New York, NY 10036

COMPUTER GRAPHICS (Newsletter)
ACM Special Interest Group
11 West 42nd Street
New York, NY 10036

COMPUTERS IN EDUCATION
American Society Engineering Edu-
   cation
Computers in Education Division
P.O. Box 308 W
Long Branch, NJ 07764

C.U.E. NEWSLETTER
Computer-Using Educators
c/o Don McKell
Independence High School
1776 Educational Park Drive
San Jose, CA 95133

INSTRUCTIONAL   INNOVATOR
Association for Educational Communications and Technology

1126 16th Street, N.W.
Washington, DC 20036

JOURNAL OF COMPUTER-
BASED INSTRUCTION
Association for the Development of
Computer-Based Instructional
Systems
8120 Penn Avenue South
Bloomington, MN 55431

MATHEMATICS TEACHER
National Council of Teachers of
Mathematics
1906 Association Drive
Reston, VA 22091

OREGON COMPUTER TEACHER
Oregon Council of Computer Edu-
cation
Computer Center
East Oregon State College
La Grande, OR 97850

SIGCUE BULLETIN
Association for Computing Machinery
Special Interest Group on Computer Uses in Education
1133 Avenue of the Americas
New York, NY 10036

# Appendix E
# Books on Computers

The number of books available on using computers and computer-based learning is quite large, as is the number of books on learning and using computer languages. The following list of books is provided for your convenience in locating additional sources of information.

## Books on Programming

*Applied Basic Programming*, Ageloff, R., and Mojena, R. Belmont, CA, Wadsworth Publishing, 1980.

*BASIC and the Personal Computer*, Dwyer, T., and Critchfield, M. Reading, MA, Addison-Wesley, 1978.

*BASIC Computer Programming*, Bartee, T. New York, Harper and Row, 1981.

*Computer-Assisted Instruction Using BASIC*, Huntington, J.F. Englewood Cliffs, NJ, Educational Technology Publications, 1979.

*Fundamentals of Microcomputer Programming: Including PASCAL.* McGlynn, D. New York, John Wiley and Sons, 1982.

*How to Build a Program*, Emmerichs, J. Beaverton, OR, Dilithium Press, 1982.

*Introduction to Computer Programming*, Brainerd, W. *et al.* New York, Harper and Row, 1979.

*Picture This! PILOT Turtle Geometry*, Thornburg, D. Reading, MA, Addison-Wesley, 1982.

*Programming Primer: A Graphic Introduction to Computer Programming with BASIC and PASCAL*, Taylor, R.P. Reading, MA, Addison-Wesley, 1982.

*Teach Yourself Computer Programming in Basic*, Carter, L.R., and Huzan, E. New York, Longman, Inc., 1981.

*Teaching Computer Programming to Kids and Other Beginners: A Teacher's Manual*, Van Horn, R. Austin, TX, Sterling Swift Publishing Co., 1982.

*What to Do After You Hit Return*, Peoples Computer Company. Rochelle Park, NJ, Hayden Book Co., 1980.

## Books on Computer-Based Learning

*The Author's Guide to CAI* (Fourth Edition), Burson, J. Ohio State University, 1976.

*Basic Keyboard Skills*, Volpe, J. Englewood Cliffs, NJ, Prentice-Hall, Inc., 1983.

*CAI Sourcebook*, Burke, R. Englewood Cliffs, NJ, Prentice-Hall, Inc., 1982.

*The Computer Age*, Dertouzos, M., and Moses, J. (Eds.) Cambridge, MA, MIT Press, 1980.

*Computer Assisted Instruction: Its Use in the Classroom*, Chambers, J.A., and Sprecher, J.W. Englewood Cliffs, NJ, Prentice-Hall, 1983.

*Computer Assisted Instruction in Schools: Achievements, Present Developments, and Projections for the Future*, Hallworth, H.J., and Brebner, A. ERIC Document Reproduction Service, Document ED 200 187, 1980.

*Computer Assisted Learning in Science Education*, Breech, G. (Ed.) London: Pergamon, 1979.

*Computer-Assisted Test Construction*, Lippey, G. (Ed.) Englewood Cliffs, NJ, Educational Technology Publications, 1974.

*Computer-Based Learning (Selected Readings)*, Rushby, N.J. (Ed.) New York, Nichols Publishing, 1981.

*The Computer in the School: Tutor, Tutee, Tool*, Taylor, R. (Ed.) New York, Teachers College, 1980.

*Computer Managed Instruction: Theory and Practice*, Baker, F. Englewood Cliffs, NJ, Educational Technology Publications, 1978.

*Computers for People*, Wills, J., and Miller, M. Beaverton, OR, Dilithium Press, 1982.

*Computers in the Curriculum*, Baker, J. Bloomington, IN, Phi Delta Kappa, 1976.

*The Electronic Cottage*, Deken, J. New York, William Morrow and Co., 1981.

*Elements of CAL*, Godfrey, D., and Sterling, S. Reston, VA, Reston Publishing Company, Inc., 1982.

*Exploring with Computers*, Bitter, G. New York, Messner, 1981.

*Guidelines for Evaluating Computerized Instruction Materials*, Heck, W., Johnson, J., and Kansky, R. Reston, VA, National Council of Teachers of Mathematics, Inc., 1981.

*The Handbook of Computer-Based Training*, Dean, C., and Whitlock, Q. New York, Nichols Publishing, 1982.

*Home Computers: A Beginner Glossary and Guide*, Miller, M., and Sippi, C. Beaverton, OR, Dilithium Press, 1978.

*Intelligent Tutoring Systems*, Sleeman, D., and Brown, J.S. (Eds.) New York, Academic Press, 1982.

*Introduction to Computers*, Kindred, A. Englewood Cliffs, NJ, Prentice-Hall, Inc., 1982.

*Learning Alternatives in U.S. Education: Where Student and Computers Meet*, Hunter, B. et al. Englewood Cliffs, NJ, Educational Technology Publications, 1975.

*Learning with Computers*, Bork, A. Maynard, MA, Digital Equipment Corp., 1981.

*The Making of the Micro: A History of the Computer*, Evans, C. New York, Van Nostrand Reinhold Co., 1981.

*Microcomputer Applications in the Classroom*, Hofmeister, A. New York, Holt, Rinehart, and Winston, 1984.

*Microcomputers and the 3 R's—A Guide for Teachers*, Doerr, C. Rochelle Park, NJ, Hayden Book Co., 1980.

*Microcomputers in Secondary Education*, Tagg, D. (Ed.) New York, Elsevier, 1980.

*Mindstorms: Children, Computers, and Powerful Ideas*, Papert, S. New York, Basic Books, 1980.

*One Computer, Thirty Kids*, Richardson, K. Indianapolis, IN, Meka Publishing Co., 1980.

*A Practical Guide to Computers in Education*, Coburn, P. *et al.* Reading, MA, Addison-Wesley, 1982.

*Schaum's Outline of Computers and Programming*, Scheid, F. New York, McGraw-Hill Book Co., 1982.

*Stimulating Simulations*, Engel, C.W. Rochelle Park, NJ, Hayden Book Co., 1979.

*Teacher's Guide to Computers in the Elementary School*, Moursund, D. International Council for Computers in Education, c/o Computing Center, Eastern Oregon State University, La Grande, Oregon, 97850, 1980.

*A User's Guide to Computer Peripherals*, Eadie, D. Englewood Cliffs, NJ, Prentice-Hall, Inc., 1982.

# Appendix F

# Sources of Information on Educational Software

There are a number of direct sources for software. Much software is advertised in popular magazines and in professional journals, and those sources can be utilized for up-to-date publications. The following are some of the sources of compiled information on available software. New sources appear almost daily.

## DIRECTORIES

THE APPLESOFTWARE DIRECTORY
WIDL Video
5245 W. Dempsey Avenue
Chicago, IL 60639

CLEARINGHOUSE FOR EDUCATIONAL SOFTWARE
Faculty of Education
University of British Columbia
Vancouver, B.C., Canada

CONDUIT
P.O. Box O
Oakdale, IA 52319

COURSEWARE MAGAZINE & DIRECTORY
4919 N. Millbrook, #222
Fresno, CA 93726

EDUCATIONAL SOFTWARE DIRECTORY

Libraries Unlimited, Inc.
P.O. Box 263
Littleton, CO 80160

THE EDUCATIONAL SOFTWARE SELECTOR
EPIE Institute and Teachers College Press
1234 Amsterdam Avenue
New York, NY 10027

EDUCATORS HANDBOOK AND SOFTWARE DIRECTORY
Vital Information, Inc.
350 Union Station
Kansas City, MO 64108

EVALUATION OF EDUCATIONAL SOFTWARE: A GUIDE TO GUIDES
SEDL
211 East 7th Street
Austin, TX 78701

INTERNATIONAL DIRECTORY
OF SOFTWARE
CUYB Publications
First Federal Building, Suite 401
Pottstown, PA 19464

INTERNATIONAL MICROCOM-
PUTER SOFTWARE DIREC-
TORY
Imprint Software
420 S. Howes Street
Fort Collins, CO 80521

MICROCOMPUTER EDUCATION
APPLICATIONS NETWORK
256 North Washington Street
Falls Church, VA 22046

MICRO CO-OP
P.O. Box 432
West Chicago, IL 60815

MICROSIFT
N.W. Regional Educational Labora-
tory
300 S.W. 6th Avenue
Portland, OR 97204

SOFTSIDE
P.O. Box 68
Milford, NH 03055

THE SOFTWARE CATALOG: MI-
CROCOMPUTERS
Elsevier Science Publishing Co.
52 Vanderbilt Avenue
New York, NY 10017

THE SOFTWARE DIRECTORY
Software Central
P.O. Box 30424
Lincoln, NE 68503

The SOFTWARE FINDER (Form-
erly SCHOOL MICROWARE DI-
RECTORY)
Dresden Associates
P.O. Box 246
Dresden, ME 04342

SOFTWARE REPORTS
Allenbach Industries, Inc.
2101 Las Palmas Drive
Carlsbad, CA 92008

STARBEKS SOFTWARE DIREC-
TORY
11990 Doresett Road
St. Louis, MO 63043

SWIFTS DIRECTORIES
Sterling Swift Publishing Co.
7901 South IH-35
Austin, TX 78744

VANLOVES APPLE II/III SOFT-
WARE DIRECTORY
Vital Information, Inc.
350 Union Station
Kansas City, MO 64108

## CATALOGS AND REVIEWS

CIE SOFTWARE NEWS
Computer Information Exchange
P.O. Box 159
San Luis Rey, CA 92068

COURSEWARE REPORT CARD
Educational Insights
150 W. Carob Street
Compton, CA 90220

CREATIVE DISCOUNT SOFT-
WARE
256 S. Robertson, Suite 2156
Beverly Hills, CA 90211

CURRICULUM PRODUCT RE-
VIEW
530 University Avenue
Palo Alto, CA 94301

THE DIGEST OF SOFTWARE RE-
VIEWS: EDUCATION
Suite C, 1341 Bulldog Lane
Fresno, CA 93710

EDUCATIONAL TECHNOLO-
GY MAGAZINE
Product Reviews Section
140 Sylvan Avenue
Englewood Cliffs, N J 07632

EPIE/CONSUMER'S UNION
P.O. Box 620
Stony Brook, NY 11790

HIVELY'S CHOICE
Continental Press
Elizabethtown, PA 17022

HUNTINGTON COMPUTING
CATALOG
P.O. Box 1297
1945 S. Dairy
Corcoran, CA 93212

K-12 MICRO MEDIA
172 Broadway
Woodcliff Lake, N J 07675

MARCK
280 Linden Avenue
Brandon, CT 06405

MICROCOMPUTERS CORPO-
RATION CATALOG
34 Maple Avenue
P.O. Box 8
Armonk, NY 10504

OPPORTUNITIES FOR LEARN-
ING, INC.
8950 Lurline Avenue
Chatsworth, CA 91311

PEELINGS II
P.O. Box 188
Las Cruces, NM 88004

QUEUE
5 Chapel Drive
Fairfield, CT 06432

SOFTWARE REVIEW
Microform Review, Inc.
520 Riverside Avenue
Westport, CT 06880

# Index

Analysis of learning, 87-88
Applications packages, 42-43
Arcade games, 25-27
Attitudes, as learning outcomes, 152-154
Authoring languages, 219-220
Authoring systems, 223-224

BASIC, 216-219
Behavior, of computer, 93
Bloom's Taxonomy, 152
Briggs, L., 117, 151, 159

CAI, 30-32
    contrast with CMI, 172
    integration with CMI, 189-191
    lesson designs, 65
CAL (see CAI)
CBI (see CAI and CMI)
CBT (see CAI AND CMI)
Characteristics of well-trained computer, review of, 134
Class, of test items, 80
Class lists, 198-199
CMI (see also Computer-managed instruction)
    a basic system, 181-184
    a powerful system, 185-189
    a simple system, 174-177
    blank systems, 194
    closed systems, 193-194
    contrast with CAI, 172
    defined, 31-32
    integration with CAI, 189-190
    menu-driven, 195-196

    open systems, 193-194
    power of, 206-207
    purpose of, 172
    recordkeeping, 177-181
    structural elements, 187, 189
    system set-up, 196-198
    value of, 32
Cognitive strategies, 152, 154
Computer (see Microcomputers)
Computer competence, levels of expertise, 9-10
Computer components, 16
Computer dialog, 42
Computer games, 39
Computer instruction, development of, 149
Computer languages
    examples of, 215-216
    learning of, 219-220
    nature of, 215
    spectrum of, 219
    teacher considerations, 220, 224-226
Computer lesson, defined, 71
Computer network, 15
Computer objective, writing of, 83-86
Computer objectives, 77-83
    by learning category, 154-155
    examples of, 86, 131-132
Computer program, 19
Computer programming
    as phase of training computer, 54
    considerations for teachers, 212-213

Computer screens, limitations of, 113-114
Computer simulation, 40
Computer testing, 99-101 (*see also* Testing)
Computer-assisted instruction (*see* CAI)
Computer-based instruction (*see* CAI and CMI)
Computer-based training (*see* CAI and CMI)
Computer-managed instruction (*see also* CMI)
    defined, 30-32, 172
    functions, 173-174
Computer-teacher, characteristics, 134
Computer-teacher training, 55
Computereze, 6
Concept learning
    and computer objectives, 157-158
    teaching for, 164-166
Course, defined, 71
Courseware, defined, 21
Courseware evaluation
    criteria, 235, 238, 240-241, 243, 246-248
    elements of, 232
    for effectiveness, 244-245
    process of, 230-233
    teacher considerations, 228-229, 250
Criterion-referenced measurement (*see* Objective-referenced testing)

Data entry, 10
Defining lesson purpose, 58-60
Diagnosis and prescription, 41-42
Diagnostic teaching, with CMI, 185
Dialog, with computer, 42
Discrimination learning
    and computer objectives, 156-157

teaching for, 163-164
Disk drive, 13-14
Disk operating systems, 219, 224
Diskette, 13
Domains of learning, 151-153
Drill and practice, 33-34

Educational intent, 68-94 (*see also* Goals and Objectives)
Effective presentation, 116-118
Effectiveness, of computer lesson, 113, 116
Efficiency, of computer lesson, 113, 118
Evaluation
    of CAI design, 333
    of CMI design, 244-247
    of courseware (*see* Courseware evaluation)
    of lesson content, 238-239, 242-243
    of measures, 236-237
    of objectives, 233-236
Events of instruction
    defined, 64
    identified, 117
Examples, in computer instruction, 124-125

Feedback
    examples of, 144-145
    in computer instruction, 126
Floppy disk, 13-14
Formative evaluation, 228, 244-245, 248

Gagné, R., 117, 151
Games, 39
Goal analysis, process of, 69-71, 87-89
Goal development, considerations, 72
Goals
    examples of, 131

from broad to specific, 70
nature of, 71-73
Graphics tablet, 15

Hard disk, 13
Hardware, v, 19
Helps, in computer lesson, 124
History of testing, 96-98

Information input, 13-15
Information inquiry, 40-41
Information storage, 12-13
Instruction, by computer, 118
Instructional design, 54
Instructional development model, 65
Instructional intent (*see* Purpose or Goals)
Instructional roles, of microcomputer, 30-31
Intellectual skills
defined, 152
examples of, 154
hierarchy of, 159-160
Item class, 80-84

Joysticks, 15

Keyboard
as microcomputer component, 8
for data entry, 10
Keypad, 15
Krathwohl, Bloom, and Masia, 152

Learning
categories of, 150-155
defined, 73
supported by computer, 117
Learning maps
example of, 89-90, 92, 132
for goals, 87-91
for objectives, 91-92
Lesson, defined, 71, 110

Lesson design
components of, 62
model of, 65
rules, 120-128
Lesson objectives, definition of, 74
Lesson presentation, aspects of
answer feedback, 126
examples, 124
helps, 124
motivation, 121
practice, 125-126
pretesting, 123
purpose, 121
retention and transfer, 127
review, 123
screens, 123-124
testing, 123, 127
Lesson presentation rules, 161
Lesson purpose and motivation, 121
Light pen, 13
Limitations, of computers, 43-46, 53
LOGO, 214-215, 219-220

Mastery learning
and performance levels, 105
facilitation with computer, 35
used with CMI, 177
Measurement, 60-61 (*see also* Testing and Objective-referenced measurement)
Memory, 8, 11-12
Menu
example of, 116, 136
value of, 114-116
Menu-driven format, 195-196
Microcomputer accessories, 13, 15-16
Microcomputer capability
auditory, 28
decision-making, 29
manipulation, 29

mathematical, 29
memory, 28
time-telling, 28
visual, 28
Microcomputer components, 8, 15
Microcomputer networks, 15, 18
Microcomputer role
adjunct, 30, 32
instructional, 30-31
Microcomputers
and instructional effectiveness,
57
as similar machines, 17-19
as simple machines, 5
as teacher's aides, iv
classroom roles of, 30
limitations of, 43-46
purchase of, vi
set-up of, 21-23
technical power of, 27
Microprocessor, 8
Modem, 17
Motivation, 121
Motor skills, 152-154

Network, 15, 18
Norm-referenced testing (*see* Testing)

Objective testing, 34-36
Objective-referenced measurement,
98
Objective-referenced test (*see also*
Testing)
defined, 61, 63
performance level, 106
related to objectives, 106
reliability, 103-106
validity, 101
Objectives (*see also* Computer objectives)
characteristics, 74
clarity versus value, 76
examples of, 131-132
function of, 93

Paddles, 15
Parent report, 181
Performance levels, 104-105
Performance objectives, 74 (*see also*
Computer objectives)
characteristics of, 74
defined, 63
related to computer objectives,
78
Personal computer (*see* Microcom-
puters)
PILOT, 219-223
Practice, in computer instruction,
125-126
Precise objectives, 74
Presentation features, 116-118
Presentation rules, modification of,
160-161
Printer, 15
Process of instruction, 61-62
Process of learning, 117-118
Program, computer, 19
Programming
considerations of, 212
process of, 54
Purpose
example of, 137
need to define, 68-69

Recordkeeping, 36-37
Reliability, of test, 103-104, 106
Retention, 127
Rule-using learning
and computer objectives,
158-159
teaching for, 166

Screen, as microcomputer component, 8
Simulation, 40
Software (*see also* Courseware)
importance of, 19
problems with, 19, 21
purchase of, 21

Student performance
  records of, 179-181
  review of, 204-206
Summative evaluation, 228

Teaching
  as task of computer, 112-113
  defined, 52
Terminal objective, for computer
  lesson, 91-92
Test item
  as representative of item class,
    80
  presentation of, 79
Testing (*see also* Reliability and
  Validity)
  by comparing students, 96-97
  by objectives, 98
  for two types of instructional
    decisions, 100
  in computer lesson, 123, 127
  on computer, 35-36
  traditional, 96-98
  varieties of, 96
Testing decisions, in a computer
  lesson, 100
Testing situation
  item presentation, 78
  limitations, 83

TICCIT computer, 118
Training a computer
  premises, 57
  process of, 54
  systematic framework for, 58-59
Transfer of learning, 127
Tutorial
  interaction pattern, 139, 143
  response pattern, 145
Tutorial lesson, example of,
  129-148

Unit, defined, 71, 110
Unit goals,
  complexity of, 110
  examples of, 131
User expertise, 9

Validity, of test, 101-102, 106
Verbal information, 152, 154
Verbal information learning
  and computer objectives, 156
  example lesson, 130
  teaching for, 163
Videogames, 25-26

Wager, W., 117, 159
Weizenbaum, J., 42
Word processing, 37-39